A.R. GURNEY, JR., was born in Buffalo, New York, in 1930. He received his B.A. from Williams College and his M.F.A. from Yale University. He is the recipient of many awards and honors, including a Drama Desk Award, a Rockefeller Playwriting Award, and a National Endowment Playwriting Grant. Mr. Gurney is currently teaching literature at the Massachusetts Institute of Technology. He is married and has four children.

FOUR PLAYS:
Scenes from American Life

Children

The Middle Ages

The Dining Room

by
A.R. Gurney, Jr.

A BARD BOOK/PUBLISHED BY AVON BOOKS

AVON BOOKS
A division of
The Hearst Corporation
1790 Broadway
New York, New York 10019

Published by arrangement with the author
Library of Congress Catalog Card Number 84-091259
ISBN: 0-380-89498-X

First Bard Printing, May 1985

BARD TRADEMARK REG. U.S. PAT. OFF. AND IN
OTHER COUNTRIES, MARCA REGISTRADA,
HECHO EN U.S.A.

Printed in the U.S.A.

OPB   10 9 8 7 6 5 4 3 2 1

To Gilbert Parker

TABLE OF CONTENTS

Introduction

The discovery that these four plays by A. R. Gurney, Jr., are almost as good to read as they were to see should come as no surprise. Mr. Gurney is a deft and lively writer, whose scripts are able to make clear the theatricality, vivid and innovative, that meant so much to the productions: the ingenious ways in which he records the passage of time—sequential time or broken chronology—as one scene melts into the next; the ingenious ways in which, in *The Dining Room* and *Scenes from American Life*, he uses actors in multiple roles; and the ingenious ways in which he uses light and shadow in the simplest of settings to underline or actually to make his points.

One notes immediately the clarity and depth of Gurney's characters and his acute ear for their speech, the humor and tempo of his dialogue that somehow enhance emotion, and the underlying seriousness and irony of the true satirist. Over and over, he proves that humor and sadness, even tragedy, are not incompatible. These characters are, of course, the well-born, well-bred, and well-heeled—in short, the white Protestant gentry or, as someone in *The Dining Room* puts it, "the Wasp culture of the Northeastern United States." The erosion of that culture over the past forty or fifty eruptive years is the source of the fun and the feeling in Mr. Gurney's comedy: the erosion of guidelines and standards and self-esteem, and the effects of that erosion—dismay, bafflement, indignation, as well as relish and gallantry—on the members of the club. Seldom can one dramatist have rung more changes on snobbery. Seldom can one dramatist have more heartily celebrated the rebellious spirit, in whatever guise or circumstances it appears.

Sifting through my old reviews (and memories) of his work, I keep running across the word *unconventional;* that the most conventional and convention-ridden people on earth should appear in the most unconventional of plays is one paradox among several. It is also one good joke among many. For what I best remember, as a member of the audience, is laughing as much with surprise as amusement, and feeling immediate sympathy for the characters, even when they get their comeuppance. I also remember, on every occasion, my admiration for a writer who never allows his gravity or even, in the case of *Scenes from American Life,* his deep pessimism to dim his wit or dampen his spirits. And who never forgets, incidentally, to entertain the customers.

EDITH OLIVER

Scenes from American Life

SCENES FROM AMERICAN LIFE was first presented in a workshop production at Tanglewood, Massachusetts, in the summer of 1970, under the auspices of Boston University, with the following cast:

Rue McLanahan
Michael Moriarty
Steve Nelson
Patricia O'Connell
Kurt Peterson
Lisa Richards
and others.

It was directed by Jared Barclay.

It was first produced in New York City by the Repertory Theatre of Lincoln Center at the Forum Theatre in March of 1971, with the following cast:

James Broderick
Herbert Foster
Martha Henry
Elizabeth Huddle
Lee Lawson
Priscilla Pointer
Robert Symonds
Christopher Walken

It was directed by Daniel Sullivan.

It was also produced at the Studio Arena Theatre, Buffalo, New York, in 1970.

CAST

The size of the cast may vary. The play is probably impossible to do with less than four men and four women. To do it with more might diminish some of the sense of virtuosity which should emerge. It is very important that the roles be evenly and variously distributed, that sons play fathers, that mothers play daughters, and so forth. This will mean that sometimes the director will have to cast against the grain. Otherwise, the play will seem to be the story of one or two families, whereas it should be the story of many. However, the same actor and actress should play the mother and father in the first and last scenes of the play.

SET

The set should be attractive, simple and functional, without seeming stark or cold: a few flats, a few levels, easy entrances and exits. The space should conform easily to whatever a scene requires. Centrally located is a burnished, baby grand piano, around which the action should flow. Simple wooden chairs are brought in and out as needed.

COSTUMES

Basic costumes, enhanced by various props and accessories, should be worn throughout: the women in simple, clean-lined dresses, the men in dark gray suits. Accessories, such as hats, gloves, ties, collars, jewels, should then become crucial to establish both the era and the character in a particular scene.

PROPS

Props, similarly, should be used sparingly but pointedly. A baby carriage or a telephone, for example, must help anchor the date of a particular scene.

MUSIC

The music, like the props and accessories, is essential in indicating the time and tone of a particular scene. The script indicates, wherever possible, what music to be used. The pianist will be required to bridge scenes, to improvise on occasion, and even to compose music of his own for those scenes that take place in the future.

CONTINUITY

Finally, it is absolutely imperative that the scenes metamorphose naturally, one into the other. Therefore, lighting blackouts should be used only rarely. The director should find as many ways as he can to blend the end of one scene into the beginning of the next, by having actors set up the stage, carry on or carry off their props and costumes, and so forth. Only some of these blends are suggested in the script.

ACT I

No curtain. Empty stage, but for the piano. The PIANIST *can play a sort of prelude, composed of songs from all the periods of the play, before the houselights dim.*

As the houselights dim, the PIANIST *should modulate into songs from the early thirties. As he does so, a* MAID, *indicated simply by her white apron and white cap, places a tray of martinis on the piano. A* GODMOTHER *and* GODFATHER *enter. Other guests begin to drift in, with appropriate accessories to suggest 1930. Finally, as the houselights are out and the stagelights up, the* PIANIST *begins to play a lively version of "You Must Have Been a Beautiful Baby." The* MOTHER, FATHER, *and* BISHOP *enter. The* BISHOP *has a clerical collar with a purple dickey blouse; the* MOTHER *carries a doll with a long and lacy christening dress.*

FATHER: [*With an arm around the* BISHOP]. He's a happy baby, Bishop. He laughed all during the christening.
BISHOP: [*Taking a cocktail from the* MAID] So did his father.
FATHER: I'm a happy man. [*Kisses his wife*] With a lovely wife . . . [*Pats the doll*] And a fat, sleek son and heir . . . [*Indicating the group*] And a fine, loyal, attractive group of friends! Let me toast you all! [*Raises his glass*] In the name of the Father, the Son, and the best gin ever smuggled across the Niagara River!
BISHOP: [*Drinking*] Now, now.
[*The* MAID *brings out a chair for the* MOTHER.]

7

MOTHER: We've *got* to find a nickname. We have no nickname. We've all got to *think* of something.

GODFATHER: [*Steps forward*] While we're thinking, here's a present from his godfather.

[*Hands her a small box. She sits in the chair and opens it.*]

MOTHER: Why . . . it's a sterling silver pusher. [*Holds it out*]

FATHER: A sterling silver what?

MOTHER: A pusher! For manners at meals! [*Demonstrates*] To keep his hands clean! [*Busses the* GODFATHER] Oh, thank you, Bill!

GODFATHER: He can pawn it if Roosevelt is elected.

[*Laughter; the* PIANIST *plays a musical comment.*]

BISHOP: He gets a Bible from me. It's being engraved in New York.

FATHER: [*Waving a piece of paper*] And a rather sizable check from his grandmother.

[*Cheers; the* PIANIST *plays a fanfare.*]

MOTHER: [*Hugging the baby*] Oh, baby: You're riding on the gravy train.

FATHER: [*Raising his glass*] I'll drink to that.

GODMOTHER: [*Steps forward*] I won't. [*Is a little drunk. Everyone looks at her.*] I won't drink to that.

ANOTHER GUEST: The fairy godmother wants to make a prediction!

[*Laughter*]

GODMOTHER: [*Going right on*] I'm sorry. I just want to say one word, please, to my godson.

FATHER: [*Tolerantly*] Fine, Grace. Say it.

GODMOTHER: [*Picking up the baby; looking at it*] Responsibility. That's what I want to say to you. Responsibility. [*Pause*]

A WOMAN: Well, go on, Grace.

GODMOTHER: [*Boozily*] Well, I mean he has a responsi*bil*ity. To himself. And to, well, us. And to his country.

[*The* PIANIST *starts "The Star-Spangled Banner." Someone salutes. The* GODMOTHER *plugs on.*]

I'm *serious.* We're in difficult times. There's a depression going on. People are hungry and out of work.

[*Ad-libs: "Oh, God. Here we go again."*]

Well, it's true. And I want to propose a toast. To responsibility! [*Waves her glass; her drink spills on the baby.*] Oh, dear. Did I— Oh, I'm terribly sorry.

MOTHER: [*Taking the baby, wiping it off*] It's nothing. . . . Look: He's asleep. He's having a little snooze. Oh, now I know what we'll call him. Snoozer! We'll call him Snoozer!

FATHER: [*Arm around the* GODMOTHER, *who is crying*] A second christening, Grace.

MOTHER: Exactly. Snoozer. Because he sleeps through everything.

[*The* PIANIST *plays "Rockabye Baby." Everyone gathers around the chair and sings.*]

EVERYONE: [*Singing*] ". . . When the bough breaks the cradle will fall, and down will come Snoooooozer, cra—[*The* MAID *takes a picture with a box Brownie. They all hold still*]—dle and all. . . ."

[*The piano modulates into a contemporary rock version of "Low Bridge, Everybody Down." The* MAID *takes the baby offstage, and the others follow, with the exception of one of the male guests, who begins to address the audience with great earnestness.*]

SPEAKER: I just want to make one point, please. The real issue, it seems to me, is whether Buffalo can survive as a major city in the nineteen-seventies! I say we can! And I say it's our responsibility as businessmen to see that we do! Listen: Snoozer and I did a little research in the Erie County Library. We found out about our name, Buffalo. We weren't named after that damned bison! No, sir! Buffalo comes from the French. Beau Fleuve. Beautiful river. The Niagara! The bison is almost extinct, but that beautiful river is still rolling along! And we had the Erie Canal! We were the Queen City of the Great Lakes! We were the largest fresh water port in the world! So now let's float a big new bond issue right out onto that beautiful river! Let's build a new stadium we can be proud of! Let's keep our hockey team and our football team right here in Beau Fleuve, and cheer this city on into the future! Come on, fellas! It's high time we realized who we are!

[*The piano shifts to another thirties song. As the* SPEAKER *goes off, he winks at* NELLIE, *a nurse, who wears a white hat and collar. She enters wheeling an elaborate English baby carriage. She bends over the carriage, fussing with the baby within. A* MOTHER *enters, wearing hat and gloves as if she were going out. She carries a telephone from the thirties.*]

MOTHER: Now, Nelly: You and I both have lots of things to do this morning, but I'm afraid there's something we've got to discuss.

NELLY: [*Irish accent; still tucking the child*] Yes, ma'am?

MOTHER: Nelly, I'm going to ask you point-blank: Did you have a man in your room last night?

[NELLY *stops tucking.*]

Nelly, I'm asking you a question.

NELLY: No, ma'am.

MOTHER: Now, Nelly, are you sure? When Mr. Pratt and I got home last night, we heard some very strange footsteps sneaking down the back stairs.

[*Pause*]

NELLY: Just to listen to my Victrola, ma'am.

MOTHER: Ah-hah.

NELLY: Just to listen to my records from Ireland, ma'am.

MOTHER: I won't have it, Nelly.

NELLY: Just to—

MOTHER: I simply won't have it. What if the baby had needed you?

NELLY: I could hear the baby.

MOTHER: Oh, Nelly, *honestly!* This is a big *house.* With lots of closed doors.

[*Pause*]

NELLY: I get lonely, ma'am.

MOTHER: That's not the point. We all get lonely. But we don't have strange men in our rooms. That we don't do.

NELLY: He wasn't strange, ma'am.

MOTHER: Nelly, I'm not going to argue. I do not want men in this house, nor do I want you meeting them when you walk the baby.

NELLY: I don't—

MOTHER: Nelly, you *do.* The Wheelers' Bertha said you were talking to a man in the park. Nelly, haven't you heard of the Lindbergh *kid*napping?

NELLY: He wouldn't—

MOTHER: I'm just terribly disappointed, that's all. I liked you so much during your interview. You were clean, and

10

neat, and sweet. You were right off the boat, and I've trained you from scratch. And you're very good, Nelly, in so many ways. [NELLY *begins to sniffle.*] You're marvelous with the baby's clothes. And the bathrooms are immaculate, and the baby adores you. [NELLY *starts to whimper.*] So we've decided not to let you go, Nelly. We're going to see this thing through, all of us. I've called your priest, and he's going to arrange it so you can meet some other Irish girls. . . .

[NELLY *begins to blubber.* MOTHER *takes a neat hanky out of her purse, hands it to* NELLY.]

Here. Use this. Keep it. Now you have a crucial responsibility, Nelly. That child. He is absolutely in your hands. And if you get tied up with men, he will no longer get your undivided attention. And then we're *all* in trouble. [*Begins to dial the telephone*] So we'll say no more about it. Give him plenty of fresh air. Cod-liver oil at lunch. Long nap. I'll be back at four to read him "Pat the Bunny."

[NELLY *returns to carriage.* MOTHER *begins to talk, a little furtively, on the telephone.*]

Hi.

NELLY: [*To child in carriage, bitterly*] Ah, ye've kicked yer covers off, have ye? And yer soakin' wet.

MOTHER: Everything's all right in the Nelly department. I can meet you for lunch after all.

NELLY: Now I'll have to change ye.

MOTHER: Good God, no! People will see us there.

NELLY: No, no. Nelly said no-no. Don't touch that. Touch that again and Nelly will cut it off.

MOTHER: [*Still on telephone*] That's better.

NELLY: Dirty, dirty, dirty . . . .

MOTHER: I'll see you there. . . . Mmmm. Good-bye. . . .
[*She hangs up. They go out separate ways, as the piano shifts to a dissonant version of "Auld Lang Syne." A* MAN *in a ski parka enters carrying a very modern telephone. He is finishing dialing.*]

MAN: Hello, Judge? This is Tyler Moffat. . . . Happy New Year, and all that. . . . Listen, Judge, could you do me a favor? I was caught in the curfew the other night. Yes, I was driving home from the club and they stopped me cold. I shouldn't have had that last drink with

11

Snoozer. . . . [*Laughs*] I know. It's not the fine I mind, but it means showing up in court, and we're taking the kids skiing over New Year's. . . . Hold it. [*Gets the ticket out of his pocket*] The officer's name is Pulanski. One of our more serious Polish citizens, I'm afraid. [*Laughs*] Many thanks, Judge. . . . I know, dammit. Seven o'clock is just plain too early for a curfew. I was just in Philadelphia, and they don't start their curfew till nine! [*Laughs*] Ah, tempora; ah, Buffalo! . . . Well, thanks again, Judge, and I'll see you in the sauna when we get back. Goodbye. [*He hangs up and goes off. The piano plays a sprightly tune, perhaps "America the Beautiful." A* WOMAN *comes on briskly, carrying a folder and a small can. She puts her finger out as if to ring a doorbell. The piano sounds door chimes. A* MAN *in his undershirt comes to the "door." He carries a beer can.*]

WOMAN: Hello. I'm Mrs. Arthur Bigelow from over on Middlesex Road. And I'm collecting money to save the elms.

[*Rattles her can; we hear very few coins. The* MAN *looks at her.*]

The elms. The American elms. [*Looks around*] I guess you don't have any on this particular street, but they're one of the things Buffalo used to be famous for, and now they're dying like mad. [*No response*] If you drive down Richmond or Delaware, you can see huge bare patches where the elms once were. It's awful. And those streets used to be like great, green cathedrals. [*No response; she shows him her folder.*] You see, what happens is that a tiny beetle gets under their bark and lays its eggs in their capillaries, and that stops their sap from flowing. So they die. Unless we all chip in to save them. [*Pause*]

MAN: You want money for trees?

WOMAN: Yes! Exactly!

[*The* MAN *points. The* WOMAN *follows his glance.*]

Oh, is that your tree? That's a nice little tree. What is it? A scrub oak or something? But it's not an American elm. No, you see the elm is perfect for the city. Their shade gives lovely lawns. And they have shallow roots which never interfere with the sewers. And their branches

12

A. R. GURNEY, JR.

More sounds from the machine. She reads a dial.]
u have to bring it up to date.,
ll, how do I do that?
You apply through the District Registry after the
f the year.
od Lord. When was this decided?
Oh, it wasn't de*cid*ed, sir. It just happened.
st happened?
Well, with all these young people voting no , we
to keep track of who's who.
t I want to vote *today!*
So do we all, sir!
t this is an important election. I have a responsi-
.
tient ad-libs from the people in line]
Sir, you are keeping other people waiting.
. I'm sorry. This is quite disturbing. I'm not going
this happen again!
[*As he leaves, calling to him*] Next time, stay a Re-
can. And don't go to Canada!
*crowd goes off as the piano plays a hymn: "Praise
rom Whom All Blessings Flow." A* MINISTER, *indi-
by a clerical collar, comes on, carrying a Bible. He
to the* PIANIST, *who ends the hymn.*]
R: [*To audience*] The Gospel for today is taken from
Matthew, chapter nineteen, beginning at the six-
h verse: "And behold, one came unto Jesus and said
him, 'What good thing shall I do that I may have
al life?' And He said unto him, 'Keep the Com-
lments.' And the young man saith, 'All these have I
from my youth. What lack I yet?' And Jesus said,
nd sell what thou hast, and give to the poor, and
shalt have treasure in heaven.' But when the
g man heard that saying, he went away sorrowful,
had great possessions. Then Jesus said to his disci-
'It is easier for a camel to go through the eye of a
e than for a rich man to enter the Kingdom of
" [*Closes the Bible; a pause*] Of course, recent schol-
p tells us that there actually was a place in
alem called "The Eye of the Needle." And presum-
amels *could* go through it. So Jesus simply meant

16

arch over the telephone wires. So to save them we all
have to get together.
[*Pause*]
MAN: Would you like to come in for a beer?
[*Pause*]
WOMAN: Um. No. Thank you just the same.
[*They stand staring at each other a moment. The piano
plays a light rhythmic beat. Then they and the other actors arrange chairs into bleachers. They put on suggestions of sporty clothes: a tennis hat, a white sweater, a
tennis racquet here and there. They all sit in the bleachers, their heads going back and forth in time to the music
as if they were watching a match. Meanwhile, a* REFEREE
*has brought on a high stool and a large silver trophy,
which he places beside him as he sits on the stool.*]
REFEREE: Game. Mr. and Mrs. Curtis. They lead, five
games to three.
[*Applause.* UNCLE JOHN *comes out, leading a small* BOY.
The BOY *has socks pulled up over his trousers to suggest
knickers, and a sailor suit collar.* UNCLE JOHN *wears a
blazer and straw hat.*]
UNCLE JOHN: [*To* BOY, *as people make room for them*] Now
you sit here with your Aunt Helen and watch your
mummy and daddy play tennis, and your Uncle John
will be in the bar.
AUNT HELEN: [*In the bleachers*] John! stay right here! You
promised.
UNCLE JOHN: [*Reluctantly sitting down, the* BOY *between
them*] I hate the goddamn game.
AUNT HELEN: That's because you can't play it.
REFEREE: [*Calling out*] Fifteen-love!
AUNT HELEN: [*To the* BOY] These are the finals, Timmy. If
your parents win, they win that great, big, shiny cup
over there. . . .
UNCLE JOHN: That battle trophy, Timmy. . . .
AUNT HELEN: And they get their names on it, Timmy. Per-
manently engraved. . . . My name is on it, actually. I
won it once.
UNCLE JOHN: Before she was married, Timmy. As I am
being constantly reminded.
AUNT HELEN: Never mind, Timmy. You watch.
REFEREE: [*Calling out*] Thirty-love!

13

AUNT HELEN: See, Timmy? Your parents are beating Snoozer's parents! Your parents have thirty, and Snoozer's parents have love.

UNCLE JOHN: And love means nothing.

[*She glances at him. Another long point. Heads go back and forth. Applause at the end.*]

AUNT HELEN: There. Mummy won that point. And I'll tell you why. When she went to the net, Daddy stayed with her. They stayed parallel all the way. If your Uncle John would stay parallel with me . . .

UNCLE JOHN: We could win that cup.

AUNT HELEN: Exactly.

UNCLE JOHN: We could keep it for one year.

AUNT HELEN: Exactly.

UNCLE JOHN: I could use it to mix martinis. . . .

AUNT HELEN: Oh, God, John.

[*Another point is played.*]

REFEREE: Out. Forty-fifteen.

UNCLE JOHN: That was a bad call.

AUNT HELEN: Oh, John . . . .

UNCLE JOHN: [*To* REFEREE, *standing up*] That was a bad call! The shot was good!

REFEREE: The shot was out, John.

CROWD: [*Ad-libbing*] Sit down, John. . . . Come on, John. . . . This is a tournament, John . . . .

AUNT HELEN: John, for heaven's *sake!* What are you teaching the C-H-I-L-D! [*Turns to* TIMMY] Your uncle John is wrong, Timmy. The referee is always right. Now notice mummy. She is not complaining. She is going right on with the game, even though she may be very unhappy inside. That's what it means to be a good sport. That's what life is all about.

[*Another point is played. Lots of head movement. Then applause; and everyone stands up at the end and applauds politely.*]

REFEREE: Game, set, match. To Mr. and Mrs. Curtis.

[*Gets off his stool, brings the cup over to* AUNT HELEN] Would he like to give the cup to his parents?

AUNT HELEN: [*Taking it*] Oh, yes. What a wonderful idea, Bill! [*Takes the cup*] Here, Timmy. See? Here's my maiden name, when I won with Mr. Rogers. [*Blows on it; wipes it off with her sleeve*]

14

UNCLE JOHN: What're you doing?

AUNT HELEN: Yes. Well. Now, Timr mother. Go on. Walk right out on with everyone. Good, firm grip. friends at the end of the game.

[*Under her breath, to* UNCLE JOHN This is it, John. I swear . . . . [*T* Timmy. Do it. Good boy.

[*Everyone claps and beams as the out, holding up the cup. The piano m like music. The crowd shifts into a g ing in line. A* WOMAN *now sits in the R with great apologies, pushes his way of the line, as others ad-lib protests.* WOMAN.]

MAN: [*breathlessly*] Excuse me. They said you my Identification Card.

[*Holds it out to her*]

WOMAN: Thank you, sir. I'll just put it in here. [*Pantomimes inserting the card* The piano plays strange noises; then stops. S the card, reads the results.*] It says you' an Independent.

[*Hands the card back, smiling*]

MAN: That's wrong. I'm a Republican.

WOMAN: Well, you seem to come out as a [*The crowd in line ad-libs impatience.*]

MAN: Oh, my gosh. Maybe I am. My child two years ago for a disarmament ca last year I was in Canada duck hunti shifted back.

WOMAN: There you are.

MAN: Well. Then I'm forced to vote as a

WOMAN: Oh, you can't do that without certificate. Do you have your pre-r cate?

MAN: I don't believe I do. No.

WOMAN: Wait a minute. [*Puts his I.D. c chine. More noises from the piano*] one and don't even know it. [*More the card.*] Yes! You *do* have one. Th

15

we must be generous, we must be charitable with our
money. . . .

[*He smiles; the piano provides a coda as he goes slowly
out. The piano plays children's music.*

A BOY, *indicated by his sailor collar, throws a big rubber ball
high in the air. A* GRANDFATHER *comes out, wearing a stiff collar, carrying a cane. He stands on a platform, to give the suggestion of height. He clasps his hands behind his back.*]

GRANDFATHER: You there! Andy! I say, Andy! Come here
and see your grandfather!

[*The* BOY *keeps his distance, frightened.*]

Come here, boy. Come closer.

[*The* BOY *comes closer.*]

I left the bank early especially to see you, Andy. Your father tells me you have a stammer. Is that true?

[*The* BOY *nods.*]

Your father also tells me you like money. Is *that* true?

[*The* BOY *nods.*]

All right. I will give you five dollars if you will tell me a
story. [*Takes a wad of money out of his pocket, removes a
five dollar bill from it, and holds up the bill temptingly.
Pause*] Begin, lad.

BOY: [*Stammering*] Once . . . once . . . once . . .

GRANDFATHER: Don't stammer.

BOY: Once upon a . . . upon . . . upon a . . .

GRANDFATHER: Don't stammer!

BOY: Once . . . once . . . once . . . once . . .

GRANDFATHER: [*Shouting; shaking him*] I said DON'T
STAMMER!

[*Long pause; they eye each other.*]

BOY: [*Very slowly and carefully*] Once . . . upon . . . a . . .
time . . . there . . . was . . . a big, mean . . . [*Pause*] . . .
ugly GIANT!

GRANDFATHER: Good. That will do. Here's your five dollars.
I'm putting it in the bank for you. [*Puts it in another
pocket*] When you're twenty-one, it will be worth seventeen dollars and sixty cents. Now run along. Play with
your chums. And don't stammer again.

[*The* GRANDFATHER *exits. The* BOY *exits slowly and perplexedly in the opposite way, as the piano plays a bossa
nova.* MRS. BIDWELL *comes out, carrying a glass of liquor,
holding a sixties telephone.*]

MRS. BIDWELL: [*Coldly*] Good morning. This is Mrs. Bidwell.
. . . Let me speak to Doctor Taubman, please. . . . Yes,
I'd say this was important. Not crucial, but important. . . . Thank you. [*Pause; then very brightly*] Hi! . . .
Listen I'm sorry I missed yesterday's appointment. It
completely slipped my mind. What with one thing and
another. [*Pause*] No, no. Listen. What I'm calling about
is . . . What I want to say is . . . No, Doctor Taubman, I
really do think this psychotherapy business is not for
me. We're simply not getting anywhere, you and I. You
keep wanting me to talk about the most personal things.
I can't. No, I just plain can't. It seems so—so whiney. No,
I mean it. I'll just have to call on the old willpower to
solve the drinking thing. I'll just have to pull myself together, that's all. . . . No, I mean it. . . . No, now send
me a bill, please. I assume I don't have to pay for the session I missed. . . . I do? I do have to pay? Now that
doesn't seem quite sporty, does it? . . . All right, all
right. Just send the bill. Good-bye.

[*Hangs up. A moment. She looks at her glass; then goes
off as the* PIANIST *modulates to hard rock music.* A HUS-
BAND *and* WIFE *bring out two chairs, set them up as the
front seat of a "car." The* HUSBAND *pantomimes driving;
after a moment, the* WIFE *turns off the "radio." The music
stops; a moment of silence as they drive along.*]

WIFE: [*Suddenly*] I want another baby.

HUSBAND: A baby!

WIFE: No, I do. I really do.

HUSBAND: What did you drink tonight?

WIFE: Freeze-dried coffee in styrofoam cups. Oh, I hate,
hate, HATE, these community action meetings! Everyone just sits around and inter*rupts*.

HUSBAND: "Wake up, America! Engage in politics at the
local level!"

WIFE: I didn't see you engaging. You didn't say anything.

HUSBAND: I almost fell asleep.

[*Pause*]

WIFE: I really do want another baby, Nick.

HUSBAND: We've got five babies.

WIFE: They're not babies. And they're not mine.

HUSBAND: Two of them are.

WIFE: They're not. Howard gets *at* them every weekend.

They're all brainwashed. They come back waving the flag at me. Laurie wants to be a drum major*ette* now! [*Looks at him*] And your children: They miss Ellie. They keep asking me where their *real* mother is. [*Pause*] Well, *I* want to be a real mother just once more. Before I . . . dry up completely.

[*A whistle from offstage*]

HUSBAND: [*Pantomiming stopping the car*] Now what?

[*A helmeted* POLICEMAN *comes on, with flashlight and nightstick. He flashes the light in their faces, speaks as if through car window.*]

POLICEMAN: Let's see the I.D. cards.

[*They hand him their I.D. cards. He reads them by flashlight, checks their faces with the photographs, hands them back.*]

Gotta take a detour, folks.

HUSBAND: [*Dryly*] What seems to be the trouble, Officer?

POLICEMAN: They've blown up the water main. You can get through on Elmwood.

HUSBAND: Thanks.

POLICEMAN: And lock your doors. It's a new city ordinance.

HUSBAND: Thanks.

[*They pantomime reaching back and locking the car's rear doors. The* POLICEMAN *goes off. The* HUSBAND *pantomimes making a turn; he shakes his head.*]

Still want a baby?

WIFE: Yes.

HUSBAND: Oh, come on.

WIFE: I'm serious.

HUSBAND: Too late for babies.

WIFE: Not for me it isn't.

HUSBAND: We're too old.

WIFE: I'm not. Maybe you are. But I'm not.

HUSBAND: What's that supposed to mean?

WIFE: I'm pregnant.

[*The* HUSBAND *pantomimes slamming on the brakes.*]

Please don't stop the car, Nick. It's dangerous to stop the car here.

[*He angrily starts up again.*]

HUSBAND: You're not pregnant.

WIFE: I am. I ought to know.

HUSBAND: In you go. The hospital. Tomorrow.

WIFE: Oh, no.

HUSBAND: Oh, yes.

WIFE: I want a baby, Nick. I've got nothing to *do* now. No one needs me. I can't get a job that means anything. And these hysterical meetings—oh, I hate it, Nick. I want to stay home and start again, with a new baby.

HUSBAND: Into the hospital.

WIFE: Says who?

HUSBAND: Says me. It's my baby, too.
[*Pause*]

WIFE: [*Impulsively*] How do you know?

HUSBAND: [*Slams on the brakes; they both jerk forward. He looks at her.*] Say that again.

WIFE: [*Doggedly*] I said how do you know?

HUSBAND: Lookit—

WIFE: You had that thing with Katie McGowan. I had to sit that one out.

HUSBAND: There was no "thing" with Katie McGowan!

WIFE: Everybody does it these days. Why can't I have some fun if I want to? Why can't I have a baby if I want one?

HUSBAND: Who? Name the guy.

WIFE: Why should I?

HUSBAND: [*Suddenly*] Get out of the car!

WIFE: You slept with Katie McGowan!

HUSBAND: Out! Get out!

WIFE: Oh, not *here*, Nick. Honestly.

HUSBAND: [*Starting to shove her*] Will you get out of my car, bitch!

WIFE: All right. [*He shoves her.*] ALL RIGHT! [*Gets out, stands by "door." A little plaintively*] How will I get home, Nick?

HUSBAND: Call your lover! [*Shouts at her as if through a closed car window*] I should have stuck with Ellie!
[*She winces and moves a little away from the car. He watches her, then leans over and pantomimes rolling down the window. He shouts out to her.*]
We were almost there! No kidding! I thought we were almost there! I thought we'd make it! I thought that soon both sets of kids would be out of our hair, and we'd have some time to ourselves, and you and I could . . . [*Softly*] We were almost there.

arch over the telephone wires. So to save them we all have to get together.

[*Pause*]

MAN: Would you like to come in for a beer?

[*Pause*]

WOMAN: Um. No. Thank you just the same.

[*They stand staring at each other a moment. The piano plays a light rhythmic beat. Then they and the other actors arrange chairs into bleachers. They put on suggestions of sporty clothes: a tennis hat, a white sweater, a tennis racquet here and there. They all sit in the bleachers, their heads going back and forth in time to the music as if they were watching a match. Meanwhile, a* REFEREE *has brought out a high stool and a large silver trophy, which he places beside him as he sits on the stool.*]

REFEREE: Game. Mr. and Mrs. Curtis. They lead, five games to three.

[*Applause.* UNCLE JOHN *comes out, leading a small* BOY. *The* BOY *has socks pulled up over his trousers to suggest knickers, and a sailor suit collar.* UNCLE JOHN *wears a blazer and straw hat.*]

UNCLE JOHN: [*To* BOY, *as people make room for them*] Now you sit here with your Aunt Helen and watch your mummy and daddy play tennis, and your Uncle John will be in the bar.

AUNT HELEN: [*In the bleachers*] John! stay right here! You promised.

UNCLE JOHN: [*Reluctantly sitting down, the* BOY *between them*] I hate the goddamn game.

AUNT HELEN: That's because you can't play it.

REFEREE: [*Calling out*] Fifteen-love!

AUNT HELEN: [*To the* BOY] These are the finals, Timmy. If your parents win, they win that great, big, shiny cup over there. . . .

UNCLE JOHN: That battle trophy, Timmy. . . .

AUNT HELEN: And they get their names on it, Timmy. Permanently engraved. . . . My name is on it, actually. I won it once.

UNCLE JOHN: Before she was married, Timmy. As I am being constantly reminded.

AUNT HELEN: Never mind, Timmy. You watch.

REFEREE: [*Calling out*] Thirty-love!

13

AUNT HELEN: See, Timmy? Your parents are beating Snoozer's parents! Your parents have thirty, and Snoozer's parents have love.

UNCLE JOHN: And love means nothing.

[*She glances at him. Another long point. Heads go back and forth. Applause at the end.*]

AUNT HELEN: There. Mummy won that point. And I'll tell you why. When she went to the net, Daddy stayed with her. They stayed parallel all the way. If your Uncle John would stay parallel with me . . .

UNCLE JOHN: We could win that cup.

AUNT HELEN: Exactly.

UNCLE JOHN: We could keep it for one year.

AUNT HELEN: Exactly.

UNCLE JOHN: I could use it to mix martinis. . . .

AUNT HELEN: Oh, God, John.

[*Another point is played.*]

REFEREE: Out. Forty-fifteen.

UNCLE JOHN: That was a bad call.

AUNT HELEN: Oh, John . . . .

UNCLE JOHN: [*To* REFEREE, *standing up*] That was a bad call! The shot was good!

REFEREE: The shot was out, John.

CROWD: [*Ad-libbing*] Sit down, John. . . . Come on, John. . . . This is a tournament, John . . . .

AUNT HELEN: John, for heaven's *sake!* What are you teaching the C-H-I-L-D! [*Turns to* TIMMY] Your uncle John is wrong, Timmy. The referee is always right. Now notice mummy. She is not complaining. She is going right on with the game, even though she may be very unhappy inside. That's what it means to be a good sport. That's what life is all about.

[*Another point is played. Lots of head movement. Then applause; and everyone stands up at the end and applauds politely.*]

REFEREE: Game, set, match. To Mr. and Mrs. Curtis.

[*Gets off his stool, brings the cup over to* AUNT HELEN]

Would he like to give the cup to his parents?

AUNT HELEN: [*Taking it*] Oh, yes. What a wonderful idea, Bill! [*Takes the cup*] Here, Timmy. See? Here's my maiden name, when I won with Mr. Rogers. [*Blows on it; wipes it off with her sleeve*]

14

UNCLE JOHN: What're you doing? Wiping off the blood?

AUNT HELEN: Yes. Well. Now, Timmy, give this cup to your mother. Go on. Walk right out on the court. Shake hands with everyone. Good, firm grip. See? Everyone's good friends at the end of the game.

[*Under her breath, to* UNCLE JOHN *bitterly*]
This is it, John. I swear . . . . [*Then all smiles*]
Go on, Timmy. Do it. Good boy.

[*Everyone claps and beams as the* BOY *reverently walks out, holding up the cup. The piano modulates to machine-like music. The crowd shifts into a group of people standing in line. A* WOMAN *now sits in the* REFEREE *stool. A* MAN, *with great apologies, pushes his way through to the head of the line, as others ad-lib protests. He confronts the* WOMAN.]

MAN: [*breathlessly*] Excuse me. They said out there to give you my Identification Card.

[*Holds it out to her*]

WOMAN: Thank you, sir. I'll just put it into the computer here. [*Pantomimes inserting the card into a machine. The piano plays strange noises; then stops. She removes the card, reads the results.*] It says you're registered as an Independent.

[*Hands the card back, smiling*]

MAN: That's wrong. I'm a Republican.

WOMAN: Well, you seem to come out as an Independent.
[*The crowd in line ad-libs impatience.*]

MAN: Oh, my gosh. Maybe I am. My children made me shift two years ago for a disarmament candidate, and then last year I was in Canada duck hunting, and so I never shifted back.

WOMAN: There you are.

MAN: Well. Then I'm forced to vote as an Independent.

WOMAN: Oh, you can't do that without a pre-registration certificate. Do you have your pre-registration certificate?

MAN: I don't believe I do. No.

WOMAN: Wait a minute. [*Puts his I.D. card back into the machine. More noises from the piano*] You probably have one and don't even know it. [*More sounds. She removes the card.*] Yes! You do have one. They gave you one anyway. [*More so*...*unds from the machine. She reads a dial.*]

But you have ...to bring it up to date.

MAN: Well, how ...do I do that?

WOMAN: You appl...y through the District Registry after the first of the yea...r.

MAN: Good Lord. ...When was this de...?

WOMAN: Oh, it wa...sn't decided, sir. It happened.

MAN: Just happen...ed?

WOMAN: Well, wit...all these you...ple vo...ing no...w, we have to keep tra...ck of who's wh...

MAN: But I want t...o vote *today!*

WOMAN: So do we a...ll, sir!

MAN: But this is a...n important e... have a responsibility.

[*Impatient ad-lib*...*s from the peo...ne*]

WOMAN: Sir, you ar...e keeping oth...e wait...ing.

MAN: Oh. I'm sorry - ...This is quite o...ng. I'm...n not going to let this happe...r...again!

WOMAN: [*As he leave*...*s, calling to hi...time...* stay a Republican. And do...n't go to Canad...

[*The crowd goes* ...*ff as the piano...a hym...n: "Praise God from Whom* ...*All Blessings Fl...* A MINISTER, *indicated by a clerical...collar, comes on...rying a Bible. He nods to the* PIANIST...*, who ends the h...*]

MINISTER: [*To audien...ce*] The Gospel for...ay is taken from Saint Matthew, ch...apter nineteen, b...nin...at the sixteenth verse: "And...behold, one came...to Jesus and said unto him, 'What g...ood thing shall I d...that I may have eternal life?' And...He said unto him, 'Keep...the Commandments.' And t...he young man...ith, 'A...these have I kept from my yout...h. What lack I yet?' And Jesus said, 'Go and sell what...hou hast, and give to the poor, and thou shalt have t...easure in heaven.' But when the young man heard t...at saying, he went away sorrowful, for he had great pos...sessions. Then Jesus said to his disciples: 'It is easier fo...ich man to enter the Kingdom of God!' " [*Closes the B...ble; a pause*] Of course, recent scholarship tells us th...t there actually was a place in Jerusalem called "T...e Eye of the Needle." And presumably camels *could* go...through it. So Jesus simply meant we must be generous, we must be charitable with our money. . . .

[*He smiles; the piano provides a coda as he goes slowly out. The piano plays children's music.*

A BOY, *indicated by his sailor collar, throws a big rubber ball high in the air. A* GRANDFATHER *comes out, wearing a stiff collar, carrying a cane. He stands on a platform, to give the suggestion of height. He clasps his hands behind his back.*]

GRANDFATHER: You there! Andy! I say, Andy! Come here and see your grandfather!

[*The* BOY *keeps his distance, frightened.*]

Come here, boy. Come closer.

[*The* BOY *comes closer.*]

I left the bank early especially to see you, Andy. Your father tells me you have a stammer. Is that true?

[*The* BOY *nods.*]

Your father also tells me you like money. Is *that* true?

[*The* BOY *nods.*]

All right. I will give you five dollars if you will tell me a story. [*Takes a wad of money out of his pocket, removes a five dollar bill from it, and holds up the bill temptingly. Pause*] Begin, lad.

BOY: [*Stammering*] Once . . . once . . . once . . .

GRANDFATHER: Don't stammer.

BOY: Once upon a . . . upon . . . upon a . . .

GRANDFATHER: Don't stammer!

BOY: Once . . . once . . . once . . . once . . .

GRANDFATHER: [*Shouting; shaking him*] I said DON'T STAMMER!

[*Long pause; they eye each other.*]

BOY: [*Very slowly and carefully*] Once . . . upon . . . a . . . time . . . there . . . was . . . a big, mean . . . [*Pause*] . . . ugly GIANT!

GRANDFATHER: Good. That will do. Here's your five dollars. I'm putting it in the bank for you. [*Puts it in another pocket*] When you're twenty-one, it will be worth seventeen dollars and sixty cents. Now run along. Play with your chums. And don't stammer again.

[*The* GRANDFATHER *exits. The* BOY *exits slowly and perplexedly in the opposite way, as the piano plays a bossa nova.* MRS. BIDWELL *comes out, carrying a glass of liquor, holding a sixties telephone.*]

MRS. BIDWELL: [*Coldly*] Good morning. This is Mrs. Bidwell.
. . . Let me speak to Doctor Taubman, please. . . . Yes,
I'd say this was important. Not crucial, but important. . . . Thank you. [*Pause; then very brightly*] Hi! . . .
Listen I'm sorry I missed yesterday's appointment. It
completely slipped my mind. What with one thing and
another. [*Pause*] No, no. Listen. What I'm calling about
is . . . What I want to say is . . . No, Doctor Taubman, I
really do think this psychotherapy business is not for
me. We're simply not getting anywhere, you and I. You
keep wanting me to talk about the most personal things.
I can't. No, I just plain can't. It seems so—so whiney. No,
I mean it. I'll just have to call on the old willpower to
solve the drinking thing. I'll just have to pull myself together, that's all. . . . No, I mean it. . . . No, now send
me a bill, please. I assume I don't have to pay for the session I missed. . . . I do? I do have to pay? Now that
doesn't seem quite sporty, does it? . . . All right, all
right. Just send the bill. Good-bye.

[*Hangs up. A moment. She looks at her glass; then goes
off as the* PIANIST *modulates to hard rock music.* A HUS-
BAND *and* WIFE *bring out two chairs, set them up as the
front seat of a "car." The* HUSBAND *pantomimes driving;
after a moment, the* WIFE *turns off the "radio." The music
stops; a moment of silence as they drive along.*]

WIFE: [*Suddenly*] I want another baby.

HUSBAND: A baby!

WIFE: No, I do. I really do.

HUSBAND: What did you drink tonight?

WIFE: Freeze-dried coffee in styrofoam cups. Oh, I hate,
hate, HATE, these community action meetings! Everyone just sits around and inter*rupts*.

HUSBAND: "Wake up, America! Engage in politics at the
local level!"

WIFE: I didn't see you engaging. You didn't say anything.

HUSBAND: I almost fell asleep.

[*Pause*]

WIFE: I really do want another baby, Nick.

HUSBAND: We've got five babies.

WIFE: They're not babies. And they're not mine.

HUSBAND: Two of them are.

WIFE: They're not. Howard gets *at* them every weekend.

They're all brainwashed. They come back waving the flag at me. Laurie wants to be a drum major*ette* now! [*Looks at him*] And your children: They miss Ellie. They keep asking me where their *real* mother is. [*Pause*] Well, *I* want to be a real mother just once more. Before I . . . dry up completely.

[*A whistle from offstage*]

HUSBAND: [*Pantomiming stopping the car*] Now what?

[*A helmeted* POLICEMAN *comes on, with flashlight and nightstick. He flashes the light in their faces, speaks as if through car window.*]

POLICEMAN: Let's see the I.D. cards.

[*They hand him their I.D. cards. He reads them by flashlight, checks their faces with the photographs, hands them back.*]

Gotta take a detour, folks.

HUSBAND: [*Dryly*] What seems to be the trouble, Officer?

POLICEMAN: They've blown up the water main. You can get through on Elmwood.

HUSBAND: Thanks.

POLICEMAN: And lock your doors. It's a new city ordinance.

HUSBAND: Thanks.

[*They pantomime reaching back and locking the car's rear doors. The* POLICEMAN *goes off. The* HUSBAND *pantomimes making a turn; he shakes his head.*]

Still want a baby?

WIFE: Yes.

HUSBAND: Oh, come on.

WIFE: I'm serious.

HUSBAND: Too late for babies.

WIFE: Not for me it isn't.

HUSBAND: We're too old.

WIFE: I'm not. Maybe you are. But I'm not.

HUSBAND: What's that supposed to mean?

WIFE: I'm pregnant.

[*The* HUSBAND *pantomimes slamming on the brakes.*]

Please don't stop the car, Nick. It's dangerous to stop the car here.

[*He angrily starts up again.*]

HUSBAND: You're not pregnant.

WIFE: I am. I ought to know.

HUSBAND: In you go. The hospital. Tomorrow.

WIFE: Oh, no.

HUSBAND: Oh, yes.

WIFE: I want a baby, Nick. I've got nothing to *do* now. No one needs me. I can't get a job that means anything. And these hysterical meetings—oh, I hate it, Nick. I want to stay home and start again, with a new baby.

HUSBAND: Into the hospital.

WIFE: Says who?

HUSBAND: Says me. It's my baby, too.
  [*Pause*]

WIFE: [*Impulsively*] How do you know?

HUSBAND: [*Slams on the brakes; they both jerk forward. He looks at her.*] Say that again.

WIFE: [*Doggedly*] I said how do you know?

HUSBAND: Lookit—

WIFE: You had that thing with Katie McGowan. I had to sit that one out.

HUSBAND: There was no "thing" with Katie McGowan!

WIFE: Everybody does it these days. Why can't I have some fun if I want to? Why can't I have a baby if I want one?

HUSBAND: Who? Name the guy.

WIFE: Why should I?

HUSBAND: [*Suddenly*] Get out of the car!

WIFE: You slept with Katie McGowan!

HUSBAND: Out! Get out!

WIFE: Oh, not *here*, Nick. Honestly.

HUSBAND: [*Starting to shove her*] Will you get out of my car, bitch!

WIFE: All right. [*He shoves her.*] ALL RIGHT! [*Gets out, stands by "door." A little plaintively*] How will I get home, Nick?

HUSBAND: Call your lover! [*Shouts at her as if through a closed car window*] I should have stuck with Ellie!
  [*She winces and moves a little away from the car. He watches her, then leans over and pantomimes rolling down the window. He shouts out to her.*]
  We were almost there! No kidding! I thought we were almost there! I thought we'd make it! I thought that soon both sets of kids would be out of our hair, and we'd have some time to ourselves, and you and I could . . . [*Softly*] We were almost there.

[*Huddles down as if leaning over the steering wheel. The* WIFE *walks slowly back to the car. She stands by the door.*]

WIFE: I was lying, Nick. It's your baby. [*Opens the door*] I'll go to the hospital. I promise. Tomorrow. [*Gets into the car*] I was just . . . I just wanted to . . . I was just dreaming. [*Tentatively touches his shoulder*] Oh, Nick, I love you. Oh, sweetie, I'm so sorry. Oh, Nick, oh, sweetie, please. . . .

[*Another helmeted* POLICEMAN *comes up with flashlight. He shines it on the* HUSBAND, *who is still slumped forward over the wheel.*]

POLICEMAN: [*To* WIFE] Is he wounded? [*To* HUSBAND] Buddy, are you wounded?

HUSBAND: [*Sitting up; shaking his head*] No. . . . Just tired.

POLICEMAN: Well, move on, folks. Get home. This is a Red Zone.

[*He Goes off. The* HUSBAND *and* WIFE *sit facing forward as the lights dim on them. The piano modulates to "Little Old Lady" as they go offstage. A* CHAUFFEUR, *in a chauffeur's hat, comes out carrying more chairs and a lap robe. He adjusts the "car" so that it becomes a "limousine," as the* GRANDMOTHER *enters, perhaps in a fur piece and turbaned hat. The* CHAUFFEUR *assists the* GRANDMOTHER *into the car and pantomimes tucking a lap robe around her. He takes the driver's seat as a* BOY *and* GIRL *run on. The* GIRL *wears a big bow or sash; the* BOY, *a little boy's hat.*]

CHILDREN: Hi, Granny. . . . Hi, Granny. . . .

[*They squeeze into chairs on either side of her.*]

GRANDMOTHER: Say good morning to Edward, children.

[*Pantomimes handing them a car phone*]

CHILDREN: [*Into car phone*] Good morning, Edward. . . . Good morning, Edward. . . .

[*The* CHAUFFEUR *tips his cap. The* GRANDMOTHER *takes the car phone.*]

GRANDMOTHER: Now, Edward: First we are going to the cemetery to see the swans; then downtown to the corset woman; and then home . . . [*Hangs up the car phone; turns to* CHILDREN] . . . where Annie is fixing us a nice luncheon with prune whip for dessert.

[*The* CHILDREN *groan.*]

Prunes? Nonsense. They're good for your insides. . . .
And after luncheon we're all going to lie down for fifteen
minutes, and then Edward will drive us down to the
Erlanger Theatre where we will see Katharine Cornell,
who comes from Buffalo, and whose father I knew very
well.

BOY: Is this a Packard, Granny?

GRANDMOTHER: It is not. It's a Pierce Arrow, made right
here in Buffalo. Mrs. Warren has a Packard, and her
chauffeur can't get it to park. Now bundle up under the
lap robe, children.

[*They snuggle up next to her.*]

We don't want your mother and father to come back
from Bermuda and find you with the sniffles.

GIRL: What's a corset woman, Granny?

GRANDMOTHER: It's a woman who makes corsets.

BOY: What are corsets?

GRANDMOTHER: They are articles of women's underclothing.

[*The* CHILDREN *giggle.*]

Carleton, look at your fingernails. They're filthy. Your
grandfather just fired a man at the bank for dirty fingernails.

GIRL: Do you like the corset woman?

GRANDMOTHER: I don't like her or dislike her. But I am always polite to her. Because she is one of the people who
help us live. Like Annie. Or Edward.

BOY: [*Looking out the window*] Hey. Look at the nigger.

GRANDMOTHER: That's very rude, Carleton. He is a darky.

GIRL: We play Nigger Baby. Is that all right?

GRANDMOTHER: It is not. The children of darkies are called
pickaninnies.

[*The* CHILDREN *repeat the word. The* BOY *picks his nose.*]

Carleton, don't do that. Whenever you have to touch
your nose, go into the bathroom and lock the door. [*Looks
out*] Ah. Here's the cemetery. And there are the swans.
[*Into the car phone*] Stop the car, Edward.

[*Everyone looks out.*]

Aren't they beautiful? Now there is a play, children, by
a Hungarian, about a princess called The Swan. And the
Hungarian says she must never, never leave her castle.
Because that would be like a swan going on dry land.

Which swans don't do. No. She must stay in the middle of the lake all her life, because that is where swans belong. [*A moment. They all watch. Then she speaks into the car phone.*] All right, Edward. Drive on to the corset woman.

[*The piano plays the theme from "Swan Lake," as the lights dim on them. They go off as a* MAN *addresses the audience hastily and nervously.*]

MAN: May I have the floor, please? . . . I hear that a number of the younger men in this club—George and Snoozer, for example—are indignant over the fact that the David Goldfarbs were blackballed from membership. Well, I want to say right now that I was the one who blackballed them. And Dave Goldfarb is probably one of my closest friends. I'll wager I've done more business with Dave than anybody else in this room. He comes to our house for dinner, and we go to his. Peggy and I and Dave and Ronna all met in Jamaica together last winter. But I blackballed the Goldfarbs because I don't want to see them hurt. I know darned well what could happen in the Grille Room at six-fifteen in the evening when a few of our anti-Stevenson people have finished their second martini. They'd start on Dave. And I won't have that. I don't want Dave and Ronna embarrassed in any way. I'd feel personally responsible for it. Some people say I should resign if that's the way I feel. But I won't. Because I think we're just going through a phase now. And I'll bet that by 1960 my friend Dave Goldfarb can play tennis here, and have a shower, and join us for a drink in the grille, and not have to worry about a damn thing.

[*As he goes off, the piano plays "Good King Wenceslas." A* FATHER, *wearing a hat and overcoat, paces back and forth. After a moment, a helmeted* POLICEMAN *brings in* NANCY, *who wears a poncho and a floppy hat.*]

POLICEMAN: Here she is, sir. Take her away. Merry Christmas.

FATHER: Thank you, Officer.

[*The* POLICEMAN *stands aside, working on a clipboard. The* FATHER *takes* NANCY *downstage.*]

Now tell me what happened.

NANCY: I was picked *up,* Daddy. Just for hitchhiking home from college.

FATHER: We wrote you specifically not to hitchhike.

NANCY: Well, I did.

FATHER: I sent you plane fare.

NANCY: Well, I hitchhiked.

FATHER: We offered you a car in September.

NANCY: I like to hitchhike.

FATHER: It's against the *law,* Nancy!

NANCY: Some law. You hitchhike home for Christmas to save on pollution, and the pigs pick you up.

FATHER: We don't call people names.

NANCY: I do.

[*Pause*]

FATHER: All right. Let's go home. Everyone's waiting. Where's your bag?

NANCY: I don't have a bag.

FATHER: You don't have a—

NANCY: I don't need a bag.

FATHER: [*With a sigh*] Come on, then.

NANCY: [*Standing pat*] What about Mark?

FATHER: Mark?

NANCY: He was with me. And he's still in the cell.

FATHER: Mark who, for God's sake?

NANCY: Oh, Daddy, I don't know his *last* name. I met him on the road outside of Albany.

FATHER: Where's *his* father?

NANCY: He lives in *Detroit,* Daddy. I told Mark he could spend the night with us.

FATHER: Nancy, it's Christmas Eve!

NANCY: Exactly. Do you want to just *leave* him here, rotting in jail, on Christmas *Eve?*

[*Pause*]

FATHER: [*To* POLICEMAN] Officer! I'll stand for the boy that was with her.

POLICEMAN: On recognizance?

FATHER: On recognizance.

POLICEMAN: Suit yourself.

[*Exits, shaking his head*]

NANCY: [*Hugging her* FATHER] Thank you, Daddy.

FATHER: We will take Mark What's-his-name home, and we will introduce him to your mother, and your grandmother, and your Uncle Snoozer, and your brothers, and Alice in the kitchen. We will have cocktails with Mark

What's-his-name. We will eat roast turkey with Mark
What's-his-name. We will sing carols, and hang up our
stockings with Mark What's-his-name, whom you happened to meet hitchhiking on the New York State
Thruway outside of Albany, and it won't be Christmas
at all.

NANCY: Oh, Daddy, honestly. . . .

[*The* POLICEMAN *returns with a grubby, bedraggled-
looking youth.* NANCY *goes to him.*]

Daddy, this is Mark.

MARK: Hiya.

FATHER: Get in the car, both of you.

MARK: [*To* NANCY, *under his breath*] Heavy. . . .

[NANCY *and* MARK *go out. The* POLICEMAN *hands the* FA-
THER *a paper.*]

POLICEMAN: Sign here, sir. Have them back on Monday for
court.

FATHER: [*Signing*] You mean we've got him till Monday?

POLICEMAN: You're too easy on them, sir.

FATHER: [*Sighing*] It's Christmas Eve.

[*Reaches into his pocket, offers a bill to the* POLICEMAN]
Merry Christmas, Officer.

POLICEMAN: [*Coldly; refusing the tip*] Same to you, sir.

[*They exit in opposite directions, as a woman comes out
and begins to make strange snorting noises. Then she begins to slap herself all over. The rest of the cast comes on,
doing the same: grunting, slapping, stretching. The
woman is the* GROUP LEADER *for an Encounter Group and
these are limbering-up exercises. After a brief spell of this,
she claps her hands.*]

GROUP LEADER: All rightee. Everyone sit on the floor,
please.

[*Everyone does, awkwardly. The* GROUP LEADER *lectures
them.*]

Now let me explain exactly what I'm up to. . . . I firmly
believe that one of the reasons our young folk are up in
arms is that we, their parents, can no longer reach them.
If we can learn to communicate without relying on a
dead language, and dead stereotypes of behavior, then
perhaps this country can pull itself together again.
Right?

[*The others ad-lib agreement.*]

Good. That's why we're here. To learn new techniques of relating to each other. So let's begin. Everybody on their feet. Up, up. Let's mill around the room. [*Goes to* PIANIST] Play some of that milling music, please.

[PIANIST *plays the "Moonlight Sonata"; the* GROUP *follows her orders awkwardly.*]

Good. Everyone mill around the room, please. . . . Just mill. . . . Shhh. Shhhh. No talking! . . . Just move through space. . . . That's it. . . . Feel the ground under your feet. . . . Feel the blood pulsing through your veins. . . . Feel your heart beating. . . .

[*Notices a* MAN *standing aside, angrily trying to get the attention of his* WIFE.]

You're not milling, friend. What's your name?

MAN: Wheelright. Steven Wheelwright.

GROUP LEADER: [*Loosening his tie.*] Loosen up, Steve. [*To* GROUP] It's first names here, people, by the by. Including me. I'm Pat.

GROUP: [*Mechanically*] Hi, Pat.

GROUP LEADER: Good. Now mill, Steve.

[STEVE *mills, reluctantly.*]

Good, Steve boy. You're milling now. . . . All right, we'll have pairing: Everyone select a partner—random, random, no husbands and wives, whoever's nearest—good— now: All pairs kneel down on the floor and face each other. . . . I said, NO TALKING. . . . Stevie, get away from your wife. . . . [*To* WIFE] What's your name?

WIFE: Marge.

GROUP LEADER: Well, Marge, you go pair off with . . . Who are you?

ANOTHER MAN: Gordon.

GROUP LEADER: Go with Gordon. And you, Steve. You kneel opposite me.

[*All pairs kneel, facing each other.*]

Now. Shhh, shhh. Everyone look into his or her partner's eyes, and just try to say something to each other without words.

[*A long moment. People stare. Then a* WOMAN *begins to giggle.*]

Please, people . . .

WOMAN WHO GIGGLED: I'm sorry. Bert was being silly.

BERT: What do you mean?

WOMAN: You were wiggling your nose.

BERT: I was not wiggling my nose.

WOMAN: Well, you were doing peculiar things with your face.

BERT: I was not doing peculiar . . .

GROUP LEADER: Try again, please. I know it's hard. But it's worth it.

[*They all kneel again. A longer moment. Then—*]

ANOTHER MAN: That's no fair, Marge.

MARGE: [*Who is opposite him*] What? What? What's no fair?

OTHER MAN: [*To* GROUP LEADER] She was looking down.

MARGE: Well, I felt em*barr*assed.

[*Everyone ad-libs agreement.*]

A WOMAN: Perhaps if we all had a couple of good stiff drinks.

[*The* GROUP *ad-libs agreement.*]

GROUP LEADER: No alcohol! Please! That never works! Everyone on their feet. . . . Up, up.

[GROUP *gets up.*]

Form a circle. . . .

[*They do.*]

You . . . Marge . . . in the center.

MARGE: Why me?

GROUP LEADER: Because you're the embarrassed one, Marge, and we've got to get over that hurdle. . . . Everyone in a circle? . . . Marge, please. . . . In the center. . . . Good. . . . Now. Everyone do to Marge what he or she feels like doing.

[*Nervous reaction from* GROUP.]

A MAN: [*Laughing*] Within reason.

GROUP LEADER: No, Chuck. *Not* within reason. We are trying to get *around* reason. Everyone do to Marge what he or she feels like doing. Clockwise. You start, Steve. After all, she's your wife.

[STEVE *steps into the circle, looks angrily at* MARGE *for bringing him here, and then steps back.*]

Next.

[*A* WOMAN *steps into the circle. She can't decide what to do. Finally, she tickles* MARGE. MARGE *jumps, shrieks. Group laughs.* LEADER *gestures for the next. A* MAN *steps into the circle, looks at* MARGE, *reaches out for her hair. She cowers back.*]

27

A. R. GURNEY, JR.

STEVE: Hey!

GROUP LEADER: Relax, Steve. Relax, Marge.

[MARGE *braces herself. The* MAN *takes the hairpins out of* MARGE's *hair; her hair falls loose. Group goes "Ahhhhh."* *She quickly starts to pin it up.*]

Leave it, Marge.

[MARGE *leaves it. A* WOMAN *steps in and gives* MARGE *a sweet little hug. Group smiles "ohhhhh."*]

Exactly! Next.

[*A* MAN *steps in and gives* MARGE *a more sexual hug.* STEVE *controls himself.*]

Good, Marge. Good, Steve.

[ANOTHER MAN *steps in and kisses* MARGE's *neck. The atmosphere gets tense. Now it is the* LEADER's *turn. She steps into the circle, faces* MARGE. *Then she carefully touches* MARGE's *face. Then her hands move down over* MARGE's *breasts. A long moment.* STEVE *then moves in angrily and grabs the* LEADER's *rear. She wheels around and slaps him frantically, and then gasps as she realizes that she has broken the rules. General consternation and confusion as the piano starts playing "Brahms' Lullaby." The* GROUP *modulates into a party, saying good night to two children, a* BOY *and a* GIRL, *indicated by the fact they wear bathrobes or carry blankets or teddy bears or a doll. The adults are ushered off by the* MOTHER, *with lots of ad-libs about the children. The* MOTHER *then turns back to the children, who remain on a platform as if it were a staircase.*]

MOTHER: Now, kiddie cars, as a special treat, you can listen to "I Love a Mystery," and then lights out. That's an ultimatum. [*She hugs them.*] Good night, lovebugs.

GIRL: You look so beautiful, Mummy.

BOY: And you smell so sweet.

MOTHER: [*Releasing them*] Off you go. Upstairs.

[*They separate. The children get on the platform. The* MOTHER *starts toward the party, then turns again to the children.*

Oh, children!

[*They look at her. A moment*]

I just want to say . . . I just think you should know . . . that you both behaved beautifully just now. You went up to people, and shook hands, and called them by *name,*

28

and you spoke right up when you were spoken to. [*Glances off toward the party*] They're all talking about you now. And . . . and, well, daddy and I are just very, very proud, that's all. Now good night.

[*Whooshes off. The* BOY *and* GIRL *wait till she's gone, and then quickly sit on the stairs.*]

BOY: Didn't mummy smell sweet?

GIRL: [*Listening to the offstage talk*] Sssshhh. . . . They're saying I'm going to be beautiful. Mr. Irwin is saying I've got a beautiful nose. I'm going to be as beautiful as mummy. [*More listening*]

BOY: But I'm the cutest. Hear that? And I'm going to be a great hockey player. [*Yawns*] Now let's hear "I Love a Mystery."

GIRL: [*Still listening*] Wait! Hey, I'm getting a doll house, from Schwartz, for Christmas. Oh, I knew it!

BOY: That's because you heard it at the last party.

GIRL: [*Standing up; stretching*] I used to hate being polite to them. I used to feel so shy and awful. But now I think it's worth it.

BOY: [*As they go off*] Gosh, didn't mummy smell sweet!

GIRL: And I'm going to be just like her!

[*They exit as the piano plays a sturdy World War II marching song. A* FATHER *comes out carrying one old wooden ski. He props it on a chair and begins to wax it meticulously. A* SON *watches his* FATHER. *The music subsides.*]

SON: Please, Dad. . . .

FATHER: [*Patiently waxing*] Did you, or did you not, promise Miss Watson you would walk her cocker spaniel this afternoon?

SON: But I didn't know there'd be snow.

FATHER: That makes absolutely no difference. You made a promise.

SON: But I want to go skiing with you.

FATHER: I don't give a tinker's damn what you want or what you don't want. When we make a promise in this family, we keep it. That's the trouble with Hitler. He doesn't keep his promises.

SON: I can get Snoozer to walk the dog.

FATHER: [*Always waxing*] I don't believe Snoozer was part of the understanding with Miss Watson. I don't believe

Miss Watson knows Snoozer. I don't believe Miss Watson's dog knows Snoozer.

SON: The dog does know Snoozer.

FATHER: Don't get fresh.

SON: You made me get these jobs with Miss Watson.

FATHER: That's right.

SON: To pay for my new ski boots.

FATHER: That's right. To learn what money means.

SON: And now there's skiing, I can't even go. I can't even use them.

FATHER: That's right. Not this weekend anyway.

SON: [*Quietly; walking away*] Shit.

FATHER: [*Stopping waxing; looking up*] What did you say?

SON: I didn't say—

FATHER: [*Walking directly to him*] WHAT DID YOU SAY?

SON: [*Defiantly*] I said "shit."

FATHER: [*Gives him a tremendous cuff, sending him reeling*] I NEVER want to hear that word again! Ever! Your mother is right in the next ROOM! I am thoroughly disGUSTed with you!

[*The* SON *stands with his back to the audience, obviously crying. The* FATHER *looks at him and then returns to waxing his skis.*]

Now. There is nothing—nothing in the world—more valuable to me than my family. I mean that. Hitler could attack us tomorrow and I wouldn't care—just as long as mummy and you and Tinkie and Bobby were safe. These are precious years for all of us. Time moves so fast. In two years you'll be away at school. And so there is nothing I'd like more than to ski with all my family. The singing in the car, the fresh air, the exercise, the listening to The Shadow and Jack Benny on the way home—Oh, there is nothing I like more in this world. [*Stops waxing, turns to him*] And so when my son, my eldest son, isn't there with us, then half the fun goes out of the day. [*Goes to* SON] But you made a deal. And you've got to stick to it. If we don't stand by our word, then the world falls apart and people start using foul language to get what they want. [*Looks at him*] OK?

[*The* SON *nods.*]

Good. Now go help your sister with the ski-rack.

[*They exit either way as a* WOMAN *named* MISSY *comes out*

*to address the audience. She carries note cards, which
she refers to continually.*]

MISSY: [*Nervously*] Um. I want to make three quick points
about this whole business of the fence. [*Glances at first
card*] Point one. Appearance. I don't like the looks of it. I
know we've been having a lot of fires and robberies and
terrorism, but I still don't like putting one of those ugly
chain fences around the entire neighborhood. Even in
the brochure, it looks terribly unattractive. That awful
barbed wire. Those ghastly gates. I don't care how much
planting or landscaping we do, we are still going to look
like a concentration camp. And that's point one. [*Next
card*] Point two. Inconvenient. The whole thing is going
to be terribly inconvenient. I hate the idea of having to
get out of the car, to put my I.D. card into those gates
just so they'll open and I can get home. And what about
deliveries? How do the cleaners, and the milkman, and
the eggman get in? The brochure simply doesn't say.
[*Next card*] Point three, and then I'll sit down. What
about dogs? This fence is electrified, remember. We can
train our children to stay away from it, but what about
dogs? Or do we have to tie them up? I refuse to do that,
frankly. You know our Rosie, our old Lab. It would kill
her to be tied up. I won't do it. And yet if Rosie should
run up against this fence, she could be electrocuted. So
what I suggest we do is, I suggest we call our friends in
Shaker Heights, and Concord, and Palo Alto, and all the
other places which have put in these fences, and we find
out a few more details. I mean, I'm just not sure a fence
is the best solution.

[*The lights shift as* TED, *her* HUSBAND, *joins her and
hands her a brandy snifter; he has another for himself.
We are now at another party, the sounds of which we hear
offstage. Their host,* HOWARD, *guides them downstage.*]

HOWARD: Now come into the library, you two, where we can
talk seriously for two minutes.

MISSY: [*Gesturing offstage*] What about your other guests,
Howard?

HOWARD: They'll survive. . . . Now, Ted, I think you're
sound asleep! And, Missy, so are you! And as an old
friend, I'm going to try to wake you up!

TED: [*Patiently*] Why am I asleep, Howard?

HOWARD: Because you are sitting on all those old-fashioned stocks your father left you! He's *sit*ting on them, Missy, and he's sitting on *yours*. He hasn't done a goddamn thing to his portfolio in twenty years, and I'm giving him a chance to bring things up to date!

MISSY: What is it? Some new company?

HOWARD: It is not a new company. It is a wholly owned subsidiary of one of the largest companies in this country. And the stock is going to go sky-high. And I'm giving him a chance to get in on the ground floor, and he won't touch it.

TED: Yeah . . . well . . .

MISSY: What do they make?

TED: Guns.

HOWARD: No, Teddy. Not guns. Machine guns. They've invented a machine gun—pocket-*size!*—a goddamn *toy*, for Chrissake—which can be carried by any foot soldier and which shoots eight hundred rounds a minute! The government has already signed the contract. And Ted's walking away from it.

TED: [*Shrugs*] I'll stay with what I've got.

MISSY: Yes. I mean, machine guns, Howard. . . .

HOWARD: That's where it's at, my love. Do you like this house? Do you like that painting? Do you like this new rug? Did you like that dinner, and that wine, and that brandy you're drinking right now? Well, I like it. And I'm going to hold onto it. So wake up, my friends. Invest in the future, or you'll be left out in the cold! [*Walks out, calling offstage*] Now who out here wants a highball? [*He exits. Pause.* TED *and* MISSY *look at each other.*]

MISSY: Machine guns. How awful.

TED: I know.

MISSY: I should have argued with him. The children would have argued it out.

TED: I know.

MISSY: We should have said the whole thing is absolutely wrong, wrong, wrong.

TED: He's my friend. I'm drinking his liquor. He's my host. [*Suddenly*] Oh, WHY are we always so goddamn *polite?* [*Impulsively and deliberately spills his brandy on the floor. Then he looks at her.*]

MISSY: Oh, my gosh . . . Sweetie!

[*She frantically begins mopping it up with his handkerchief as the* PIANIST *begins to play elaborate renditions of Richard Strauss. The* DANCING MASTER *comes out, in tails and with a black walking stick, and arranges three chairs, neatly in a row. Then he interrupts the* PIANIST.]

DANCING MASTER: Well, Mr. Cromeier: And how do you like playing for a dancing school in Buffalo? It's not Vienna, is it? Oh, no: It's not Vienna. But at least we're in a free country.

[*Taps his stick. The* PIANIST *plays the Grand March from* Aida. *Separate lines of* BOYS *and* GIRLS *march out from either side of the stage, all doggedly trying to stay in step and in line with each other. The* GIRLS *wear big bows and sashes; the* BOYS, *stiff collars and white gloves. When the music stops, the* GIRLS *sit demurely in the chairs, the* BOYS *standing rigidly facing them across the stage. The* DANCING MASTER *taps his stick. The* DANCING MASTER *consults with the* PIANIST. *Two* BOYS *whisper.*]

FIRST BOY: Let's sneak out.

SECOND BOY: How?

FIRST BOY: I'll go to the john. You follow.

SECOND BOY: Then where will we go?

FIRST BOY: Downtown. To see Hedy Lamarr. In *Ecstasy.* You can see her boobs!

SECOND BOY: Hey, yes! Say when.

DANCING MASTER: [*German accent*] The young gentlemen will ask the young ladies to dance.

[*All boys dash across the stage and slide to a stop in front of the prettiest* GIRL.]

Go back!

[*The* BOYS *go back to their chairs.*]

The young *gentle*men will ask the young *ladies* to dance.

[*The* BOYS *walk militarily across the stage; each stands in front of a* GIRL.]

Bow!

[*The* BOYS *bow, one hand behind their backs.*]

Young ladies rise and curtsey. [*The* GIRLS *do, in rigid order.*]

Handkerchiefs out.

[*The* BOYS *take clean white handkerchiefs out of their pockets.*]

Music, Mr. Cromeier, if you please.

33

[*The* PIANIST *begins to play "I'm Always Chasing Rainbows" slowly and methodically. The* BOYS *put their handkerchiefs behind the* GIRLS' *waists. Couples dance stiffly. The* DANCING MASTER *taps with his cane.*]

One and two and one and two and . . . al-ways small steps . . . care—ful— . . . care—ful— . . .

[*A* COUPLE *dances downstage.*]

BOY: I'm the boy. I'm supposed to lead.

GIRL: Then *lead*, please.

BOY: You've got Beeeee-ooooooooooow.

GIRL: Just *lead*, please.

[*He leads her stiffly away.*]

DANCING MASTER: [*Calling out*] Step and two and turn and two and . . .

[*Another* COUPLE *dances downstage.*]

BOY: Are you a Jewess?

GIRL: No.

[*They turn.*]

BOY: My mother says you are.

GIRL: Well, I *was*. We were. But we gave it up. We changed our name and everything.

BOY: Hey. Wow.

GIRL: I know it.

[*They turn.* FIRST BOY *dances downstage with his* PARTNER.]

FIRST BOY: I'm ducking out. Say I'm in the john.

GIRL: I will not.

FIRST BOY: Come on. I'll give you a dollar.

GIRL: Oh, no.

FIRST BOY: Come on. . . .

[*Starts furtively offstage*]

GIRL: [*Calling out*] Mr. Van Dam! Mr. Van Dam!

[DANCING MASTER *notices her.*] I don't have a partner!

[DANCING MASTER *pounds the floor rapidly with his cane. The music stops. Everyone stops dancing.* FIRST BOY *is heading offstage by now.*]

DANCING MASTER: [*Calling out*] Mr. Wickwire!

[FIRST BOY *slides to a stop.*]

Approach me!

[FIRST BOY *hesitates; everyone giggles.*]

APPROACH ME!

[FIRST BOY *walks toward him.*]

BOW TO ME!

[FIRST BOY *does.*]

LOWER!

[FIRST BOY *does.* DANCING MASTER *walks slowly around the* BOY, *raising his cane as if to strike him. Then, facing the* BOY, *he says very quietly.*]

Dance with me.

[THE BOY *looks up slowly, with horror.*]

I said, dance with me. [*To* PIANIST] A waltz, please, Mr. Cromeier.

[*Holds out his arms to the* BOY.]

Now dance with me.

[*The music begins; the* BOY *takes out his handkerchief again. They dance, as everyone watches and giggles.*]

I am a lovely young lady. . . . Lead me carefully. . . . I am glass. . . . Turn, turn. . . . I am fine Meissen china. . . . I am a fairy princess. . . .

[*Then he pushes the* BOY *away.*]

Now go dance properly with Miss Jones. [*To others*] Dance, everyone! Dance!

[*Everyone does.* FIRST BOY *dances downstage with* MISS JONES.]

FIRST BOY: [*Between his teeth*] OK for you.

MISS JONES: [*frightened*] What do you mean?

FIRST BOY: I said OK for you, pal.

MISS JONES: What are you going to do?

FIRST BOY: Next week I'm going to get my boys together. Freddy, Snoozer, the whole bunch. And when you're walking to your music lesson, we're going to grab you. And take you behind Miss Watson's garage. And strip you. All the way. And then we're going to piss all over you.

[*She looks at him in terror as they dance away.*]

DANCING MASTER: [*Calling out*] Dance, everybody! Dance! The night is young, and you are beautiful! Dance! Dance! Dance!

[*Everyone dances offstage.*]

END OF ACT ONE

ACT II

The piano plays rock music. The lights come up on a WOMAN *in a ski parka, sidestepping as if she were in line for a chair lift, which is indicated by two chairs to one side. She pantomimes the encumbrances of boots, skis and poles. A* MAN *"slides" onto the stage.*

MAN: Are you a single?

WOMAN: Am I ever.

[*The* MAN *engineers his way alongside her.*]

MAN: Then we'll ride up together.

WOMAN: Fine.

[*They move slowly along, side by side, as if in a ski-tow line.*]

Isn't the skiing marvelous?

MAN: Superb. It's worth it, isn't it?

WOMAN: Exactly.

MAN: I drove all the way up from Buffalo.

WOMAN: Then you had to get one of those travel permits—to cross a state line.

MAN: Oh, sure.

WOMAN: So did I. What a goddamn bore! I had to swear—even my *nine*-year-old had to swear—that we were not going to Stowe to incite riot!

[*Both laugh.*]

MAN: Ah. You've got a family here.

WOMAN: Just the children. I'm divorced. And you?

36

MAN: I'm alone. My children are away at school. My wife's had a breakdown.

WOMAN: Oh, dear. Who wouldn't, these days.

[*They reach the lift and side by side prepare for the ride up. They settle back into the chairs, adjusting their skis and poles.*]

MAN: Where're you from?

WOMAN: Connecticut . . . Greenwich.

MAN: Do you know Patty and George Tremaine?

WOMAN: I knew Patty quite well. She's dead, you know. [*Pause*] She got caught in the September Insurrection. She was shot. [*Pause*] They were rocking her car or something, and she got out, and one thing led to another. You know.

MAN: [*Quietly*] Oh, wow.

WOMAN: Thank heavens for this. I took the children out of school for it. It gives them some perspective.

MAN: My kids say I'm crazy to spend all my time and money just to slide down a hill. They say I'm acting out the death wish of the upper middle class.

[*Both laugh.*]

WOMAN: Here's the top.

[*They adjust their skis and poles and go through the contortions of getting off and getting ready to go down the hill.*]

You tell your children, for me, that the trouble with their generation is they don't know how to have fun.

MAN: That's right. If we're doomed, let's at least do a few graceful turns on the way down.

WOMAN: [*Laughing*] Exactly! And meet in the bar afterwards?

MAN: Why not?

[*They pantomime pushing off in different directions down the hill. The* PIANIST *plays "'Come, Ye Thankful People, Come." A* FATHER *and* MOTHER *place the two chairs opposite each other, to indicate a long table.*]

FATHER: [*Pantomiming sharpening a carving knife*] I would hope—at least on Thanksgiving—that someone around here is polite enough to push in his mother's chair.

MOTHER: [*Sits down, slides her chair in. Over her shoulder, as if to a child*] Thank you, Billy.

FATHER: [*Pantomiming carving a turkey*] All right now. I

want everyone to listen carefully, and to remember what I say.

MOTHER: I'll have the wing, Ralph.

FATHER: [*Carving*] Our nation is at war. . . . Pass that down to your mother, Tootsie. . . . We are fighting a death struggle against the Germans and Japanese. You children have no idea what war is, but you're going to learn. And very quickly.

MOTHER: Give Tootsie some dressing, Ralph.

FATHER: [*Carving*] To begin with: I won't be around much. I'm going into the Army, and I doubt if I'll be able to get up from Washington more than once or twice a month. Which means that *someone*, without being told, has got to start pushing in his mother's chair!

MOTHER: [*Pantomiming serving vegetables*] Who does *not* want gravy on their potatoes?

FATHER: And we are going to have no more maids. For the duration. Agnes will still come in to clean, but that's *it.* Which means everyone makes his own bed and helps with the dishes.

MOTHER: Billy likes the drumstick, Ralph.

FATHER: As far as food goes, only one butterball per person. Did you hear that, Tootsie? If you put more butter on your potato, then you can't have any more for your roll. And no more finger bowls. Finger bowls are out.

MOTHER: Begin, children. While it's hot.

FATHER: [*Sitting down*] The boys will collect tin cans, and the girls will knot Bundles for Bri— . . . [*Stops, stands up*] Who told you to pick up that drumstick, Billy?

MOTHER: It's all right, Ralph.

FATHER: It is not all right. Put it down, Billy. I said, put it DOWN! Is this what war does to us? Are we reduced to gnawing at bones like jackals?

MOTHER: Oh, Ralph . . .

FATHER: We use knives and forks around here!

MOTHER: But he'll waste half the meat!

FATHER: We use knives, we use forks!

[*Pause*]

MOTHER: Use your knife and fork, Billy.

FATHER: [*Sitting down*] More rules. [*Eats lustily*] We're going to do very little driving. Everyone takes the bus.

Even your mother. When we go skiing, we'll take the train. Let no one forget; this is *war!*

MOTHER: Sally, don't feed the dog at the table.

[*Fade-out on the dinner table. The piano plays "There's No Place Like Home" in a rock style. A* YOUNG MAN *is getting into a barber's chair.* CHARLIE, *the barber, in a white jacket, is arranging a sheet around him and pumping the chair back. They eye each other for a long moment in the mirror in front of them.*]

YOUNG MAN: [*Settling back*] Remember me, Charlie?

CHARLIE: Sammy? Sam Curtis?

YOUNG MAN: Good for you, Charlie.

CHARLIE: I gave you your first haircut. I still cut your father's hair. I just cut your grandfather's hair. What there is left. Oh, I know all the Curtises. [*Begins to pantomime cutting*] You're the one who's a painter.

YOUNG MAN: Right, Charlie! Good for you. . . . Take some off the top, Charlie.

CHARLIE: Sure. You're the painter. You won a painting prize at Nichols School. You came in here and showed me your painting prize.

YOUNG MAN: [*Beaming*] God, Charlie. You remember everything.

CHARLIE: Sure. I keep in touch. Your father tells me. Let's see. You went away to school, and then Princeton, and then the Army, and now you're in New York, being a painter. Right?

YOUNG MAN: Well, I'm back now, Charlie.

CHARLIE: Just to visit, huh?

YOUNG MAN: No, no. I'm back. In Buffalo.

CHARLIE: You going to paint here, huh?

YOUNG MAN: Well, no. I'm going to be a stockbroker, actually, Charlie.

CHARLIE: You mean, work for your father?

YOUNG MAN: Right, Charlie. [*Pause*] Better take a little more off the back, Charlie.

CHARLIE: I thought you was going to be our painter.

YOUNG MAN: Yeah, well, you know New York, Charlie. Nobody . . . cares.

CHARLIE: You used to come in here, and tell me you were going to be—

YOUNG MAN: Hey, Charlie. How about one of those shaves?

Like the ones you give my father. With hot towels and all the trimmings. How about it? Oh, boy. I just want to relax.

[*Leans back, luxuriously.* CHARLIE *puts a towel around his face.*]

CHARLIE: I thought you was going to be my painter.

YOUNG MAN: [*Closing his eyes*] Mmmmmm. That feels good. I might just . . . catch . . . forty winks . . . Charlie.

CHARLIE: [*Sadly; massaging his face; looking at him directly for the first time.*] My painter. . . .

[*The piano plays a few bars of party music. Female giggles from offstage. A* WOMAN *comes on, carrying a telephone and a drink, to get away from the noise, gesturing that they be quiet.*]

WOMAN: [*On telephone*] Buzzy? It's your mother! . . . Listen, sweetie, I'm sorry to bother you at college, but Mrs. Rothenberg and Mrs. Kreb are here, and daddy's out of town, and we've decided to try it, and we want to know where it is. . . . It, Buzzy. It! I'm not going to mention it over the phone. . . .

[MRS. ROTHENBERG *and* MRS. KREB *come on at this point and hover around the phone.*]

No, we've decided to find out what it's like, before we continue to criticize, so where is it? . . . It is not in your top drawer. We looked in your top drawer—Oh, you mean *that*. . . . *That*, Buzzy? That little bag? . . . All right, all right, now what do we do? Hold it, hold it. . . .

[*Frantic fumblings and gestures for pencil, paper. Problems of who is to hold whose drink*]

Do we have to strain it, or what? [*Writes things down*] All right. . . . Yes. We found the water pipe.

[*Someone produces it.*]

Can we just use regular water? . . . I see. And do you recommend any music? Let it what? Let it *bleed?*

[*Someone knows it.*]

All right. Let it bleed. . . . All right, Buzzy. Yes, I'll pay you. I'll *pay* you, Buzzy. I'll send you a check. . . . Goodbye, sweetie. Work hard. And don't you dare tell daddy!

[*Hangs up; they all go off.*]

It *was* in the top drawer. It was that ratty old bag of fish food.

[*They exit. The piano plays "Now the Day Is Over." A*

RECTOR, *in a purple stole, marches slowly in, followed by* THREE CHOIRBOYS *in a line, wearing surplices and carrying hymnals. All sing.*]

ALL:

Now the day is over,
    Night is drawing nigh.
Shadows of the evening
    Steal across the sky. . . . Amen.

RECTOR: [*Comes forward.*] Let us pray silently for Saint Luke's School, remembering to thank God for our nation's victory in war and asking for His guidance in peace.

FIRST CHOIRBOY: [*Praying quietly*] Oh, God: thanks for beating the Germans and Japs. . . . And please help us beat the shit out of Andover tomorrow.

SECOND CHOIRBOY: Oh, God: Please let me get over eighty in the Latin test so I can get out of study hall, and see the Saturday night movie. And please make it a good movie. For once.

THIRD CHOIRBOY: Please let there be a letter from Snoozer's sister in my mailbox tomorrow, saying she'll come to the midwinter dance. And please, if she comes, get her to put out.

FIRST CHOIRBOY: And please, God, make me a better guy, and keep me from picking on Fat-Pig Hathaway at breakfast. . . .

SECOND CHOIRBOY: And please don't let there be a nuclear war with the Russians. . . .

THIRD CHOIRBOY: And please, please, please, God, get rid of my hard-on before I have to stand up and march out.
[*The* PIANIST *strikes up "Oh, God, Our Help in Ages Past." The* RECTOR *leads them out, all singing, the* THIRD CHOIRBOY *protecting himself with his book.*]

ALL:

Oh, God our help in ages past,
    Our hope for years to come,
Our shelter from the stormy blast,
    And our eternal home. . . .

[*A very distinguished, very* OLD LADY *is escorted to the edge of the stage by her* GRANDDAUGHTER.]

OLD LADY: [*Addressing the audience*] On behalf of the Lockwood family, I wish to make the following announcement to the newspapers. I am hereby donating my house and grounds in East Aurora to be a permanently endowed summer camp for Negro children from the Eighth Detention Area. These children will now have the opportunity to swim in the pool, play in the gardens, learn tennis and croquet, and do all the things my children and grandchildren once did. It is my firm belief that if colored children can spend their summers in the country, they will cease throwing fire bombs from their cars, and detention areas will no longer be necessary.

[*Her* GRANDDAUGHTER *escorts her out. The* PIANIST *plays cocktail-y music as a* WAITER *carries in a small table and two chairs. A* HEADWAITER *leads on a* MOTHER *and* DAUGHTER. *They sit down at the table. There is the usual business of taking off gloves, powdering of noses, and so forth.*]

DAUGHTER: Oh, mummy! Thank you, thank you, thank you for the tennis dress, and the bathing suit, and the Bermuda shorts. They're just yummy, Mummy.

MOTHER: Well, they *fit.* Which is why we come to New York. [*To the* WAITER.] We'll have Eggs Benedict, green salad, fresh strawberries and coffee. And two Daiquiris. Now.

WAITER: Is the young lady eighteen?

MOTHER: Yes, she is, thank you.

[*The* WAITER *goes offstage.*]

DAUGHTER: Oh, Mummy, you lied.

MOTHER: I did not lie, Pookins. And I don't like that expression. I *fibbed.* And I fibbed for a very good reason. [*Leans forward*] You have got to learn to drink.

DAUGHTER: I don't really like it.

MOTHER: That's not the point. You've got to *learn* to like it. The way you learned to like riding. The way you learned to like Westover. Most of life is learning to like things. [WAITER *brings drinks.*]

Now drink it slowly.

[DAUGHTER *sips.*] For heaven's sake, don't stick your pinkie out. You look like a dental hygienist.

[DAUGHTER *sips again.*]

Good. Now. If you get tipsy, make the most of it. Tell people you're tipsy. And then you can say and do almost

anything you want. [MOTHER *takes out cigarette.*] And
when you smoke—

DAUGHTER: I don't like smoking, Mother.

MOTHER: Good for you. It's a vile habit. It's messy, and unhealthy, and expensive. And I love it.

[*The* WAITER *lights her cigarette.*]

And so will you. And now, sweetie pie, you've got to
make a decision, and you've got to make it in the next
hour, because *Kiss Me, Kate* starts promptly at two.

DAUGHTER: What decision?

MOTHER: Probably *the* most crucial decision of your entire
life. [*Leans forward*] I talked to your father long distance, and for the first time since the divorce, we *agreed*
on something. We agreed to leave the decision up to you.

DAUGHTER: *What* decision, Mummy?

MOTHER: About next *year,* Pookins. After you graduate
from that nunnery. You've got to decide whether you
want to go to college, or have a coming-out party. Your
father will pay for one or the other, but not both.

[*Pause*]

DAUGHTER: Oh, I'll take college then.

[*Long pause*]

MOTHER: I see.

DAUGHTER: I mean, what's the point of coming out anyway?
I already know everybody. I'm already out.

MOTHER: Now don't get smart, Barbara. That's just smarty-
pants stuff.

DAUGHTER: Well, then *explain* it to me, Mother.

[*Pause*]

MOTHER: All your friends are coming out. All. And if you
don't, you'll miss all the parties over Christmas and in
June.

DAUGHTER: Oh, I'll be invited.

MOTHER: But you can't GO! Unless you give a party. It's
just not fair. And I will not try to squeeze you onto the
list with a cheap little tea, either. You will have a good
party of your own, with Lester Lanin or Harry
Marchard, or you will not go to anyone else's. And that's
final.

[*Pause*]

DAUGHTER: I'll go skiing over Christmas then.

MOTHER: With whom?

43

DAUGHTER: I don't know. I want to go to college, Mummy.
[*Pause*]

MOTHER: Why?

DAUGHTER: Why?

MOTHER: *Why?* I said, why?

DAUGHTER: I want to . . . further my education. I want to
have something to *do*.

MOTHER: Oh, Barbara, you sound like some immigrant. [*To*
WAITER] Martini on the rocks, please. [*To* DAUGHTER] *I*
didn't go to college.

DAUGHTER: I know that, Mother.

MOTHER: I came *out.* And so did all my friends.

DAUGHTER: I know that, Mother.

MOTHER: None of us went to college. We never even considered it. We were having too much fun.

DAUGHTER: I know, Mother.

MOTHER: And I've done all right in the world. Without college.

DAUGHTER: Yes, Mother.

MOTHER: Or do you think I haven't? Do you think I'm stupid?

DAUGHTER: No, Mother.

MOTHER: I *read* more than you do.

DAUGHTER: I know.

MOTHER: I read all the time. I don't go to the movies twice a
week like some people I know. I like to think I can carry
on a decent conversation. I don't keep saying uh-huh and
uh-uh like some people I know around here.

DAUGHTER: Oh, come on, Mummy.

MOTHER: Who's going to college from Westover, answer me
that.

DAUGHTER: Lots of people.

MOTHER: Who? Who? Name names. *That I know.*

DAUGHTER: Betsy Wettlauffer wants to go to Wellesley.

MOTHER: She's a babe.

DAUGHTER: She's not a—

MOTHER: She's a *babe,* Pookins. She's a pew. Look at her
hair sometime.
[*Pause*]

DAUGHTER: I still want to go to college.
[*Pause*]

MOTHER: I'll tell you what: We'll give a smallish party.

Local orchestra. Close the bar at one. And you can go to
Bennett or Briarcliffe for two years.

DAUGHTER: They're not—

MOTHER: They're very good. Wendy Pratt is going to one of
them.

DAUGHTER: I want to go to—

MOTHER: No, no. Bennett. And a small coming-out party.
And then listen—oh, here's the solution. We'll pass the
hat and you can go to Europe for a year. You can go to
Florence. *There's* your education, Pookins. And you'll
learn more in the next three years, I promise, than you'll
ever learn with Betsy Wettlauffer at Wellesley. Right?
Right.

[WAITER *brings in plates.*]

Good. Here's food. [WAITER *sets plates down.*]

Now. One other thing.

[*Waits until the* WAITER *goes; then speaks softly*]

Have you got a diaphragm?

DAUGHTER: A what?

MOTHER: A diaphragm. Now you're coming out, you should
be fitted for a—

DAUGHTER: Oh, *M*other!

MOTHER: Just asking. Skip it. Now eat up or we'll be late
for *Kiss Me, Kate.*

[*The* WAITERS *take off the table, as a* FATHER *and* SON *take
the two chairs downstage, placing them so as to indicate a
sailboat, and then executing a sailing maneuver. The piano plays a wry arrangement of "Sailing, Sailing." The*
FATHER *pantomimes working the tiller, adjusting the
mainsheet. The* SON *looks off dreamily.*]

FATHER: [*After a moment*] This old boat is always at her
best running with the wind. [*Pause*] Look under your
seat. I brought a thermos of gin-and-tonics.

SON: No, thanks, Dad.

FATHER: Oh, come on. You always used to love gin-and-
tonic. Even when you were tiny, you always wanted a
taste of my gin-and-tonic.

SON: [*With a shrug*] All right.

[*Pantomimes taking a sip, then hands it to his* FATHER]

FATHER: [*Taking a slug*] Now admit it. Doesn't this bring
back happy memories?

SON: I guess. . . .

FATHER: This boat, poor, sad, dying old Lake Erie. They still work. You can still sail. Life's not so bad now, is it?

SON: Dad. . . .

FATHER: I mean, can't we *talk?* Can't we even do *that?* Why did you come sailing with me? I didn't pay your bail just so we could sit here and stare at each other. Your mother can't talk to you, but I thought maybe I could.

SON: OK. Talk, talk, talk.

FATHER: I want to know where you're going to go.

SON: I can't tell you.

FATHER: Oh, look, Skipper. We're in the middle of Lake Erie. Or do you think they've bugged this *boat?* I want to know where you're going to *be.*

SON: I don't know.

FATHER: Will you telephone us? When you know?

SON: You know I can't.

FATHER: Well, write then. They don't open mail.

SON: Don't they?

FATHER: This is like some bad dream. My own son going into *hiding.* Behaving like some criminal.

SON: Which I am.

FATHER: Which you are *not!* You haven't even come to trial yet.

SON: Some trial. Name someone who's gotten off.

FATHER: If only we had *pull.* We don't have any *pull* anymore. I called twenty lawyers in Buffalo, but they won't touch your case with a ten-foot pole.

SON: I could have told you that.

FATHER: [*Takes another slug from the thermos, then spits it overboard.*] This is awful, isn't it? Without ice. Don't drink it if you don't want to. [*Pause*] I'm coming about. We'll tack against the wind.

[*Pantomime of shifting seats, tightening lines, etc. After they're settled*]

Your mother and I strongly feel that you should show up for your trial on Monday morning.

SON: And get nailed with three years.

FATHER: How do you know?

SON: Read the new security laws, Dad. *Read* them.

FATHER: Don't shout, please. [*Pause*] What's three years, in the long run? I spent three years in the Navy during Korea.

46

SON: That wasn't prison.

FATHER: Oh, what's prison these days? It's not a stigma anymore. Teddy Miller just got out. His family gave a small party for him.

[*The* SON *laughs sardonically.*]

All right, all right. I know. But I talked to him at great length. He said he read a lot of good books and got very good at baseball.

SON: I'm not Teddy Miller.

FATHER: At least talk to him.

SON: I've got better things to do.

FATHER: Such as what? Hiding in the hills? Living with that little Jewish girl? Blowing up buildings?

SON: You want to go through all the old arguments?

FATHER: No, thank you. [*Pause*] We'll never see you again. You'll be killed. [*Reaches out to touch his son's shoulder*] You're our oldest son!

SON: [*Pulls away, looks off. Pause*] We're getting close to those shoals.

FATHER: [*Tightening a line*] We are not getting close to those shoals. Don't tell me about sailing. You never won a race in your life. You never stuck to anything. You ducked out, just the way you're ducking out now.

SON: Let's go in, huh?

FATHER: We gave you the finest education in the country. We sold stock. We rented our house here for three summers—we sweltered in the city—just so you could learn how to break laws and jump bail.

SON: I want to go in now, Dad.

FATHER: You have no idea what duty means. You have no conception of what the word duty means. We don't just quit. We don't desert the ship. Or scuttle it. Which is what you're doing. When your mother got into that non-sense with Mr. Fiske, I stuck *by* her. I stuck by the rules. And so should you. Now stand up at that trial and take your punishment like a man. Do it. No arguments. Just do it.

SON: Fuck you.

[*The* FATHER *slaps him across the face. The* SON *hits his father. They struggle, knocking over a chair. The boat is in trouble. The* FATHER *frantically pantomimes grabbing lines.*]

47

FATHER: Grab the tiller! . . . I said GRAB THE TILLER!
. . . Head her off! I said OFF! . . . Oh, my God, you can't
even sail!

[*The lights dim on them, as the* PIANIST *plays a series of
scales.* MRS. HAYES, *a woman of about fifty, comes in and
speaks to the* PIANIST. *She wears a hat and gloves. He
stops playing and looks at her.*]

MRS. HAYES: [*Sweetly, shyly to the* PIANIST] Before we begin,
you probably want to know, don't you, why I'm taking
up singing lessons at my age. I mean, I'm no spring
chicken. [*Laughs embarrassedly*] Well, you see, the
thing is . . . I've always wanted to sing. I've always had
this . . . music . . . in me, and now I've just got to let it
OUT. Before it's too late. I've always had this dream of
standing on a stage, with other singers all around me,
and we're singing the sextet from *Lucia di
Lammermoor.* You're the first person I've ever told. I've
never even told my husband.

[*The* PIANIST *begins to play the sextet.*]

Yes! Oh, yes! That's it! Oh, I *dream* of it! Everyone singing a different thing, nobody out of tune, and everything
fitting together so perfectly at the end. Oh, what heaven,
what bliss to be able to sing that!

[*The* PIANIST *plays flamboyantly.*]

Yes! And I'd be Lucia, a young girl, with long blonde
hair, and I've made a terrible mistake. I've done just
what my family wanted me to do and married the wrong
man and now I'm going mad and I'm singing my heart
out!

[*The* PIANIST *begins the second chorus of the sextet. She
tries to sing along with the piano. She almost makes a
high note. Then she stops.*] Oh, dear. [*Quiet tears*] Oh,
dear. [*Shakes her head*] I'm sorry. I'm terribly sorry. I'm
terribly, terribly sorry.

[*She runs out, as a* MAN *dictates a letter to a pretty* SECRE-
TARY, *who sits on a chair, taking shorthand.*]

MAN: [*Dictating*] Dear Brad. [*Pause*] Thanks for your note.
[*Pause*] I'm very sorry, but this year I don't think I'll
cough up another nickel for Yale. I'm distressed that the
library was burned but why should I keep Yale up when
even its own students persist in dragging her down?
[*Gets angrier*] Indeed, why do people like you and me and

Snoozer, Brad, have to keep things *up* all the time? It seems to me I spend most of my time keeping things up. I keep the symphony up. I keep the hospital up. I keep our idiotic local theatre up. I keep my lawn up because no one else will. I keep my house up so the children will want to come home someday. I keep the summer house up for grandchildren. I keep up all that furniture mother left me because Sally *won't* keep it up. I even keep my morals up despite all sorts of immediate temptations.

[*The* SECRETARY *glances up at him.*]

I keep my chin up, I keep my faith up, I keep my dander up in this grim world. And I'm sick, sick, SICK of it. I'm getting tired supporting all those things that maybe ought to collapse. Sometimes all I think I am is an old jock strap, holding up the sagging balls of the whole goddamn WORLD! [*Pause*] Strike that, Miss Johnson. Obviously. And excuse me. [*Pause*] Strike out the whole letter, Miss Johnson. [*Pause*] Begin again. [*With a sigh*] Dear Brad. Enclosed is my annual check for Yale. I wish it could be larger. Sally joins me in sending love to you and Jane. Sincerely. And so forth.

[*The* PIANIST *bursts into a fast medley of Lester Lanin-type songs: "From This Moment On."* COUPLES *twirl onto the stage, the actresses can wear long skirts, the actors black bowties. A* COUPLE *twirls downstage.*]

BOY: Fabulous party.

GIRL: I know it.

[*They turn.*]

BOY: Fabulous music, fabulous decorations, everything's fabulous.

GIRL: I know it.

[*They turn.*]

BOY: Who's giving it, do you know?

GIRL: I am.

[*They turn. An* OLDER COUPLE *dance by—doing the sliding fox-trot of their generation.*]

WOMAN: It's a lovely party, Howard.

MAN: Better be. Cost me a cool ten thou.

WOMAN: What is it you do again?

MAN: We make parts for rockets.

WOMAN: You mean, for Korea?

MAN: For all over the world!

[*They turn. Another* BOY *and* GIRL *dance by.*]

GIRL: Why were you kicked out of Williams?

BOY: I refused to go to compulsory chapel on Sunday nights.

GIRL: How brave! Don't you believe in God?

BOY: Oh, sure. But I could never get back from Vassar in time.

[*They dance offstage. Another* COUPLE *dances in, followed by a* BOY WITH GLASSES.]

BOY WITH GLASSES: [*Calling to them*] Hey! They've got a TV set here. You can see the McCarthy hearings!

OTHER BOY: [*Breaking away from his partner*] No kidding!

GIRL: [*Standing pat*] Don't tell me you're going to sit around and watch the boob tube!

OTHER BOY: [*Looking at* GIRL] I guess I'll stay and dance.

BOY WITH GLASSES: [*Going offstage*] Suit yourself.

GIRL: [*Looking after him*] How shallow can you get! Watching TV when you can be with *people!*

[*She dances offstage with the* OTHER BOY. TWO BOYS *stand downstage, back to audience, as if at urinals. The* SECOND BOY *makes a loud burp.*]

FIRST BOY: I'll bet you say that to all the girls.

[*They pantomime washing their hands, adjusting ties, combing hair, now facing audience.*]

SECOND BOY: Janie put out for me tonight.

FIRST BOY: Oh, yeah?

SECOND BOY: Sure. I took her out by the pool. And she really came across.

FIRST BOY: How much did you get?

SECOND BOY: [*Spreading his arms*] Yay much.

FIRST BOY: Oh, well. I've had that.

SECOND BOY: Janie?

FIRST BOY: Oh, sure. She drops on a dime.

SECOND BOY: Janie? My Janie?

FIRST BOY: Oh, sure. She's got round heels from the word go.

SECOND BOY: [*Sadly*] It figures.

[*Pause*]

FIRST BOY: Well, I've got to go dance with my mother.

SECOND BOY: Ditto.

[*They exit.* TWO GIRLS *meet in the ladies' room One* GIRL *is wiping off the other's dress.*]

FIRST GIRL: He suddenly just leaned over and barfed all over my goddamn dress.

SECOND GIRL: How awful.

FIRST GIRL: Seventy-five dollars at Peck and Peck. Down the drain.

SECOND GIRL: Send him the bill.

FIRST GIRL: It doesn't matter. I'm on the shelf, anyway. No one will invite me to a thing next year.

SECOND GIRL: What are you going to do?

FIRST GIRL: Oh, God. Go to New York. Parlay my art major into a job at some museum. Live in a grubby apartment with a bunch of gals, where everyone gets the curse at the same time. Unless . . .

SECOND GIRL: Unless what?

FIRST GIRL: Well . . . He asked me to marry him before he barfed on me.

SECOND GIRL: Oh, Susie!

[*They both squeal and embrace and jump up and down and exit. Music up. A* COUPLE *dances by. A* GRANDMOTHER *marches up to them and cuts in.*]

GRANDMOTHER: Drive me home, Billy.

BILLY: Aw, Gram! The night is young!

GRANDMOTHER: I have to get up early and memorize Milton.

BILLY: Memorize *Milton?*

GRANDMOTHER: Otherwise my mind will go. Drive me home. [*Starts out.*]

BILLY: [*Starting after her; to* GIRL] She doesn't memorize Milton. . . .

GRANDMOTHER: [*Reciting as she walks out*]
"Hence! Vain deluding joys,
The brood of folly, without father bred!
How little you bested,
Or fill the fixed mind with all your toys!
Dwell in some idle brain . . ."

[*She is out by now.* BILLY *looks at his* GIRL *and then trots after his* GRANDMOTHER. *The piano plays a Bunny Hop. Everyone available dances it. A* BOY *and* GIRL *break away. The* BOY *wears a naval officer's hat.*]

GIRL: I love your uniform.

BOY: Thanks.

GIRL: Will the Navy get you to Europe this summer?

BOY: Oh, sure.

GIRL: I'll be in Paris. And so will Nancy, and Tookie, and Honey, and Muffy, and Squeakie. Can you get leave?

BOY: Oh, sure.

GIRL: I just think it's fantastic what you boys are doing about the Korean War. I just think it's superb, frankly.

BOY: Well. Somebody's got to hold the line against Communism.

[*They rejoin the Bunny Hop.*]

A FATHER: [*Coming onstage, holding telephone*] Hello. . . . Roger? . . . Can you hear me? . . .

[*The* MOTHER *rushes in, stands anxiously by the* FATHER *as he talks.*]

We got your letter. Yes. Your mother is sick about it. She can't talk. We're here at the Gardners' coming-out party, and we can hardly face people. . . . No, now you listen to me, Roger. If you insist on marrying that Japanese girl, I'm going to fly down to Washington and speak to an admiral and have you committed to a mental institution. . . . That's ridiculous. You are not happy. You can't be happy. . . . No. Now take a leave and come home and think about it. I'll pay your fare. . . . Roger? Roger?

MOTHER: What? *What?*

FATHER: He hung up.

MOTHER: Oh, Lord; oh, Lord!

FATHER: Relax. I got through to him. Let's get back to the party!

[*Joins two boys, beginning to harmonize around the piano. Another* BOY *tries to make out with a* GIRL *downstage.*]

SINGERS: "We're poor little sheep who have lost our way. . . . Baaa, baaaa, baaaaa. . . ."

GIRL: [*Fending off the* BOY] But why won't the Negroes sit in the back of the bus?

BOY: It's the principle of the thing.

SINGERS: "Little black sheep who have gone astray, baaaaa, baaaa, baaaa."

GIRL: [*Desperately fighting him off*] I like the back of the bus.

BOY: [*Pantingly*] But it's the principle of the thing. . . .

SINGERS: "Gentleman songsters off on a spree . . . damned from here to eternity . . ."

GIRL: [*One last stab*] Can they sit next to the window?

BOY: [*Losing control*] Yes.

GIRL: Then what are they complaining about?

[*He rolls her back onto the floor.*]

SINGERS: "Lord have mercy on such as we . . . baaaa, baaaa, baaaa."

[*The piano modulates to the "Wedding March." A* BRIDE *comes on, now wearing a bridal veil. A* GROOM *joins her. Everyone else congratulates them.* TWO PEOPLE *bring on a table with champagne glasses on a white tablecloth. The* BRIDE *and* GROOM *pantomime cutting the cake. She feeds him a piece, then they kiss. Cheers, applause, cries of "Speech." Everyone shushes everyone else. The* GROOM *speaks nervously, perhaps even with a stutter.*]

GROOM: I understand it's the custom among the rich for the groom to toast his bride. [*Laughter*] Before he deflowers her. [*Laughter*] I'm nervous. I shook like a leaf all during the ceremony. [*Laughter*] Gosh. And here I am marrying a girl I danced with at dancing school! [*Laughter*] Here I am, marrying a girl I've known all my life! [*Laughter; pause*] Why? Why am I doing it?

BEST MAN: For her body!

[*Laughter*]

FATHER-IN-LAW: For her money?

[*Laughter*]

A BRIDESMAID: For her soul!

[*General laughter*]

GROOM: No, no. Really. Why am I marrying her? Why am I, from an old family, marrying a girl from another old family to live in this dying city under these dying trees on this dying lake? [*A moment of silence and sadness. He pulls out of it.*] Why, because I love her! I love her and you and this city and these trees and this lake! And so let's have one final frantic toast to all of us here today!

BEST MAN: And gone tomorrow!

[*Laughter, raising of glasses.* PEOPLE *line up. The* BRIDE *pantomimes throwing her bouquet. Then the* BRIDE *and* GROOM *run through two lines as* PEOPLE *pantomime throwing rice at them. The piano plays the "Wedding March" in fast time.* PEOPLE *follow the* BRIDE *and* GROOM *offstage, ad-libbing "Give my regards to Bermuda" and so forth. Someone removes the white tablecloth from the*

table, revealing a stark desk underneath. A MAN *remains
on stage, and from under the desk takes out a sheaf of papers and an Army officer's hat. The* PIANIST *plucks the
bass strings of the piano to give a sharp, menacing, mechanical sound. The* ARMY OFFICER *sits at the desk, shuffling through his papers. An* ENLISTED MAN *comes in,
followed by* RAMSAY, *a civilian.*]

ENLISTED MAN: Excuse me, Colonel. This guy says he knows
you.

[COLONEL *looks up.*]

RAMSAY: [*Brightly*] Hi.

COLONEL: I'm very busy.

ENLISTED MAN: He's very busy.

RAMSAY: I'm Phil Ramsay, from Yale.

COLONEL: Phil . . . Ramsay?

RAMSAY: Sure. And you're Bucky Kratz. You were on the
Dartmouth hockey team. Right wing, third line. I played
goalie for Yale, same year. [*Pause*] Sure! And we met
again at Peggy Niles's coming-out party here in Buffalo.
Oh, sure, Bucky Kratz. When I heard that you were the
new district commander, I said I *know* that guy. I *know*
Colonel Kratz. I played hockey with him. [*Moving to
desk; holding out his hand*] Hi, Bucky.

COLONEL: [*Getting up, a little reluctantly; shaking hands*]
Phil. . . .

RAMSAY: Ramsay. Don't you remember? We beat you three-
to-two in overtime. I think I stopped a slap-shot of yours,
Bucky. From the blue line. I think we talked about it afterwards. In the shower.

COLONEL: Maybe. . . .

RAMSAY: Sure! And then, the day after the party, I think I
beat you in tennis, Bucky. We drove over to the Tennis
Club, and I think I whipped your ass. [*Laughs nervously*]

COLONEL: Phil Ramsay . . .

[*He nods; the* ENLISTED MAN *goes out.*]

RAMSAY: Sure. And now you're district commander. Wow,
Bucky! All this from—what? Army ROTC, at Dartmouth?

COLONEL: We can all thank God that it's only temporary.

RAMSAY: That's right. That's right, Bucky. You had to do it.
The Army had to take things in hand. Things were falling apart. We all realize that. All of us here.

[*Pause*]

COLONEL: Well, what's on your mind, Phil Ramsay?

RAMSAY: Bucky, I want my job back.

COLONEL: Where do you work?

RAMSAY: At the Buffalo City Bank. I was vice-president there, Bucky.

COLONEL: I can't—

RAMSAY: No, no. Now listen. Your man, Bucky, the man you put in there, he fired me, Bucky. Point-blank. Just called me in and canned me. My grandfather started that bank, Bucky. I've been there twenty-three years.

COLONEL: We don't normally tinker with civilian jobs unless there's a good reason.

RAMSAY: Of course you don't! I mean, where are we? Nazi Germany? There's some stupid mistake.

COLONEL: [*Pantomiming pushing a buzzer*] Let's look at your file.

RAMSAY: My . . . file?

COLONEL: Yes. Your file.

[ENLISTED MAN *comes in.*]

Would you bring in this gentleman's file, please? Mr.— what is it?—

RAMSAY: Philip R. Ramsay. The Third.

ENLISTED MAN: [*As he exits*] Philip the Third.

[COLONEL *laughs.*]

RAMSAY: [*Nervously laughing*] My file, eh? I've got a file, huh?

COLONEL: Everyone's got a file.

RAMSAY: Wow, Modern efficiency, eh? Computers and all that stuff, eh?

[*The* ENLISTED MAN *returns with the file, hands it to the* COLONEL, *exits. The* COLONEL *begins to look it over.* RAMSAY *crosses behind desk, and tries to look over his shoulder. Genially*]

Can't wait to see my own file.

COLONEL: [*Closing if immediately*] Hey, hey, hey! This is private *stuff!*

[RAMSAY *looks at him, nods and sits down.* COLONEL, *reading, flipping pages*]

Hmmmmmm. . . . Hmmmmmmmm. [*Looks at* RAMSAY, *and then reads some more*] Ummmmm-hm.

RAMSAY: What? What?

COLONEL: I see you signed a petition to stop the bombing back in sixty-six.

RAMSAY: Oh, well. Who didn't sign one of those, Bucky?

COLONEL: I also see you protested against the security laws in 1978.

RAMSAY: I didn't march.

COLONEL: Ramsay, you MARCHED! You carried a sign, saying "Stop Fascism in America." There's a picture here. Do you want to see your own picture?
[*Pause*]

RAMSAY: No.

COLONEL: [*Reading*] And you've got a son in detention camp, and a daughter in Canada. [*Closing the file*] There you are, Phil.

RAMSAY: Where am I?

COLONEL: You're not a V.P. at the bank, buddy. I can tell you that. Money's important, pal. We're devaluating. It's a tricky business.

RAMSAY: I know money, Bucky. I've worked with money all my life.

COLONEL: Yeah, well, we're talking about new money, Phil.

RAMSAY: I served in Korea, Bucky. Does my file say that? I was in the Navy during Korea. I was in the service, Bucky!

COLONEL: Sorry.

RAMSAY: I need money, Bucky.

COLONEL: Dig into grandpa's.

RAMSAY: There's none *left*, Bucky.

COLONEL: Oh, come on. Sell some antiques.

RAMSAY: I need a job, Bucky. Really.

COLONEL: I'm not the Yale Placement Bureau, friend.

RAMSAY: No, you're NOT! [*Pause*] No. You're not. [*Pause*] So what do I do now?

COLONEL: You go.

RAMSAY: [*Nods mechanically, starts out, and then suddenly turns and explodes*] We all laughed at you, you know. When you played tennis. You wore black socks and basketball shoes, and we all laughed, and I whipped your ass!

COLONEL: Get the hell out of here!

RAMSAY: I should punch you right in the nose!

COLONEL: [*Calling offstage*] A little help here!

[*An* ENLISTED MAN *comes in.*]

Get him out of here!

[*The* ENLISTED MAN *takes* RAMSAY's *arm.*]

RAMSAY: [*Shaking his arm loose*] And now I suppose your goons will put me in detention!

COLONEL: Hell, no. You're harmless. All of you guys. Harmless. [*To* ENLISTED MAN] Go on. Get him out of here.

[*He returns to his work as* RAMSAY *is dragged out. The piano continues the metallic noise. A* GIRL *appears speaking into a modern telephone, isolated in light.*]

GIRL: Daddy? . . . Did I wake you up? . . . I'm sorry, but you said to call. . . . Anyway, we made it, Daddy. We're here, and we're safe. . . . Dave already has a job, and I've got one lined up, and the commune helps care for the baby. . . . We feel like pioneers. . . . Pio*neers.* No, Daddy, we don't *need* money. You'll never get it out and we don't need it. We're all right. We're fine. . . . No, I don't think we'll ever come back. Not unless things change. Really change. . . . [*Suddenly*] Who's that? . . . Is someone cutting in? . . . Daddy, we're being cut off! . . . Daddy? [*Very quickly*] Good-bye, Daddy. . . . Good-bye, good-bye, good-bye. . . .

[*The piano takes up once again the rhythmic, metallic beat. A* MAN *enters from the opposite side, and addresses the audience.*]

MAN: [*To audience*] I'll be very brief because we've gotten word that they've revoked the club's license, and so we are technically illegal. [*Glances at notes*] Bill Satterfield has sent out Christmas cards with a resistance message. Apparently they can be used as evidence, so when your card arrives, burn it. [*Glances again at notes*] Pug Washburn's boat is available for people who want to get across the river to Canada. As far as I know, they haven't touched it because of Pug's connections with the military. So if you want to emigrate, see Pug. Before they confiscate the boat. [*Another glance*] Chuck Spaulding has a few extra guns. He's broken up his father's gun collection, and says there are some excellent firearms in it. Chuck needs the money, so check with him if you want a gun.

[*A loud knocking offstage. He remains calm.*]

There they are. [*Glances at notes*] Snoozer's funeral services will be at Trinity Church next Thursday at four.

[*More knocking; then the sound of someone running*]

Poor Esther has yet to receive an adequate explanation of how he died. . . . [*Speaks as if to soldiers directly offstage*] We are having a meeting here. This is a private club, founded in 1893, and we are having a meeting, and you have no right to break in on us. . . .

[*Lights change on him. He sits on the edge of a platform, we hear* BOYS *singing offstage: "In the Evening by the Moonlight." The piano is now silent. A* MOTHER, *played by the same actress who played the mother in the first scene, comes out, as if onto a terrace.*]

MOTHER: [*Quietly*] Oh, look at the lake! [*Calling back in*] Bring your coffee out here, everybody, and look at the lake!

[*The rest of the cast begins to come out, some carrying coffee cups. The* BOYS *are still singing: ". . . You can hear their banjos ringing." The* MOTHER *speaks to the* MAN *sitting on the edge of the porch.*]

Have you ever seen it so calm? And there's the harvest moon. . . . [*Turns to the others, now on the terrace*] Listen, everybody. I'm issuing an ultimatum: No more talk about the moon landing tonight. Not a word!

MARY: [*A daughter*] It was a lovely dinner, Mother.

MOTHER: It was fair. That creature in the kitchen can't cook corn.

ESTHER: [*A daughter-in-law*] The leaves are going. You can see the lights from the city.

MOTHER: Well. Tomorrow's Labor Day. And then we'll be gone. [*Pause*] Where's your father?

SIBBY: [*A daughter*] Getting the tennis balls.

MOTHER: Oh. Right.

TOM: [*A son-in-law looking out, with* MARY, *his wife*] This was the time the fish used to jump. Remember?

MOTHER: Don't remind me. It's so sad. Oh, while we're all here, I don't think the children should swim in the lake next year. It's just not healthy. I think we should build a pool. Down by the tennis court. You can all chip in and your father and I will cough up a thousand apiece.

[FATHER *comes in carrying a large old wicker basket. He*

*is played by the same actor who played the father in the
first scene.*]

Ah. Here's the master of the hounds.

FATHER: Who's first?

MOTHER: Wait, wait. We have to explain things to Ray
here. [*Turns to* RAY *who has been standing silently upstage*] Now, Ray, if you're going to marry Sibby, you've
got to learn our annual family ritual. Just as Sibby is
going to learn about grace before meals, and saluting
the flag, and all those things *your* family does.

SIBBY: Oh, Mo-thurrrrr.

MOTHER: Aaaaaaaaanyway, Ray, on the Sunday night before
Labor Day, we take all the old tennis balls of the entire
summer, and the children take turns throwing them
into that canoe. And the first one to get a tennis ball in
the canoe . . .

MARY: . . . which *stays* in the canoe. And doesn't bounce
out . . .

MOTHER: . . . gets first choice of when he or she can have
the house next summer.

RAY: You throw away all those tennis balls?

SIBBY: They're useless, Ray. They've lost their weight.

FATHER: And this is a burning year. We burn the canoe.
I've doused her with kerosene, and, after the tennis
balls, I'll give the signal to Chipper down there on the
dock, and he'll light her up, and push her out, and we'll
watch her burn.

MOTHER: And it looks perfectly lovely.

RAY: You burn that boat?

FATHER: It leaks like a sieve. Its ribs have all rotted. I can't
repair it anymore.

SNOOZER: [*A son, laughing*] Well, we sort of let it go, Dad.

FATHER: Not true. There's a certain point in the life of a
boat when it's better to burn it.

RAY: [*Scratching his head*] I'll bet I could fix it.

SIBBY: Oh, Ray, re*lax.*

MOTHER: All right. Ladies first. One at a time. Sibby, you're
the youngest.

[SIBBY *pantomimes throwing. Everyone laughs. Ad-libs:
"Sibby, you're hopeless."* SIBBY: *"I never could hit it and I
never will."*]

Next, Mary.

[*Ad-lib from* TOM: *"You're throwing for two this year, baby."* MARY *bends down awkwardly to get the tennis ball, throws clumsily.* MARY: *"And both of us missed." Laughter*]

Now, Esther.

[ESTHER *throws with great vigor. Everyone groans. Ad-libs:* "You aiming for Canada, Esther?" *etc.*]

Now the guest. Your turn, Ray. [*Ad-lib from* SNOOZER: *"Let's see a good old Amurrrican throw."* RAY *gets set carefully and throws the ball. Cheers and congratulations. The* MOTHER *intervenes, shouting them down.*]

No, no, no. That doesn't count. You stepped over the line, Ray.

[*Groans from* GROUP]

RAY: What line?

MOTHER: That line. That old line. Can't you see that line? Snoozer carved it twenty years ago with his jackknife. Sorry. Who's next? You, Snoozer. The eldest son.

[*Ad-lib from* ESTHER: *"Don't you want to sober up first?"* SNOOZER *throws neatly, with a backspin, obviously using an old system. Cheers. He gets it in.*]

Snoozer wins! Snoozer and Esther get their choice!

FATHER: [*Calling out*] OK, Chipper! Light her up and push her out!

SNOOZER AND ESTHER: [*confer briefly*] We'll take the first two weeks in July!

[*Groans, ad-libs:* "You luckies." "You get the Fourth of July Tournament."]

MOTHER: [*To* RAY] Better luck next year, Ray. Learn where the line is.

ESTHER: [*Pointing offstage and out*] Look, look. The canoe. It's burning.

EVERYONE: Ahhhh. . . .

[*They all look. A reddish glow begins to light their faces.* SNOOZER *and* TOM *begin to sing very quietly. Others join in, except for* RAY *who stands apart, watching the canoe.*]

THE FAMILY:

It was sad,

It was sad,

It was sad when the good ship went down,
  to the bottom of the,

Husbands and wives,

Little children lost their lives,
It was sad when the great ship went down. . . .
[*They repeat the song. One by one they stop. Everyone watches, transfixed, as the red glow slowly fades and leaves them in darkness.*]

THE END

[*The piano should play a lively version of "The Good Ship," both during the curtain calls and as the audience is leaving.*]

CHILDREN

Suggested by a story
by John Cheever

CHILDREN was first presented in New York City by the
Manhattan Theatre Club, Lynne Meadow, Artistic Director, on October 20, 1976. It was directed by Melvin
Bernhardt; the set designer was Marjorie Kellogg; costumes were by Patricia McGourty; the lighting designer
was Arden Fingerhut; the sound designers were George
Hanson and Chuck London; and the production stage manager was Mark Paquette. The cast, in order of appearance,
was as follows:

BARBARA ...., Holland Taylor
RANDY .... Dennis Howard
MOTHER .... Nancy Marchand
JANE .... Swoosie Kurtz

CHILDREN received its American premiere on January
30, 1976, by the Repertory Company of the Virginia Museum Theatre. It was directed by Keith Fowler.

The play was first produced at the Mermaid Theatre in
London, opening on April 8, 1974. It starred Constance
Cummings and was directed by Alan Strachan.

CAST OF CHARACTERS

BARBARA
RANDY
MOTHER
JANE

*The action of the play takes place during the morning, after-
noon, and evening of a Saturday on a July Fourth weekend,
on the terrace of a large, old summer house, overlooking the
sea, on an island off the coast of Massachusetts. The year is
1970.*
*The terrace occupies most of the stage. It is surrounded by a
low sitting wall, and contains primarily old terrace furniture, wicker, metal, and wood, thick with many coats of
white paint. There is only an occasional concession to alu-
minum and vinyl. Behind, there is the side of the house,
composed of weathered shingles. Ground-floor windows,
framed by shutters, graced with window boxes containing
geraniums and petunias, open onto the terrace, and of
course a large screen door, which slams closed by means of
a rusty, sagging spring.*
*To the right, screened by shrubs, a path leads off and down
to the driveway and the tennis court. To the left, around the
corner of the house, another path leads to wooden steps
down the bluff to the beach.*

NOTES

*Everyone in this play should look thoroughly tanned. The
clothes they wear—and they are the kind of people who*

66

change their clothes a lot—should be bright, summery, expensive looking, and conservatively stylish.

The songs should not be considered isolated interludes, but rather should contribute to the flow of the play. They should begin as a scene is ending, and fade out only after the next scene has begun. Similarly the light changes should be carefully modulated.

Finally, the house should be used almost as a character in the play. The upstairs shades should be closed for the first scene. The leafy shadows change over its surface during the day. Before the final scene, the lights come on inside, and for the first time we can see something of the interior.

SPECIAL NOTE ON SONGS

For performance of such songs mentioned in this play as are in copyright, the permission of the copyright owners should be obtained; or other songs in the public domain substituted.

Permission to perform the song "Secrets," must be secured from Broadcast Music, Inc., 580 Fifth Avenue, New York, N. Y. 10036.

SYNOPSIS OF SCENES

ACT I

SCENE 1: 7 A.M.
SCENE 2: Mid-morning
SCENE 3: Late morning
SCENE 4: Before lunch

ACT II

SCENE 1: After lunch
SCENE 2: Late afternoon
SCENE 3: Early evening
SCENE 4: Night

ACT I

The sound of a group of amateur voices singing, in good, close, genial harmony, as if at a beach party. They might be singing a song about morning, or the sun, or even "Show Me the Way to Go Home." The lights come up on the terrace. It is very early in the morning. Bright sunlight has begun to slant across the stage, which will become brighter as the scene continues. No one is in view. We hear various sounds: birds chirping offstage right, the slow pound of the sea offstage left. Then, offstage right, the motor of a car getting closer, and the crunch of its wheels on a gravel driveway. The crunch stops, the motor stops. Car doors are heard slamming. Then, closer at hand, but still offstage right, a woman giggles. Finally we can make out some of her words.

WOMAN'S VOICE: Ssshhhh. You'll wake mother. . . . All right, this is far enough. . . . Mmmmmm. . . . You'd better go. People will see you. . . . Good night—oops, I mean, good morning. . . .
[BARBARA *comes on from upstage right. She is tan, lean, and attractive, in her late thirties. She wears a stylish summer outfit which looks slightly disheveled, as is her hair. She tiptoes on, carrying her shoes in one hand. Then she turns back, and waves offstage, down right. When the car door slams again, she cringes and puts her finger to her lips. She waves as the car is heard driving off. She sighs and turns toward the house. Stealthily, she*

69

*makes her way on tiptoes toward the screen door. She
opens it very carefully, trying not to make its spring
squeak. She is about to enter the house when suddenly the
strident sound of a telephone is heard ringing within.
She starts, jumps back, catches the screen door before it
slams shut, and looks around, frightened, at a loss for
what to do. The telephone rings two or three times, then
stops in the middle of a ring, indicating that someone
within has picked up the receiver.* BARBARA *stands in the
center of the terrace. Sounds begin, within the house.
First, children's voices, murmuring sleepily and petu-
lantly. Then a man's voice]*

MAN'S VOICE: [*Offstage*] What the hell was that?

WOMAN'S VOICE: [*Offstage. Sleepily*] I think it was the telephone. I think your mother answered it.

MAN'S VOICE: [*Offstage. Sleepily*] At seven o'clock? Jesus
Christ.

[BARBARA, *now unable to enter the house with all the
noise, sits down resignedly. Voices continue, ad-libbing
within. Then, after a moment, the screen door bursts
open, and* RANDY *comes out, wrapping a towel around his
waist. He is in early thirties, trim, very tan, and athleti-
cally built. He calls back into the house as he comes out.]*

RANDY: I'm going for a swim.

[*He comes onto the terrace, stops short when he sees* BAR-
BARA.]

Hey.

BARBARA: Good morning.

RANDY: You look like you just got home.

BARBARA: I did. [*lying*] Betsy's car broke down after the
movie, so I stayed over at her house.

RANDY: [*Believing her*] Oh. [*Gesturing toward the house*]
Goddamn phone woke everybody up.

BARBARA: I heard. Who was it?

RANDY: I dunno. Mother got it in her bedroom.

BARBARA: Probably a wrong number.

RANDY: [*Stretching, yawning*] No. She's still talking.
[*Starts offstage right*] I'm going for a swim.

BARBARA: No kidding.

RANDY: Hey, do you know where the oil is?

BARBARA: The suntan oil?

RANDY: [*Irritably*] No, not the suntan oil. The oil for the tennis court roller. I was looking all over for it last night.

BARBARA: Did you look in the shed?

RANDY: It's not in the shed.

BARBARA: It used to be in the shed.

RANDY: It's not there, Barbara.

BARBARA: Then I don't know where the oil is, Randy.

RANDY: [*Starting off again*] Christ, you can't find a thing around here. No one puts things back. I don't mind people using things if they put them back.

BARBARA: Oh, stop trying to be like daddy.

RANDY: [*Turning again*] You mean, because I'm taking a dip?

BARBARA: No, I mean the lecture about putting things back.

RANDY: You never do, and you never did. I have a game this morning, and the court's a mess.

BARBARA: [*Yawning*] I didn't take the oil, Randy.

RANDY: You didn't even put the roller back after Labor Day last year. It was out all winter. That's why it's rusty. That's why I have to oil the damn thing.

BARBARA: Did you ever think that the children might have taken it?

RANDY: [*Stopping and turning again*] Not my children.

BARBARA: Here we go.

RANDY: My children put things back. We've trained them.

BARBARA: So now you're blaming my children.

RANDY: Who lost the pump for the boat?

BARBARA: Oh, Randy, that's mean.

RANDY: Who lost the pump?

BARBARA: That's just plain mean. My children are naturally upset, and you start nit-picking about oil and pumps and rollers and—

RANDY: You can't run a house unless people put things back. You can't—

[*Both are talking at once. The screen door opens, and* MOTHER *comes out of the house. She is in her early sixties, and looks neat and well groomed, in her good-looking bathrobe, even at this hour of the morning.* RANDY *and* BARBARA *begin to appeal to her immediately and simultaneously.*]

A. R. GURNEY, JR.

BARBARA: Mother, now he's blaming my children because he can't find the oil for the tennis court roller. . . .

RANDY: Mother, I've got a game at ten-thirty and I can't play on that court unless I . . .

[MOTHER *closes her eyes and puts both hands over her ears.*]

MOTHER: Ssshhhh.

[RANDY *and* BARBARA *stop.*]

Just . . . sshhhh. Let me pull myself together. [MOTHER *opens her eyes.*] Guess who just telephoned from the mainland?

BARBARA: Who?

MOTHER: Guess who will be on the ten o'clock ferry?

RANDY: Who, Mother?

MOTHER: Guess who decided to join us for the Fourth of July weekend after all?

[*pause*]

BARBARA: Pokey.

MOTHER: [*Nodding*] Your brother.

RANDY: Pokey?

MOTHER: Your little brother. With Miriam. And both children. We meet them at eleven-fifteen.

BARBARA: Well, well.

MOTHER: They made up their minds yesterday. Drove all night. All the way from Washington.

BARBARA. Typical.

MOTHER: He called from Providence. At seven o'clock in the morning. He said he figured we'd all be up.

BARBARA. Typical.

[MOTHER *nods, looks at her, suddenly notices her clothes.*]

MOTHER: Barbara, where have you been?

BARBARA: [*Mechanically*] Car broke down. Stayed at Betsy's. Just got in.

MOTHER: You must be exhausted.

BARBARA: [*Stretching, yawning*] I am.

MOTHER: Well, you'll have to stay awake long enough to come to the ferry with me.

RANDY: I can't, Mother. I've got a game.

MOTHER: Oh, Randy, you always have a game when I need you.

BARBARA: Why is he coming, Mother?

72

MOTHER: I suppose because I invited him. Just as I invite both of you. Every year.

RANDY: But he refused, Mother. Remember when we called him last Christmas? He showed no interest.

BARBARA: He hasn't been near this place in—what?—four years?

MOTHER: Five.

BARBARA: That's right. Ever since daddy died.

RANDY: And now, suddenly, on the spur of the moment . . .

MOTHER: Well he's changed his mind, that's all. And of course, I'm delighted. I'm thrilled. We'll all be together for the Fourth. What fun. [*Pause*] It just requires some additional planning, that's all. [*She paces around the terrace, counting on her fingers.*] Let's see. There's Barbara, and Randy, and Jane, and me, and now Pokey and Miriam. That's six grown-ups. And Barbara's two children, and Randy's four, and Pokey's two. That's eight children. Which means a total of fourteen people in this house. We'll have to get more food on the way to the ferry.

BARBARA: And liquor, Mother.

MOTHER: Oh, they won't drink much.

BARBARA: No, but we will.

[BARBARA *and* RANDY *laugh.*]

MOTHER: [*Firmly*] There is plenty of liquor, Barbara.

[*Laughter subsides.* MOTHER *continues to plan, nervously.*]

Now please. Let me think. He'll want his old room, so we'll move all the children out onto the screen porch. Which means changing sheets. Which means stopping at the laundry. And I'll have to get the little MacKenzie girl from down the road to feed the children and help with the dishes. And of course, I've got to come up with his favorite meal tonight. Which means leg of lamb, *and* mint jelly, *and* red raspberries, if I can *find* them, and then there's the Yacht Club dance, and I suppose I should call and make two more reservations, and—

RANDY: Did he *say* why he decided to come, Mother?

[*Pause,* MOTHER *looks at him.*]

MOTHER: No. He didn't say. . . .

BARBARA: He avoids us like the plague for five years, and then suddenly . . .

RANDY: Oh, he's always doing this. Remember the time he ran away from summer camp? And just arrived, on the doorstep, in the middle of a party?

BARBARA: I remember the time he *left*. Remember that, Mother? You were having some people over for him, and right before they arrived, he walked in with his knapsack packed and said he was hitchhiking out West?

RANDY: I thought he'd settle down, now he's married. Do you think he's quit his job again, Mother?

MOTHER: He didn't say. . . . [*Pause*] But I know. I know why he's coming. He's coming because of my letter.

RANDY: Your—letter?

MOTHER: My letter. People still write letters, Randy. Occasionally. When they want to say things that can't be said on the telephone. When they want to have things sink in. That's when they write letters. [*Pause*] And knowing the United States mail, your brother just got that letter yesterday. And apparently it *didn't* sink in. It didn't sink in at all. Because he throws his poor wife and children into the car, and drives all night, and doesn't call until he's practically *here*, so that we can't say no, we can't say relax, we can't say please, before you come, at least let it sink *in*. [*Pause*] That's why he's coming. [*Pause*]

BARBARA: What did the letter say, Mother? [*Pause*]

MOTHER: Well first, I said we'd all miss him, and I wished them all a very happy Fourth of July.

BARBARA: And?

MOTHER: And then I asked him to do some serious thinking about the fall.

RANDY: The fall?

MOTHER: The fall. Because in the fall—as I wrote your brother—you three children will get this house.

BARBARA: But—why, Mother?

MOTHER: [*Taking a deep breath*] Because in the fall, in September, to be exact—now this is a secret. Nobody knows about this— [*Pause*] In the fall, in September, your Uncle Bill and I are going to be married.

[*She turns and strides into the house. Pause.* BARBARA *and* RANDY *look at each other.*]

BARBARA: Wow.

RANDY: [*Looking toward the house*] She told him first. Why does she always tell him things first?

[*Pause. They look at each other again, and then of one accord rush into the house after their* MOTHER, *calling, "That's great, Mother!"; "That's terrific"; "Why didn't you tell us?" etc. The lights dim as we hear congratulations within. The group of voices sings a song like "I Want a Girl" or "Personal Friend of Mine." The song fades as the lights have come up again. The brightness of the overhead sun indicates that it is about eleven-thirty in the morning. After a moment,* JANE *comes out of the house, a pretty woman in her mid-thirties. She wears a white tennis dress, white hair band, and white sneakers. She carries a tray with two glasses of Coke on it, which she puts on a table. Then she calls toward offstage right.*]

JANE: I'm out here, Randy.

[*Pause. Then* RANDY *comes on from around the house, now also in whites. He carries a tennis racquet. He glances at* JANE, *then walks to the edge of the sitting wall. He hauls off, about to hurl the racquet away.*]

Oh, don't, Randy! That's a new racquet.

[*He looks at the racquet, shakes his head, and tosses it aside. He slumps angrily into a chair.*]

We should have gone to the ferry with everyone else.

RANDY: We had a game.

JANE: Some game.

RANDY: All right. I stank.

JANE: You got so mad.

RANDY: They never knew. We shook hands, and all that.

JANE: They didn't even stay for a Coke.

RANDY: They couldn't, Jane. They had to get back to their children.

JANE: They *said* they had to get back to their children. Who are in camp.

[RANDY *looks at her. Pause*]

I love the ferry. All that kissing and hugging.

RANDY: Pokey and I don't hug.

[*Pause. They sip their Cokes.*]

You know why we lost?

JANE: You got mad.

RANDY: You know why I got mad?

JANE: You're upset about your mother.

RANDY: Not at all.

JANE: It makes sense, psychologically.

RANDY: I said, not at *all,* Jane.

JANE: I mean, you're very close to her. You don't want to see her go.

RANDY: She's not *going* anywhere. She'll be right here, every summer. With all of us. And Uncle Bill. Who's a great old friend of the family. Who was one of daddy's ushers in their wedding, for God's sake. It's perfect. It's ideal.

JANE: I think so, too.

RANDY: So that's not why I got mad.

JANE: All right.

RANDY: That's not why we lost.

JANE: All right, dear.

[*Long pause, they both look out to sea.*]

RANDY: You want to know why we lost?

JANE: Because of Pokey.

RANDY: No.

JANE: Well you say he always makes you nervous.

RANDY: He's not the reason.

JANE: Well you're always saying that. Everybody says it. Isn't that why you all call him Pokey? Because he's always poking around, making everybody nervous?

RANDY: We call him Pokey because he has a poker face.

JANE: Oh.

RANDY: And because he was a slow-poke. He was always holding us up.

JANE: Your mother said it was because he liked to poke around. I remember, because she said he now has the perfect job. In Washington. Working for the Department of Justice. She said now he can poke around the entire country, stirring things up.

RANDY: Oh, maybe. . . .

JANE: I'm sure she said that. She said that both her sons had perfect jobs. You teaching at a boys' boarding school because you love sports and games, and Pokey poking around for the Department of Justice.

RANDY: OK, OK.

JANE: So probably you were nervous about Pokey on the tennis court.

RANDY: Wrong.

JANE: OK.

RANDY: Just plain wrong, Jane.

JANE: OK. Skip it.

[*Pause. They look out to sea again.*]

RANDY: You want to know why we lost? Really?

JANE: I still think—

RANDY: Do you want to know why?

JANE: It's your mother. Or Pokey. Or both. I'll bet you.

RANDY: [*Shouting*] DO YOU WANT TO KNOW WHY WE
LOST THAT GODDAMN GAME OF TENNIS, JANE?

[*Pause*]

JANE: Why?

RANDY: Because of the court.

JANE: The court? What's wrong with the court?

RANDY: What's wrong with the *court*? What's wrong with
that tennis court, out there? I'll tell you what's wrong
with the court. Everything's wrong with the court. You
can't see the lines, the net is riddled with holes, the surface is like a battlefield. How can a man play under
those conditions? How can a man who is used to a decent
court play on a court like that? Daddy wouldn't have
played. Daddy would have walked right off that court. I
tell the kids, I tell the boys at school, there's no point in
playing a game unless you have good equipment. A
man's got to be able to count on certain fundamental
things. It's like Latin. That's why I like Latin. When I'm
teaching Latin, I say look for the verb. You can always
count on the verb. Find the verb, and everything will fall
into place. Now maybe those clods we played tennis with
today don't care about these things. Maybe they're used
to bad bounces, and foot faults, and wrong scores.

JANE: The score wasn't wrong.

RANDY: He called it wrong. Twice. I had to correct him. Because I care about the score. And I care about lines and
nets and smooth surfaces and bounces that I can at least
pre*dict*. And that's why we lost, if you really want to
know.

[*Pause*]

JANE: All right.

[*Pause*]

RANDY : And I'll tell you something else. We're going to re-

surface that court. That's the first thing. That's first on
the list, when the house is ours.

JANE: I think Barbara wants to winterize the house. She's
always talking about it.

RANDY: Well the court comes first.

[*Pause*]

JANE: Would you explain something to me, please?

RANDY: What?

JANE: Why do you get the house when your mother gets
married?

RANDY: It was in daddy's will.

JANE: Oh.

RANDY: It's in most wills.

JANE: Oh.

RANDY: The house is in the wife's name until she dies or
remarries. Then it goes to the children. It's standard
practice.

JANE: Oh. And Pokey understands all that?

RANDY: Of course he does. He's the executor of the will.

JANE: Oh, then that explains it.

RANDY: Explains what?

JANE: Why he's suddenly coming up. To handle these legal
things.

RANDY: I suppose.

JANE: Oh, that's a relief. You know what I thought?

RANDY: What?

JANE: I thought he was upset about your mother.

RANDY: [*Exploding*] JESUS, JANE—

[*A car horn is heard offstage right. Car doors slamming,
the sound of children's voices*]

JANE: Well. There they are.

[*She gets up.*]

RANDY: [*Getting up*] So let's get Pokey to chip in on the
court, OK?

JANE: Does he still play?

RANDY: Of course he does. He's quite good. But I can beat
him. I can beat him easily. Even on that crumby court,
with those lousy lines, and that stringy net between us, I
can still beat him. Ask mother. Mother will tell you. I
can slaughter him.

[*He is offstage right by now,* JANE *following him, as the
lights change. The group of voices might sing Stephen*

Foster's *"Old Folks at Home."* *The lights are up by now. It is high noon. The sound of children's voices can be heard occasionally offstage.* MOTHER *comes out of the house, now dressed in colorful slacks and blouse. Then* BARBARA *comes out, in a change of clothes, carrying a gin-and-tonic. She looks at her* MOTHER.]

BARBARA: Well. He's changing.

MOTHER: [*With a sigh*] Do you think so?

BARBARA: His clothes, Mother. He's changing his clothes.

MOTHER: Oh.

BARBARA: Thank God he's getting out of that dark suit. He looked like a visiting minister.

MOTHER: [*Glancing toward the house*] Sssshhhh.
[*Pause*]

BARBARA: [*Lower voice*] What did you think of *her* outfit?

MOTHER: Miriam? She's sweet.

BARBARA: Her *outfit*, Mother. What did you think of that little number?

MOTHER: I thought it was very pretty.

BARBARA: Oh, Mother. . . .

MOTHER: Very snappy.

BARBARA: Snappy? That halter job? And no *bra*, Mother?

MOTHER: That's the style these days. [*Pause*] Apparently.
[*Pause*]

BARBARA: What about the children? How did you like them getting off the ferry in their grubby little blue jeans?

MOTHER: Styles change, Barbara.

BARBARA: Oh, do they? I don't see you giving my children blue jeans for Christmas. It seems to me I remember nice little boxes from Saks Fifth Avenue.

MOTHER: People live different lives, Barbara.

BARBARA: They certainly do. He looks like a relic from the Eisenhower age escorting a bunch of hippies around.

MOTHER: That's enough, please.

BARBARA: And pale. Don't they allow the sun down in Washington? Is that one of their new laws?

MOTHER: They'll get the sun here.

BARBARA: Let's hope so. Can you imagine us all cooped up here together on a rainy day?
[*Pause.* MOTHER *shakes her head.*]

MOTHER: The first thing he did when he got here, the first thing, he walked right out on this terrace, and looked at the view, and said, "Where's the rose garden? Where's the old croquet court?" So I said, "Erosion, dear. Natural erosion. You just haven't been here."

BARBARA: If there's erosion, Pokey would notice it.

MOTHER: He says we need a seawall.

BARBARA: Oh, my God, that costs a fortune.

MOTHER: That's what he says. Otherwise, he says some night we're going to be sitting here drinking, and the whole house will slide slowly into the sea.

BARBARA: Pokey, Pokey, Pokey. . . .

MOTHER: [*With a sigh*] Well, we've just got to loosen him up, that's all.

BARBARA: How? How do we loosen up Pokey?

MOTHER: By being very affectionate and warmhearted. [BARBARA *laughs*, MOTHER *looks at her.*] What's so funny?

BARBARA: The way we were at the ferry?

MOTHER: What was wrong at the ferry?

BARBARA: Nothing. We were all on our best behavior.

MOTHER: We welcomed him with open arms.

BARBARA: A peck for a kiss.

MOTHER: I didn't peck.

BARBARA: We both pecked, Mother. And the children shook hands.

MOTHER: Well what should we have done? Are we supposed to fall all over each other, like that Italian family?

BARBARA: Not at all. We're not the type. [*Pause*] Except maybe Pokey. Remember how he cried at daddy's funeral?

MOTHER: We all cried.

BARBARA: But not so *much*. God, tears were streaming down his face. The rest of us were good old undemonstrative Wasps.

MOTHER: I hate that expression, Wasp. Everyone uses it these days, and I loathe it.

BARBARA: It's what we are, Mother.

MOTHER: We are not. We are people, like Italians or anybody else. We love our family, and we're very affectionate when we're not in public. *Hon*estly. [*Pause*] We all cried. [*Pause*] I don't like all this smart talk, Barbara. I know you're upset about your divorce, but I don't want to see you turning into a bitter, disagreeable woman.

Now you'd better learn to be nice to both your brothers, because you're going to take over in the fall.

[*Pause. She looks out to sea.*]

BARBARA: What's the matter, Mother?

MOTHER: Nothing's the matter. [*Pause*] Except that he never even mentioned my getting married.

BARBARA: No kidding.

MOTHER: Not a word. Not at the ferry, not in the car, not out here, not at all.

BARBARA: No kidding.

[*Pause*]

MOTHER: [*Carefully*] I suppose he mentioned it to you.

BARBARA: No.

MOTHER: You must have brought it up.

BARBARA: I tried. At one point.

MOTHER: What did you say?

BARBARA: Oh, I said, "What do you think of the good news, Pokey?" Something like that.

MOTHER: What did he say?

BARBARA: Nothing. He walked away. [MOTHER *sighs.*] He was fussing with his children.

[*Pause*]

MOTHER: The only way it came up with me was when I told him we were having his favorite meal tonight. Do you know what he said? He said, "I hope it's just the family." That's all he said. [*Pause*] Well. Just the family it will be.

BARBARA: Not Uncle Bill? [MOTHER *shakes her head.*] Oh, Mother, we were going to have toasts. And sing songs. I got some wine. [MOTHER *shakes her head.*] Uncle Bill's part of the family.

MOTHER: Not to Pokey. Pokey won't even call him Uncle Bill.

BARBARA: We've always called him Uncle Bill.

MOTHER: Pokey hasn't. He calls him Mister. He used to say that Uncle Bill's not his uncle, so why should he call him that. [*Pause*] Pokey doesn't like him.

BARBARA: Oh, Mother.

MOTHER: He doesn't like him. He can be very rude to him. I've seen it. [*Pause*] That's why I wrote him that letter. So he could get used to the idea. [*Pause*] I told Pokey first. Before I told any of you. Uncle Bill hasn't even told *his* children yet. But I thought I should tell Pokey.

[*Pause*] So. No Uncle Bill for dinner. No celebration. Just the family. [*She gets up, smiles, squares her shoulders.*] And maybe it's just as well. Aunt Peggy just died in March. We shouldn't be jumping the gun, should we? To be fair to her. So maybe it's just as well if we all just avoided the issue for the weekend, and had a nice family dinner, and then we'll see Uncle Bill at the Yacht Club dance. [*She starts for the house.*] And now I think I'll take a bath before lunch. [BARBARA *laughs.* MOTHER *turns.*] *Now* what's so funny?

BARBARA: Oh, Mother . . .

MOTHER: What's wrong with taking a bath?

BARBARA: Nothing's *wrong* with it. But have you noticed that since Pokey arrived, everyone makes a dash for the water.

MOTHER: Phooey.

BARBARA: It's true. I went in, Jane went in, the children went in, Randy's still in, and now you're making a bee-line for the bathtub.

MOTHER: It's a hot day.

BARBARA: Oh, sure.

MOTHER: What's wrong with people keeping clean?

BARBARA: Nothing's *wrong*, Mother. It's just who we are. I think that's why we have to be near the ocean. We have to go through these ritual cleansings.

MOTHER: People feel hot, people feel dirty . . .

BARBARA: And people feel guilty. [*Pause*]

MOTHER: Guilty? Guilty about what?

BARBARA: Oh, lots of things. Money. Having this place when poor people are sweltering in the city. Living off the stock market. All that.

MOTHER: That's ridiculous.

BARBARA: I feel guilty.

MOTHER: I don't, at all.

BARBARA: I do. I feel guilty about my divorce. I feel guilty about— [*She glances offstage right. Pause*] And Pokey always makes me feel more guilty.

MOTHER: I have nothing to feel guilty about, thank you very much.

[*She starts toward the house again.*]

BARBARA: Maybe you do, and don't even know it.

[MOTHER *turns.*]

Face it, Mother. That's who we are. We're very repres-
sive people. That's what my psychiatrist said. We survive on repression. That's how we made our money, and
that's how we've held onto it. We hold onto things. We
hold on. That's our whole bag. And it's time we realized
it.

[MOTHER *snorts, strides to the door, opens it, then turns.*]

MOTHER: I'll tell *you* what it's time we realized. It's time we
realized when to drink and when not to drink. I've noticed that glass in your hand, Barbara, and I haven't
mentioned it, but now I think it's time I did. I don't like
drinking at this hour, and I don't like drinking alone.
We have rules about drinking in this house. If your father were alive, he'd make you pour that out. You children are much too casual about alcohol. It's not a toy.
That's what it's time you realized, frankly, if you want
my opinion.

[*She goes into the house. The screen door slams behind
her.* BARBARA *looks after her, looks at the drink in her
hand, shakes her head, settles into her chair, takes a long
sip.*]

BARBARA: Oh, Pokey, Pokey, Pokey. Welcome home. . . .

[*The lights dim. The group of voices might sing "Aura
Lee" or "Tell Me Why." The lights are up again. It is
about an hour later.* BARBARA *is sound asleep in her chair,
her feet up on the wall, her empty glass beside her.* JANE
*comes out of the house, now also dressed in a fresh blouse
and slacks.*]

JANE: [*Not seeing that* BARBARA *is asleep*] There's a slight
problem with the children.

BARBARA: [*Starting, sitting up*] What?

JANE: Oh, I'm sorry.

BARBARA: That's all right. I had a late night. What's the
matter?

JANE: The children. They're using four-letter words.

BARBARA: How did that start?

JANE: I'm afraid with Pokey's children.

BARBARA: Wouldn't you know. . . .

JANE: They just started in saying them. Every word in the
book. And the other children took them up. And now
four-letter words are being tossed around the infield,

over the peanutbutter sandwiches, amid gales of laughter.

BARBARA: Did you stop it?

JANE: Oh, I tried to. But then I started to laugh. That didn't help much.

BARBARA: Oh, Jane. . . .

JANE: It was so funny. At one point, it was like a chant. All the most repulsive words. Even the sitter was doing it. I found myself roaring with laughter. [*She laughs, then checks herself.*] I hope your mother didn't hear.

BARBARA: She's taking a bath.

JANE: Whew. [*She sits down.*] Another problem. Pokey's children call me by my first name.

BARBARA: Did you ask them to?

JANE: Nope.

BARBARA: I think that might be a little fresh, don't you?

JANE: I sort of like it.

BARBARA: Then what's the problem?

JANE: Well now your children want to do it.

BARBARA: Out of the question.

JANE: Otherwise they say it's not fair.

BARBARA: They weren't brought up that way.

JANE: I told them they could.

BARBARA: I'll tell them later they can't. [*Pause*] Next thing you know, your own children will be calling you Randy and Jane.

JANE: That's what they want to do.

BARBARA: You said no, I hope.

JANE: Oh, it wouldn't kill me.

BARBARA: Randy would kill *them.*

JANE: [*Nodding*] I said that. [*Pause*] So they'll continue to call me Mummy. [*She shakes her head.*] I hate being called Mummy. I wish I were called Ma. Or Mama Mia. Or just plain old Mom. [*Pause*] Not Mummy. It reminds me of all those types I went to boarding school with. They called their mothers Mummy, and when they wrote, everything slanted backwards, and they dotted their i's with great, big, empty circles.

BARBARA: I slant backwards.

JANE: [*Sadly*] So do I. [*Pause*] It's hard to change. [*Pause*] Oh. Remind me to pick up some more Coke this afternoon.

BARBARA: There's plenty of Coke.

JANE: There was.

BARBARA: Mother just got Coke. This morning.

JANE: They've been through two big bottles.

BARBARA: Who?

JANE: The children. Just now.

BARBARA: Coke with meals? Mother planned milk.

JANE: Pokey's kids wanted *Coca-Cola.* So the sitter gave it to them.

BARBARA: Are mine having Coke? Are yours?

JANE: We had to be fair.

BARBARA: Coke is for people who play tennis. That's the rule.

JANE: Maybe it's a Jewish thing.

BARBARA: Coke? Coke is Jewish?

JANE: No, the idea of no milk with meals. Maybe it comes from Miriam. Maybe it's a Jewish rule.

BARBARA: We have our own rules around here. And one of them is Coke is for people who exercise. Think of their *teeth.* I'll tell the sitter.

[RANDY *comes in from stage left. He wears a white monogrammed terry-cloth bathrobe which is a little too big for him. His hair is wet from swimming.* BARBARA *sees him, gasps.*]

Oh, my God!

RANDY: What?

BARBARA: That bathrobe! I thought you were daddy.

RANDY: Pokey gave it to me this morning.

BARBARA: You'd better get it off before mother sees it.

JANE: Why?

BARBARA: Daddy wore it the day he drowned. She found it on the beach.

RANDY: I think she'd want me to wear it.

BARBARA: When she's getting married again?

RANDY: Pokey said that doesn't mean she wants to forget daddy.

BARBARA: [*Shaking her head*] I want to forget Fred. I can tell you that.

RANDY: That's a little different.

BARBARA: I'll say.

RANDY: Oh. Pokey brought a present for you.

BARBARA: Something of daddy's?

RANDY: Yep. He held onto a lot of his stuff.

BARBARA: [*Getting up*] I'll go see.

[*She goes into the house.*]

RANDY: [*To Jane*] Do you think she'd mind?

JANE Your mother? I don't know.

RANDY: Why should she? She gave me lots of his sport coats.

JANE: That might be a little big for you.

RANDY: It's supposed to be. You're supposed to feel free in it. Daddy would wear all these tight, stuffy clothes, but when he went swimming, this was it. Mother would try to get him to wear a bathing suit when you were around, but he wouldn't do it. He said that swimming was the one time he wanted to feel absolutely free. Remember? He'd roll around in the water like an old walrus. [*He shakes his head.*] I'm the same way. [*He looks at* JANE.] You look great. New outfit?

JANE: Your mother got it for me in the village.

RANDY: I like it.

JANE: You do?

RANDY: Don't you?

JANE: I don't know. I thought I did. But now . . .

RANDY: What?

JANE: I don't know. After seeing Miriam, I feel so . . . square.

RANDY: You look great to me.

JANE: It makes me feel like your mother.

RANDY: What's wrong with that?

JANE: I don't know. Here I am in your mother's outfit, and you're in your father's bathrobe, and we're living in your family's house. . . . [*She shakes her head.*] I don't know.

[*She walks to the edge of the wall and looks out.* RANDY *watches her, then smiles, and comes to her. He begins fiddling with the back of her blouse.*]

RANDY: Then let's take it off.

JANE: [*Giggling*] Oh, Randy, stop it.

RANDY: [*Nuzzling her*] How about it? A quickie? A little nooner, before lunch? Mmmm? Mmmm?

JANE: [*Laughing*] What's come over you?

RANDY: [*Opening his bathrobe*] This. Look. No hands.

JANE: [*Walking away, laughing*] You're repulsive!

[RANDY *follows her around.* BARBARA *comes out of the house, carrying a wristwatch.*]

BARBARA: [*Holding it out*] Look what Pokey gave me. Daddy's watch.

RANDY: Hey!

BARBARA: Daddy left this on the beach, too. [*She shakes it.*] Oh, darn! It doesn't work. [*She looks at it fondly.*] Oh, boy. I can remember this. [*Imitating her father*] Barbara, I want you in this house by ten-thirty. No and's, if's, or but's. I intend to be looking at my watch. [*Pause*] Pokey kept it. [*Pause*] I said, "Pokey, don't you want any of these things? What are you keeping for yourself?"

RANDY: What did he say?

BARBARA: Nothing. [*Pause. She sighs, settles back into her chair.*] Well. Anyway, while I was in there, I laid down the law. Milk for everyone. No exceptions. And I told our little teen-age townie to take them all out to the meadow for softball as soon as they've finished their ice cream. No children on this terrace. This is absolutely sancta sanctorum for grown-ups.

[RANDY *has begun to nuzzle* JANE *again.*]

Oh, God, Randy, stop *paw*ing the woman. It's embarrassing. Mother says you do it even in restaurants in New York. Cut it out. What are other people supposed to do when you're doing that?

RANDY: Masturbate.

BARBARA: Oh, Jesus.

[*She looks at the watch fondly, tries to shake it into running.* RANDY *continues to nuzzle* JANE. *Then* BARBARA *seems to make up her mind, and puts the watch down on the table, where it stays, in full view, till the end of the play.*]

Randy, do you think you could possibly control yourself long enough for us to have a small, serious conversation before mother and Pokey come down for lunch?

RANDY: Sure.

BARBARA: Good.

[*She smiles icily, he smiles back.*]

Do you know, for example, that when mother gets married, the house goes to us?

RANDY: I know that.

BARBARA: Good. [*Another smile*] Do you know, also, that I

am seriously considering giving up my apartment in Boston, and living down here over the winter?

RANDY: Mother doesn't think—

BARBARA: Mother will be *out* of it, Randy! Now I want to do it, and all I need is a small gas furnace to take care of the bottom floor of the house.

RANDY: We need lots of things.

BARBARA: We need that first, Randy. Now I've looked around, and I know I can get one put in for a song.

RANDY: We need a new tennis court.

BARBARA: Will you let me *fin*ish, Randy? Please. I can get one put in for about two thousand dollars.

RANDY: Two thousand!

BARBARA: That's a bargain, Randy. I've found a builder who will do it almost at cost.

RANDY: We could resurface the court for—

BARBARA: You'll *get* your court, Randy. Next year. Chip in with me for the furnace now, and next year I'll chip in with you on the court! OK?

[*Pause*]

RANDY: A thousand? Now? I don't have that kind of money.

BARBARA: Oh, yes you do.

RANDY: Do you know what they pay me at Saint Luke's School?

BARBARA: Do you know what I pay for rent in Boston? Do you know what Fred gives me for alimony? We've got to get together on this, Randy.

RANDY: I can't afford a thousand.

BARBARA: You can, Randy. You know damn well you can. You have your stocks, and Jane is privately endowed. . . .

JANE: Oh. . . .

BARBARA: You are, Jane, and both of you manage to keep four children in private school, and get them on skis every winter. You can damn well pay for a dinky little furnace, if you wanted to. And you could use it, Randy. You could all come down here. Thanksgiving. And Christmas. We'd all get together. You'd use it more than I'd ever use that court. I mean, what's more important? A home, warmth, shelter—or a goddamn game?

RANDY: You've got a home.

BARBARA: I don't, Randy. I hate Boston. Everyone there is

either a professor or a politician. Or both. It's all very
moral and earnest, and I hate it, and I want to be here.

RANDY: Mother says you'd last about a week.

BARBARA: I won't, I swear. I'll send the kids to the local
schools, and I'll do some writing. . . .

RANDY: Writing?

BARBARA: Children's books. I want to write children's
books. I've always wanted to do that. Always.

RANDY: You'd go stir-crazy, sitting around, writing about
bunnies, with nobody to see.

BARBARA: I'd see people.

RANDY: Who? Old ladies? Townies?

BARBARA: There are people.

RANDY: Who? You'd never go out, Barb.

BARBARA: I went out last night.

RANDY: With Betsy. To the movies.

BARBARA: [*Blurting it out*] Says who?

RANDY: Says you. You said so.

[*Pause*]

BARBARA: Well maybe I had a date last night. What do you
think of that?

[*Pause*]

RANDY: Who with?

BARBARA: Never you mind.

[*Pause*]

RANDY: Someone who's going to be around all winter?

BARBARA: Maybe.

[*Pause*]

RANDY: Who?

BARBARA: That's for me to know.

RANDY: Come on. Who?

BARBARA: None of your beeswax.

RANDY: And you want me to kick in a thousand bucks for
some demon lover?

[*Pause*]

BARBARA: Promise you won't tell mother?

RANDY: OK.

BARBARA: Will you chip in on the furnace?

RANDY: Maybe. It depends.

[*Pause.* BARBARA *thinks it over. Finally*—]

BARBARA: Artie.

[*Pause*]

RANDY: Artie? Artie who? Artie . . . GRIEBER?

BARBARA: [*Quietly*] Artie Grieber.

[*Pause*, RANDY *whistles.*]

JANE: Who's Artie Grieber?

RANDY: Oh, my God.

JANE: Who's Artie Grieber.

RANDY: He used to cut the *grass* around here.

BARBARA: He's a builder now.

RANDY: He cut the grass.

BARBARA: He's done very well on the island.

RANDY: I thought he was married. I thought he had kids.

BARBARA: He's getting separated.

RANDY: Artie Grieber. . . . [*To* JANE] She had a crush on him twenty years ago. [*To* BARBARA] Didn't Pokey catch you with him in the maid's room?

BARBARA: Pokey caught you doing a few things too, kid.

RANDY: [*Shaking his head*] Artie Grieber. All night, with Artie Grieber.

BARBARA: If you tell mother, Randy, I swear I'll strangle you.

RANDY: Oh, my God, I wouldn't dare tell mother. [*He sits down.*] Artie Grieber.

JANE: Is it serious, Barbara?

BARBARA: It's beginning to be.

JANE: Do you think you might marry him?

BARBARA: Maybe. I . . . see a lot of him. I'm seeing him this afternoon.

RANDY: [*Still shaking his head*] Artie Grieber . . . Old Artie the grass-cutter. . . . [*He laughs.*] So you want to be here in the winter, and have Artie come in and turn on your furnace, eh?

BARBARA: [*Angrily*] CUT IT OUT! [*Controlling herself, as he continues to chuckle*] He does tennis courts, Randy. He could put in a whole new tennis court for you, next year, at half the cost. You get your court, and I get a place to live. Please, Randy. I want this. This is very important to me. Can we get together on this, please?

[RANDY *looks at her, stops laughing, stands up, wraps his bathrobe tightly around him.*]

RANDY: Who do you think I am? Do you think I'd go along with the idea of my sister shacking up all winter in this house with Artie Grieber? Jesus, Barbara. Grow up. [*Pause*]

BARBARA: [*Grimly, quietly*] Do you know what a Wasp is, Randy?

RANDY: Yes I know what a Wasp is.

BARBARA: I don't think you do. So I'll tell you. Because you are one. A Wasp is a white Anglo-Saxon prick.

RANDY: Big joke.

BARBARA: And I'll tell you something else, brother. I'm going to be here this winter. I'm going to be right here. You wait, buster. You just wait.

JANE: [*Looking toward the house*] Ssshhh. Your mother. [*A noise within. Then* MOTHER *comes out of the house, in different clothes again. She stands at the door, and notices* RANDY's *bathrobe immediately.*]

MOTHER: Pokey gave you that.

RANDY: Yes, Mother.

MOTHER: [*Nodding, turning to* BARBARA] And what did he give you?

BARBARA: [*Indicating the watch on the table*] Daddy's old wristwatch.

[MOTHER *nods and sits down.*]

MOTHER: I wonder what he brought for me. [*Pause*]

RANDY: Do you mind, Mother? My wearing this?

MOTHER: [*Brightly*] Mind? Mind? Why should I mind? [*She looks him up and down.*] It doesn't fit at all, but why should I mind? [*To* BARBARA] And the watch, of course, doesn't work. [*Pause*] Pokey asked, he specifically asked for both those things when we were going over your father's possessions.

BARBARA: Why did he give them to us, then, Mother?

MOTHER: [*Grimly*] I think I can answer that. [*Pause*] I've just had a long talk with your brother. [*Pause*] Through the bathroom door. While I was taking my bath. [*Pause*] In *fact* . . . [*Pause*] I think we should all have a drink before lunch. [*A glance at* BARBARA] Or another drink, in some cases. [*To* RANDY] Randy, go make Bloody Marys. Barbara, there's some Brie left. Get that, and some of those Bremner wafers.

BARBARA: What did he *say*, Mother?

MOTHER: I will tell you when we all have a drink in our

91

hands. Go on, Randy. . . . And get into some clothes while you're doing it, please.

[RANDY *and* BARBARA *look at her and then go quickly into the house.* JANE *remains. Pause.* MOTHER *looks out to sea, then turns to her with a sigh.*]

You and I are going to have to work very hard this weekend, Jane. Very hard indeed. We've got a big job on our hands. . . . [*She shakes her head.*] Just keeping things going.

JANE: What do you mean?

MOTHER: [*Shaking her head again*] Wait till the others get back. [*Pause*] One thing we talked about, Pokey and I, was that outfit you're wearing.

JANE: This?

MOTHER: That. We talked about that for a while.

JANE: I don't—

MOTHER: He said it was unfair.

JANE: Unfair?

MOTHER: Unfair for me to buy you that, and unfair for me to buy Barbara her yellow sweater, when I didn't buy Miriam anything.

JANE: Oh.

[*Pause*]

MOTHER: You didn't tell him I bought it, did you?

JANE: No.

MOTHER: Of course you didn't. He just knows these things. By instinct. Always has. He can sniff out an issue like this a mile away. At Christmas, he could tell if he was one present short without even counting. [*Sighs, shakes her head*] Pokey, Pokey, Pokey. [*Pause*] So. I said I bought you that outfit because you needed one. Because you and Randy don't have much money. Because Randy just teaches school. And I said I bought Barbara that yellow sweater because Fred just gives her a pittance for alimony. And I said of course I would have bought Miriam something, but she wasn't here, and I don't dare buy her things when she's not here because I never know what she likes.

JANE: That seems fair.

MOTHER: And I said, all right. This afternoon, I'll take Miriam into the village, and she can buy whatever she wants. On me.

JANE: Did that do it?

MOTHER: No, I don't think so. All I got from that was silence, on the other side of the bathroom door. [*Pause*] There's always one. In every family. Always one child who behaves like this. Does one of yours always stir things up, Jane?

JANE: Yes.

MOTHER: Who? Which one?

[*Pause*]

JANE: I won't tell.

MOTHER: [*Smiling*] Good. Good for you. [*Pause*] But in some ways, don't you love that one most of all?

JANE: Yes.

[*Pause*]

MOTHER: Even though it's so exhausting, even though it wears you down, even though you spend more time thinking about that one than any of the others . . . there's a special feeling, isn't there?

JANE: Yes.

[*Pause. They both look out to sea.*]

MOTHER: Aaaanyway, that was the first thing we talked about, Pokey and I, while I was trying to take a bath, after a very long morning, when he hasn't been here in five years. That was just the first thing.

JANE: Didn't he talk about your getting married again?

MOTHER: [*Laughing ironically*] He didn't. So I did. Finally, I said, "Pokey, sweetheart, I'm getting *married* in the fall. I wrote you a letter, and you haven't even mentioned it. Don't you at least want to congratulate your mother? Isn't that just a little bit more important than who bought what for whom? Kind of? Maybe? Sort of? Hmmm?"

JANE: And what did he say?

MOTHER: Nothing.

JANE: Nothing.

MOTHER: Nothing. There was more silence. Endless silence. An eternity of silence.

JANE: Maybe he didn't hear.

MOTHER: Oh, he heard all right. Because then suddenly he launched into the *big* topic of discussion, and—

[*Noise from the house, clinking of glasses and ice*]

And here, thank heavens, comes something to drink.

[RANDY *enters, now in a polo shirt and khakis, carrying a tray of glasses and a pitcher of Bloody Marys.* BARBARA *follows him with a platter of crackers and cheese. As the scene continues,* RANDY *hands around the drinks, with the appropriate ad-libs.* BARBARA *puts the crackers and cheese in front of her* MOTHER, *who cuts it, puts the cheese on the crackers, and hands them out during the conversation.*]

Where is Pokey now?

RANDY: With his children.

MOTHER: That's so we can talk it over.

BARBARA: Talk *what* over?

[RANDY *hands his mother a drink.*]

MOTHER: Thank you, dear. [*She takes a long sip.*] Pokey wants you two to buy him out.

[*Startled pause*]

RANDY: Buy him *out?*

MOTHER: That's what he said. Buy out his third of the house. In the fall. When it goes to you. When I get married. . . . Have some cheese, Jane?

[*She hands* JANE *a cracker and cheese.*]

BARBARA: He doesn't want it?

MOTHER: He wants his equity. That's what he says. . . . Here, Barbara. Cheese.

[*Pause*]

RANDY: Well . . . OK. . . .

MOTHER: OK? OK? Randy, my dear love, *think* before you speak. Pokey wants one-third of a fair market value. He says that this house, with beach frontage, and a tennis court, and a barn, and five acres of valuable land, is worth at least two hundred thousand dollars. Minimum. . . . Take some cheese, dear.

BARBARA: That means . . . mmm . . . over sixty thousand each.

MOTHER: At least.

RANDY: That means we each have to pay Pokey at least thirty thousand.

MOTHER: At least and we can't sell off the land because the will won't allow it, and we can't get another mortgage, because daddy already did that after he got sick and couldn't work full-time.

[*Pause*]

RANDY: Then we can't pay Pokey.

MOTHER: Of course you can't. Nor can I. Nor can Uncle Bill.

BARBARA: Did you tell him we can't?

MOTHER: Of course I did.

RANDY: What did he say?

MOTHER: He said we can. If we sell. [*General consternation*] Oh, yes. That's what he said. Sell this beautiful place, pay a huge capital gains tax, divide up the furniture, and get out of here, lock, stock, and barrel, so that Pokey can have his money.

BARBARA: He doesn't need the money.

MOTHER: He says he does.

RANDY: He's got a good job. He earns more than any of us.

MOTHER: He wants to leave that job.

BARBARA: With the Department of *Justice?*

MOTHER: He doesn't like it. He says it's unfair.

RANDY: Unfair?

MOTHER: He's upset about civil rights. He says the Department of Justice is unfair to Negroes. I don't know. He wants to leave.

RANDY: Golly.

MOTHER: Just the way he left Andover. Just the way he left Yale Law School. Just the way he left two other jobs in the past ten years. Just the way he left *here,* summer after summer . . . [*Ironically*] whenever things are unfair. . . .

BARBARA: Oh, Lord.

MOTHER: And so he says he needs the money to live on. To support Miriam and the children. While he decides what he wants to do.

[*Long pause*]

BARBARA: So what's the solution, Mother?

MOTHER: I'll tell you what the solution is *not.* The solution is *not* to sell. That is *not* the solution.

RANDY: Of course.

MOTHER: Sell this spot? Which has been in the family for over eighty years? Why there's nothing that can compare to it on the island, in the country, in the world! I mean, look, just look at that view!

[*They all look out.*]

Pokey loves it here. In his heart of hearts, he loves it. I know it. And he knows it. . . . My glass is empty, Randy.

[RANDY *jumps up, takes her glass, and pours her another Bloody Mary.*]

It's the same old thing, with Pokey. He leaves. But he always comes back. I mean, he's here, isn't he? He's right here. And he wants us all to make a big fuss.

[RANDY *gives her her glass.*]

Thank you, dear. . . . Remember when he was little? He'd come storming in, his bag all packed, ready to run away, and we'd all have to coddle him like mad. Remember? All those trips down to the drug store for special ice cream cones? Well that's what he wants now, at thirty-one years old, and I'm afraid we're all going to have to do it. . . . Have some more cheese, Jane.

BARBARA: Do what, though, Mother?

MOTHER: Baby him, dear. Butter him up.

RANDY: Pokey's kind of a hard guy to butter up, Mother.

MOTHER: Not if we work hard. First, I think he needs sleep. He's exhausted from the trip. So I think we should persuade him to take a nap, and keep the children very quiet while he does.

RANDY: But I asked him to play tennis this afternoon. . . .

BARBARA: Oh, Randy, God!

MOTHER: Tennis can wait. Next, I think we can all loosen up. Barbara, the children *can* have Coca-Cola if they want it. He complained about that, and I told the sitter they can.

BARBARA: OK. Fine. Coke with meals. I'll send you the dentist's bills.

MOTHER: And tonight, after he's had a nap and his favorite meal, I think we should try to get him to come to the Yacht Club dance.

BARBARA: He doesn't want to go, Mother. He says he hates costume parties.

MOTHER: Nonsense. He's just forgotten what fun it can be. We'll all go together. I've decided to go as my favorite person, Eleanor of Aquitaine, mother of kings and queens. And Uncle Bill is going as the Great Gatsby. Pokey and Miriam can go as them*selves,* I don't care, but they've got to go. He'll be able to sing, and dance, and see all his old friends. So we've all got to coax him to go.

RANDY: OK.

MOTHER: And finally, I think we should ask him to stay on.

As long as he wants. All summer, if he wants. And if he wants the house to himself, he should have it.

BARBARA: Mother!

MOTHER: It's only fair, Barbara.

BARBARA: But we've made plans!

MOTHER: Change them, Barbara. Pokey comes first.

RANDY: But maybe he doesn't want to be here anymore, Mother.

[*Pause, she looks at him.*]

MOTHER: One thing I *know*. One thing I know without a shadow of a doubt. No one, and I mean no one, can live without roots. No one can cut himself off completely from his background. People are like plants. If they are cut, they last for a while, but then they wither and die. That I know. And that is Pokey's problem. And that we have got to make him realize, before it's too late for all of us. [*Pause*] Now. Change the subject. I want a picture of all of us here on this terrace together. Randy, go into the coat closet and get daddy's old *Kodak*. And please call Pokey and Miriam.

[RANDY *goes into the house.*]

BARBARA: Mother, if Pokey takes August, what'll I do?

MOTHER: Ssshhh.

[RANDY'*s voice is heard calling "Pokey" within.*]

BARBARA: But I've sublet my apartment, Mother. Where will I go?

JANE: You could stay with us, back at school.

BARBARA: But I don't want to do that.

MOTHER: Ssshhh.

[RANDY *comes back on with the camera and a package wrapped in brown paper.*]

Are they coming?

RANDY: In a while. They're reading to their kids.

MOTHER: In the middle of the *day?*

RANDY: Apparently it's their custom.

MOTHER: Oh. . . .

RANDY: [*Handing her the package*] But he told me to give you this. He says it goes with the house.

MOTHER: [*Holding it, a little nervous*] How nice.

BARBARA: Well open it, Mother.

MOTHER: All right.

[*She opens it slowly. Everyone watches.*]

BARBARA: Look out. It might explode.

[*Everyone laughs. Finally* MOTHER *gets it open.*]

MOTHER: Why it's . . .

BARBARA: [*Squealing*] It's the Family *Bi*-ble!

JANE: Bible?

BARBARA: We called it that. It's daddy's notebook. Look, Randy! [*She takes it from her* MOTHER.] All the old records. [*To* JANE] We thought it was lost, after he died. [*To* RANDY] Pokey kept this, too. [*To* MOTHER] Oh, this is a great house present, Mother!

MOTHER: [*Shaking her head, quietly to herself*] Pokey, Pokey, Pokey.

BARBARA: [*Sitting on steps, thumbing through the book, as* RANDY *looks over her shoulder.*] Look. Here's the genealogy. All the old names. Ezra, Abigail, Hepsibah. . . . Oh, and here's the account of that fabulous woman. That great, great, great, great, GREAT grandmother, who was raped by Indians, and had her stomach slit open. Remember, Mother? When daddy used to read that? And she hid herself in a hollow tree for three days, and stuffed her guts back in, and was found and sewn up by her husband, and went on to have eight children?. . . Remember, Mother?

[MOTHER *nods.*]

RANDY: [*Flipping pages, looking over* BARBARA's *shoulder*] Hey. Here are all the ministers. Look at all the Presbyterian ministers.

BARBARA: And here's one of their sermons.

RANDY: [*Reading, laughing*] "Man is conceived in sin and born in travail. . . . Seek not for salvation in the vast splendors of our bounteous land. . . . The delights of this world have been set as a bait and a snare. . . ." [*Slyly, to* BARBARA] "Forswear the pleasures of this world. . . ."

BARBARA: [*Quickly*] Isn't that *mar*velous? Isn't that marvelous, Mother?

[MOTHER *nods, a little grimly.* BARBARA *continues reading.*]

Oh, and here come the businessmen. Look at all these inventories. All this money. Look. Daddy estimated all their incomes. . . .

RANDY: And furniture. And china. And horses. And automobiles. . . . Look, even wash cloths are listed. [*To his* MOTHER] It's all here, Mother.

MOTHER: [*Impatiently*] I know it's all there.

BARBARA: [*Flipping the pages*] Oh, and now here are the games. All the old scores of all the old family tennis games. Look: in 1952, mother and daddy beat you and me 6-3.

RANDY: [*Taking the book*] Let me see that. . . . Well, here's where I beat Pokey 18-16. [*To* JANE] I told you I could beat him.

BARBARA: [*Reading over his shoulder*] Oh, Mother, look. [*She takes the book, shows it to her* MOTHER.] In 1957, you and daddy beat Fred and me, six-love. I remember that. Fred and I were engaged, and he was visiting, and he could hardly hold a racquet. God, he was horrible. Six-love. I should have read the writing on the wall.

MOTHER: [*Infinitely patient*] Do you think we can take pictures, please?

RANDY: [*Looking over their shoulder*] Look. Here's 1963. Here's where Uncle Bill started to fill in.

BARBARA: Because of daddy's bad heart.

RANDY: Let's see. In '63, mother and Uncle Bill lost to you and me 7-5.

BARBARA: I remember. Poor daddy had to watch.

RANDY: [*Taking book*] Hey, this isn't right. It says here that in 1961 Pokey beat me by default. That's not right.

BARBARA: Oh, yes it is. That was the year you threw your racquet at him. And daddy made you default.

RANDY: Oh, yeah. . . .

BARBARA: [*Taking the book, flipping through it*] Wow. Here are the sailing races, and the croquet games, and even our report cards from school. . . .

RANDY: Who won between Pokey and me in '65. [*He tries to take the book.*]

BARBARA: [*Holding onto it*] Wait a minute. Here are my marks from Westover. Look. See? An *A* in creative writing. I told you I could write.

RANDY: [*Pulling at the book*] Let me just see the tennis scores. I know I beat Pokey in '65. I'm sure of that.

BARBARA: Randy, don't grab!

RANDY: I just want to see '65!

[MOTHER *gets up, comes between them, takes the book, closes it decisively, and puts it on a table.*]

I just want to see the record for 1965, Mother.

MOTHER: [*Grimly, wheeling on him*] You won't *find* any record for 1965, dear boy. Because in the summer of 1965, your father *died.* Remember. Taking a long swim, after a big meal, on a hot day, with a bad heart. That's what happened in 1965. [*She shakes her head, tears in her eyes.*] Oh, what does Pokey think he's doing, dragging all this stuff up? The bathrobe, the watch, and now that—that stupid, stupid book! What's he trying to do?

BARBARA: It shows he cares, Mother.

MOTHER: Cares? Cares about what? A lot of old names and dates and statistics.

RANDY: These are our roots, Mother.

MOTHER: Not at all. That's just a long boring list. I used to beg your father, I used to beg him when he was working on that thing, I'd say put in the nice things we all did. Put in some of the things *I* organized. Where is a description of the blueberry picking, or the trip to Cuttyhunk, or the singing by the piano, or the time we all got together and made this terrace, stone by stone? Where are the real things? Where is the *life?* I'd beg him to include those things. But he never would. All he cared about was things you could own, and count, and pin down. [*She sits down.*] Now PLEASE! Let's take a picture of us all here together, out here on this terrace, in the sun!

[*Long pause*]

RANDY: [*Quietly*] I want a picture of you, Mother.

MOTHER: You have plenty of me.

RANDY: Not alone.

BARBARA: He wants a picture of the bride.

RANDY: I want a picture of mother.

MOTHER: [*Touched*] Oh . . . All right. [*She dries her eyes, folds her hands in her lap, puts her heels neatly together, and tries to smile.*]

RANDY: [*Kneeling, sighing, then looking up*] Gee. You're still a beautiful woman, Mother.

BARBARA: Portrait of a lady.

[*They all look at her. Pause*]

MOTHER: Oh, take the picture. Take it. Before I go to pieces completely.

[RANDY *sights, focuses, takes the picture, as* BARBARA *and* JANE *look on.*]

Now. Someone. Get Pokey.

JANE: I'll get him.

[*She hurries into the house. The sound of a car horn can now be heard honking far offstage right.*]

BARBARA: [*With a start*] Oh, my God. That's for me.

[*She starts hurriedly offstage right.*]

MOTHER: Who is it?

BARBARA: [*Glancing defiantly at* RANDY] I've—got a golf game, Mother.

MOTHER: What about the picture? What about lunch?

BARBARA: Too late, Mother. Good-bye.

[*She goes offstage right.*]

MOTHER: [*To* RANDY] Who is that? Why can't they come up and shake hands? I don't like people sitting in cars and tooting their horns. [*Shakes her head*] There goes the family picture.

[JANE *comes out of the house.*]

JANE: Miriam's made lunch. It's all ready.

MOTHER: Then we should go in.

JANE: [*To* RANDY] And Pokey wants to take you on in tennis, after lunch.

[JANE *goes in.*]

RANDY: [*Eagerly*] You mean I'll take *him* on.

[*He cuts across his* MOTHER *as she moves toward the house.*]

MOTHER: Randy!

RANDY: Oh! Sorry, Mother.

[*He holds the screen-door open for her. She goes in, shaking her head.* RANDY *follows, as the lights dim.*]

END OF ACT I

ACT II

The group of voices might sing "I Had a Dream, Dear" or "Careless Love."

Early afternoon light. Shadows are just beginning to appear on the terrace. The glasses and cheese have been cleared away, but the watch is still on the table.

From offstage right comes the occasional sound of a tennis game, and at intervals the sound of children's voices cheering.

After a moment, Barbara comes in from upstage right. She sees Jane, stops, straightens her hair, adjusts her clothes, puts on a bright smile, and speaks:

BARBARA: Hi.

    [*Jane starts, and turns.*]

JANE: We didn't expect you back so soon.

BARBARA: We only played nine holes. [*Laughs, does up a button on her blouse.*] No. He had to get back to work. Lots of summer construction. [*Pause*] People *work* on this island, if you can believe it. [*Pause*] I'm seeing him again tonight. I'll have to skip the dance. [*The sound of children cheering and clapping, offstage right*] Hey, how come you're not down there watching the big match? It looked very heated as I came by. Pokey and Randy dashing around, snorting and puffing away. And all the children were sitting in a row on the bench. Like vultures. [*She looks at* JANE.] Shouldn't you be down there, rooting for your man?

102

JANE: [*Quietly, shaking her head*] I'm tired of games.
 [*Pause*]

BARBARA: [*A little uneasily*] Where's Mother? Taking her
 nap? [*Jane nods.*] Was she—peeved at me, for ducking
 out?

JANE: She never mentioned it again.

BARBARA: Then she was peeved. [*Pause*] Was lunch awful?
 Was there a lot of bickering about the house?

JANE: Not so much . . . I don't know . . . I was talking to
 Miriam.

BARBARA: Oh, dear. You got stuck with her.

JANE: Not *stuck*. Not stuck at all. I like her.

BARBARA: So do we all, so dō we all. [*Pause*] What did you
 talk about, with Miriam?

JANE: Oh, I don't know. . . .

BARBARA: Did you talk about the house?

JANE: No.

BARBARA: No?

JANE: We never got to that.

BARBARA: Well you must at least have broached the subject.

JANE: No. I'm sorry. I didn't.
 [*Pause*]

BARBARA: What *did* you talk about, then?

JANE: Oh . . . Life, I guess.

BARBARA: [*Laughing*] *Life?* How heady.

JANE: Her life.

BARBARA: *Her* life? Does she have one? Does Pokey let her
 have one?
 [*Pause*]

JANE: She's thinking of leaving Pokey.

BARBARA: Oh, no. . . .

JANE: Unless he decides who he is. She said she wanted
 him to come up here this weekend. So he could work
 things out.

BARBARA: Work things *out?*

JANE: She said it's like being married to an elastic band.

BARBARA: Whatever that means.

JANE: I think it means that he's stretched. Between their
 life. And this.

BARBARA: And which way does she want him to go?

JANE: Either way. Otherwise, she says he'll snap. Or she will.

[*Pause*]

BARBARA: I know the feeling.

JANE: So do I.

[*Pause*]

BARBARA: Well what's her way?

JANE: Oh, her life sounds wonderful.

BARBARA: According to her.

JANE: No really. I think she has a wonderful life.

[*Pause. More noise from the tennis game is heard offstage right.*]

BARBARA: So do you. So do you have a wonderful life.

JANE: Oh, I know. [*Pause*] But she . . . does more.

BARBARA: Such as what?

JANE: She works, for one thing.

BARBARA: Busy, busy, busy. . . .

JANE: No, she's got a profession. People . . . need her. People count on her. In her work.

BARBARA: What does she call herself?

JANE: I don't even know the title. But she helps families that are falling apart.

BARBARA: [*Bitterly*] Oh, I know that type. I've been through that mill. You sit there, pouring out your soul to those ladies, and they smile, and give you a lot of lingo, or else yawn in your face.

JANE: She didn't yawn in mine.

[*Pause, more sounds from offstage right*]

BARBARA: Well you help people, too. You're on some hospital board, aren't you?

JANE: It's not the same.

BARBARA: Of course it's the same.

JANE: [*Shaking her head*] I'm just there. [*Pause*] Miriam's getting her Ph.D. That's what she's doing right now. She's upstairs studying for her Ph.D. So she can teach.

BARBARA: Oh, Jews always do that. They're frantic about education.

JANE: And she plays the viola.

BARBARA: The viola! My, my.

JANE: In a string quartet. Once a week, rain or shine, she gets together with three other people, and they play

Mozart, and Bach, and Vivaldi together, all evening
long. Oh, it sounds like so much *fun,* doing that.

BARBARA: Well you sing, Jane.

JANE: I don't sing.

BARBARA: You do, too. You sang in the Nightowls at
Vassar, and I hope you'll sing at the dance tonight. I
hope you sing *Mood Indigo.* I love the way you do that.

JANE: [*Singing softly*] "You . . . Ain't Been . . . Blue . . ."

BARBARA: [*Joining her, in harmony*] "No . . . No . . .
No . . ." [*They stop.*] See? You sing. I'll bet Miriam can't
sing that.

[*More sounds from the tennis offstage right*]

JANE: She has such a good relationship with her children.

BARBARA: What does that *mean?* A good relationship.

JANE: She lets them grow.

BARBARA: So do you. You've taught them to ski and play
tennis. . . .

JANE: But it isn't such a—struggle, with Miriam. She
doesn't make them wear things, or say things, or learn
things all the time.

BARBARA: And as a result they are spoiled little brats.

JANE: They're wonderful.

BARBARA: They're fresh, they're grubby, they use foul language. . . .

JANE: But they're so . . . open. They were there all during
lunch with us.

BARBARA: Oh, I'm sure. Interrupting mother, debasing the
conversation, while our children were out playing a good
healthy game of softball. Where are Pokey's kids now?

JANE: Watching TV, I think.

BARBARA: You see? Our children don't do that.

JANE: I know it.

BARBARA: Because we have rules about TV. I imagine Miriam lets them watch it whenever they want.

JANE: She doesn't like rules.

BARBARA: Well that's just the trouble. I think Pokey and
Miriam spend too much time giving in to their children,
and kow-towing to them, and being around them. I think
that's unhealthy. Mother says if you do that, you'll turn
into a child yourself.

JANE: I suppose. . . .

[*Pause. A big groan is heard offstage right.*]

But they fight so.

BARBARA: Who fights?

JANE: Our children. Yours and mine.

BARBARA: All children fight.

JANE: Miriam's don't. They never fight. They traveled all night, and they've been up most of the day, and they haven't fought at all.

[*Pause. Then* RANDY *comes in from upstage right, in his tennis whites, looking hot and sweaty. He looks at the two women, shakes his head, and slumps into a chair.*]

BARBARA: Well. Who won?

RANDY: [*Under his breath*] We didn't finish.

BARBARA: What do you mean?

RANDY: [*Shouting*] WE DIDN'T FINISH!

[*Pause*]

BARBARA: [*Looking at* JANE, *with a sigh*] Well. I'm going to go butter up Pokey, and get back into mother's good graces. [*Indicating* RANDY] He's all yours.

[*She goes out upstage right. Pause*]

JANE: Where's your racquet?

[*No answer from* RANDY.] Where's your racquet, Randy? [*No answer*]

Did you throw your racquet at him?

[*No answer. She shakes her head.*]

Oh, Randy. . . .

RANDY: I didn't throw it at *him*. I threw it into the poison ivy.

JANE: Oh, honestly.

RANDY: It was a crumby racquet. I hated that goddamn racquet.

JANE: In front of the children.

RANDY: I apologized. I said, Come on. I'll get another racquet. I'll get mother's racquet. Come on. Let's finish the game. But he just walked off the court.

JANE: I don't blame him.

RANDY: You don't *blame* him? For walking away? In front of all those kids?

JANE: [*Shaking her head*] Throwing your racquet. . . .

RANDY: He walked away from the game!

JANE: Oh, Randy. . . .

RANDY: Listen. You know what I think. I think he came up here just to beat me. I really think that. He's been prac-

106

ticing *up,* you know. Oh, sure. He's been playing all winter, at this jazzy club in Washington. I have to coach hockey, but he's had all winter to practice up for me. He still isn't much good, either. He's got all these cuts and lobs and drop shots, but his serve is a laugh. . . .

[*Jane sighs and starts toward the house.*]

And I could have won, too. It was my serve when he quit. Do you want to know what the score in games was? Do you—

JANE: [*Suddenly wheeling on him at the door*] Oh, Randy, I don't care! I don't CARE who beats who! I don't care whether you beat Pokey, or whether Saint Luke's School beats Exeter, or whether the Los Angeles Rams win or lose! I don't care! I don't care about scores or goals or points or batting averages! Really! I don't CARE, Randy! I just don't give a SHIT!

[*She storms into the house.* RANDY *stands up, amazed.*]

RANDY: Hey . . . HEY! . . . Hey, WAIT! . . . What's gotten INTO you?

[*He hurries after her into the house as the lights fade. The group sings a campfire song such as "A Man without a Woman" or "The Blue Tail Fly" or "When Pa Was a Little Boy." The lights have come up again. It is now late afternoon. Shadows are longer across the terrace.* MOTHER *has come out of the house. She carries a small watering can and shears, and begins to water the flowers in the window boxes, deftly snipping off the dead blossoms and leaves.* BARBARA *comes out of the house, and stands by the door, watching her.* MOTHER *ignores her, stonily working on the flowers. Finally—*]

BARBARA: Mother, I'm sorry I skipped lunch.

MOTHER: [*Blithely*] Oh, that's all right. What's lunch? Just a meal. [*She works on the flowers.*] Your brother is here for the first time in five years, it's his first meal here, the whole house is at stake—but what's lunch? Do you think you can make it for dinner?

BARBARA: [*With a sigh*] Of course, Mother.

MOTHER: You see I don't know. People come and go around here as if it were Grand Central Station. . . . Now the boys aren't speaking because of that stupid tennis. . . . I suppose now Pokey won't go to the Yacht Club dance.

BARBARA: He doesn't want to go. I've just been talking to him.

MOTHER: Why not? Because of Randy?

BARBARA: Because Uncle Bill is going.

MOTHER: And did you try to persuade him? Did you defend your Uncle Bill? Did you make even the smallest effort to keep this family together?

[*Pause*]

BARBARA: I'm not going either, Mother.

MOTHER: Oh fine. That's just fine.

BARBARA: Please don't be mad.

MOTHER: Mad? Who's mad? What makes you think I'm mad.

BARBARA: You won't even look at me.

MOTHER: [*Puttering rather violently with the flowers*] Do I have to look at you every minute of the day? Do I have to stare at you in order for you to exist? [*Pause, too casually*] Why do you care how I feel anyway? It seems to me my opinion counts for very little in your life lately.

[*Pause*]

BARBARA: What does that mean?

MOTHER: I happened to look out my bedroom window, Barbara, and see Artie Grieber's truck in our driveway this afternoon.

[*Pause*]

BARBARA: [*With a deep sigh*] Here we go.

MOTHER: I saw you give him that kiss. That was quite a kiss. *Quite* a kiss. To bestow on a yardman.

BARBARA: Not a yardman.

MOTHER: He was the yardman here.

BARBARA: He's a builder now.

MOTHER: Oh, I know what he is now. I've seen every tacky summer cottage he's put up. [*Pause*] And you said you had a golf game.

BARBARA: I didn't want an argument.

MOTHER: You've got one now.

BARBARA: I know it.

[*Pause*]

MOTHER: I suppose that's where you were last night.

BARBARA: Yes.

MOTHER: At least you're discreet about it. I'll say that.

BARBARA: Not now. I told him to drive right up to the door.
I'm glad you saw.

MOTHER: Well I don't want to see it again. I never liked
him. Neither did your father. I don't want to see him
around.

BARBARA: It's my life.

MOTHER: It's my house.

BARBARA: Not anymore.

MOTHER: Until September! And I will not have you living
here while you engage in a cheap, adulterous relationship with a local married man!

BARBARA: He's separated, Mother.

MOTHER: Because of you?

BARBARA: Yes.

MOTHER: He's leaving his family because of you?

BARBARA: Yes. If he can. They're Catholic.

MOTHER: You hardly know him.

BARBARA: I know him very well.

MOTHER: Years ago.

BARBARA: I've known him all along. Every summer.

MOTHER: While you were married to Fred?

BARBARA: Yes.

MOTHER: Don't tell me this is the reason for your divorce!

BARBARA: Yes. Partly. Yes.

MOTHER: I am appalled!

BARBARA: It's true.

MOTHER: I am simply appalled. To leave Fred for that sly,
ambitious, social-climbing Artie Grieber. I'm appalled.

BARBARA: I love him, Mother.

MOTHER: You can't love him.

BARBARA: I've loved him since I've known him.

MOTHER: What? When he was cutting our grass?

BARBARA: Even then!

MOTHER: That's impossible.

BARBARA: [*Defiantly*] He was the first boy I ever slept with,
Mother.

MOTHER: I won't hear this.

BARBARA: That's why I moved into the maid's room. So he
could come back at night. Up the backstairs. And we'd
meet on the beach.

MOTHER: I don't want to hear any of this.

BARBARA: Well it's true, Mother. And I love him. And I

want to marry him. [*Starts to cry*] And I should have married him all along. I never should have married Fred.

MOTHER: Oh, Barbara. . . .

BARBARA: I never liked Fred. I don't like my children.

MOTHER: Barbara, Barbara. . . .

BARBARA: You and daddy made me marry Fred.

MOTHER: We did no such thing.

BARBARA: [*Crying*] You did, you did. You brought him around. You turned on the charm. You kept saying he was Our Kind. You kept saying it. That's what you kept saying, Mother.

MOTHER: Stop it, Barbara.

BARBARA: He wasn't my kind. Artie is my kind. I'm going to live with him, Mother.

MOTHER: Not here, you're not.

BARBARA: Oh, yes. Right here. Because he's going to buy Pokey out. And if Randy doesn't like it, he'll buy Randy out. He's got all the money he wants, and he's going to put in a seawall, and winterize this place, and fix it all up, and we'll live here all year round. And I'll see him summers and winters and days and nights and we're going to screw any time we want!

[MOTHER *slaps her hard across the face.* BARBARA *reels back, then speaks very quietly through her tears.*]

Oh, Mother, you hypocrite! You hypocrite! Pokey just told me you did the same thing with Uncle Bill! For years! And daddy knew it! And that's why he finally killed himself!

[*She runs into the house.* MOTHER *stands aghast as the lights dim, then she strides into the house as the song comes up. The group sings a lively romantic song such as "Ain't She Sweet" or a ra-de-de-da version of "In the Evening by the Moonlight." The lights come up again, as the music fades. It is early evening. There is a rosy glow on the terrace now.* MOTHER'*s shears and watering can are still on the table where she left them. After a moment,* RANDY *comes out of the house. He wears a white, freshly laundered Yale football uniform, including the helmet. He carries a tray full of gin-and-tonic ingredients. He sets the tray down on the table, takes off his helmet, and calls toward the house.*]

RANDY: [*Calling*] Jane? . . . Are you coming out? [*No answer from within the house. He looks at the tray, looks back toward the house again.*] I'm having a drink. Won't you join me? I don't want to drink alone. [*No answer*] Come on. You'll feel better once you've had a drink. [*Still no answer. He shrugs, looks at the tray, then begins to fix himself a drink. As he does, the screen-door opens and* JANE *comes out, in her costume. It is her debutante dress, long, all white, perhaps strapless. She also wears long white gloves, has her hair done in a fancy way, and looks young and lovely.*] You. Look. Spec-*ta*cular!

JANE: I feel like a jerk.

RANDY: You look as great as the night I met you. . . . Better. . . . Even better.

JANE: I feel like a real jerk. [*Pause*] I just showed it to Miriam. She wanted to know why I was going as Little Bo-Peep. When I told her it was my coming-out dress, from my coming-out party, she said, "Ah. The Wasp Bar-Mitzvah."

RANDY: [*Returning to making the drinks*] That Miriam. I wish she'd lay off.

JANE: [*Defiantly*] She's wonderful.

RANDY: She bugs me.

JANE: I like her one heck of a lot.
[*Pause*]

RANDY: [*Looking at her*] I won't argue. You look too great. [*He starts to mix drinks. Pause*]

JANE: [*Suddenly*] I don't want to go to the damn dance.

RANDY: [*Bringing her a drink*] Oh, come on.

JANE: I don't. I look like a jerk. And everyone else there will look like a jerk. And act like one, too. Last year there were at least twenty debutantes or brides, and another twenty football players or hockey players or lacrosse players and I don't want to go. I don't want to spend a sappy evening trotting around the dance floor with all those jerks.
[*Pause.* RANDY *puts down his drink, looks at her carefully.*]

RANDY: So you think all our friends are jerks, huh?

JANE: [*Defiantly*] Yes I do.
[*Pause*]

RANDY: Do you think our children are jerks?
[*Pause. She turns away from him.*]

JANE: I think they could be. [*She turns back to him.*] I think they could turn into jerks very easily.
[*Pause*]

RANDY: Who do you think isn't a jerk?

JANE: Oh . . .

RANDY: Who? Come on.
[*Pause*]

JANE: Miriam. Miriam isn't a jerk.

RANDY: I knew it. Why?

JANE: She has a better life.

RANDY: That kook?

JANE: Sssshhh.

RANDY: [*Loud*] She's a kook! You want to wander around with your boobs bouncing and your hair in your eyes and B.O.?

JANE: She doesn't have B.O.

RANDY: She smells, my friend. She hasn't even been swimming. Smell her some time.

JANE: Sssshhh.

RANDY: That's not a better life, pal.

JANE: It is, it is. They do things, they feel things, they know what's going on. [*Pause*] We don't. We're babies. We live on an island, here and at school. What have we done with our lives? All we've done is play games. We've missed things, Randy. We've really missed things.
[*Pause*]

RANDY: You don't like your life.

JANE: No. I've wasted it.

RANDY: Do you want to change it?

JANE: Yes.

RANDY: Do you want to change—me?

JANE: I don't know.
[*Pause*]

RANDY: Do you still love me?
[*Pause*]

JANE: I guess. . . . I don't know . . . .
[RANDY *looks at her for a long time.*]

RANDY: Wait there. [*He goes into the house.* JANE *waits nervously, eyeing the screendoor. She picks up her drink, is about to take a sip, and then shakes her head and defi-*

*antly puts it down, untouched. In a moment, music can
be heard from within—a "society orchestra" recording—
bright, bouncing songs from musical comedies in the fifties.* RANDY *comes back out.*]

Hear that?

[*She nods, reluctantly.*]

Sound familiar?

[*She nods.*]

Remember your party?

JANE: [*Impatiently*] Randy—

RANDY: Remember your party?

[JANE *nods.*]

You were standing between your parents . . . holding a
huge bunch of flowers. . . .

[*He picks a flower from the window box, holds it out to
her. She hesitates, then takes it.*]

And I was visiting Bill Butler after the hockey play-offs
at Princeton.

JANE: [*Ironically*] What was the score?

RANDY: Seven to five in overtime. . . . [*He catches himself.*]
Cut it out. . . . I remember coming through the line. . . .
[*He pantomimes bowing and shaking hands.*] How do
you do? Good evening.

[*He reaches* JANE, *shakes her hand.*]

Good evening. Would you like to dance?

JANE: [*Walking away*] That's not the way it was, Randy. I
had to dance with my father first.

RANDY: Still. . . . Would you like to dance?

[*She turns, he bows very formally.*]

JANE: [*Reluctantly*] All right.

[*She holds out her arms. They begin to dance in the
waning light around the terrace, avoiding the furniture.*
JANE *is stiff and reluctant at first.* RANDY *tries a dip.*]

RANDY: Remember this?

JANE: [*Smiling*] Mmmm-hmmmm.

[*More dancing. She dances more enthusiastically now.*]

RANDY [*Trying a fancy break*] I learned this at dancing
school.

JANE: So did I.

[*They dance closer after a while, cheek to cheek, occasionally turning.*]

RANDY: This isn't so bad, is it?

JANE: Mmmm.

RANDY: Dancing on a terrace, on an island, in the sunset, overlooking the sea. . . .

JANE: Mmmm.

RANDY: [*Turning*] If this is wasting our life, baby, vive le wastefulness.

JANE: [*Eyes closed*] Sssshhh.

RANDY: [*Trying another fancy turn*] Do you think Miriam can do this?

JANE: Just . . . sshhh.

[*It is almost sunset now. And the sky is beginning to turn a deep blue behind the house.* RANDY *and* JANE *both with eyes closed, now dance very close together, very sensuously, even though the music continues its bouncy beat. Suddenly it groans to a stop, as someone has turned off the machine within.* RANDY *and* JANE *stop, still holding each other, in a dance position.* MOTHER *comes out of the house. She wears a summer jacket dress, with high heels, and carries a small traveling bag. She comes out briskly, and speaks very calmly.*]

MOTHER: Randy, I want you to do me a big favor.

[RANDY *and* JANE *stand looking at her, amazed.*]

I want you to go down to the beach, Randy, and get Pokey, bring him up here, because I want to say good-bye.

RANDY: Mother. . . .

MOTHER: Just do it, Randy. Right now. Please. Uncle Bill is picking me up in ten minutes. We're catching the eight o'clock ferry, and we're staying with the Robinsons in Boston, and we'll be married—by our*selves*—as soon as we possibly can. Go *on*, Randy. Please. Get Pokey. The house is yours. There's a lamb in the oven and spinach on the stove and you can all fight and argue over dinner all by yourselves.

RANDY: Mother. . . .

MOTHER: Do it, Randy, before I scream.

[*Pause. He looks at her, sees her determination, turns, and angrily goes offstage left toward the beach. Pause.* MOTHER *puts down her bag, looks at* JANE.]

I. AM. THROUGH. Through with this house, through with the children, through with the grandchildren, through with the WHOLE. DAMN. THING. I am free

and clear, as of right now. Take over, Jane. It's yours,
and anyone else's who wants to pay the taxes, and plant
the flowers, and fix the roof, and order the meals, and
make the gravy, and keep things UP! I've had it! Count
me permanently OUT!

[*Offstage right, a large bang*]

JANE: [*Jumping up*] What's that?

MOTHER: That was a firecracker! I just gave out all the firecrackers! To all your children! Early! I said, Go ahead.
Let 'er rip. Make as much noise as you want. This is *my*
independence day. Celebrate it, kiddoes! Make unto the
Lord a joyful noise! [*A string of bangs is heard.*] The
Mother country is cutting loose from the colonies! Long
live the Queen! [*Perhaps a Roman candle shoots across
the dark blue sky, she calls off toward stage right.*] Go on!
Get hurt! I don't care! Point those things right at the
house! Set it on fire! Who cares? We won't be here, Bill
and I! We'll be off having fun! [*More firecrackers sound.*]
Oh, such spectacular fun! We're going to spend every
nickel we've got. We're going to travel to Europe and Ja-
pan and South America. We're going to get new clothes
and new cars and a new apartment! And I'm going to forget Christmas, and Easter, and everyone's birthday, and
everyone's size and shape! If someone gets sick, I don't
want to hear! If someone loses a tooth, or wins a prize, or
needs a dress, or wants a toy, I don't want to know! I
don't want to know, I don't want to hear, I don't want to
care! I won't have anyone's telephone number, and no
one will have mine. I'm unlisted, as of now. If you find
me out, I won't be there. I'm gone, I'm finished. I'm
through! [*More firecrackers, a great barrage of Roman
candles.*] Come on, Bill! Hurry! Take me away! We've
got ten good years to go! Oh, boy; oh, boy; oh, boy! At
long last, we are about to be the most attractive older
couple in the whole, free world.

[RANDY *comes on slowly from downstage left. His white
Yale football jersey is spotted with blood and water. He
looks at his mother.*]

RANDY: Mother. . . .

[*She turns, sees him.* JANE *moves toward him.*]

I hurt Pokey, Mother.

[*They stare at him.*]

He—just walked away from me. I tried to tell him to come up, but he just walked away. So I . . . I just picked up this rock and threw it at him. I hit him in the face. . . . [JANE *gasps and starts offstage, down left;* RANDY *grabs her arm.*]

He's all right. He's bleeding, but he's all right. He's . . . kneeling in the water. He won't get up. Miriam's there, and his kids. [JANE *roughly breaks loose of his grasp and runs offstage left.* MOTHER *starts after her.*]

Mother . . . MOTHER!

[MOTHER *stops almost at the exit, her back to him.*]

He said something about you. About you and Uncle Bill. That's why I threw the rock. He told a goddamn lie about you.

[MOTHER *turns and looks at him.*]

MOTHER: Oh, sweetheart.

[*She goes to him and hugs him.*]

Oh, my little baby boy.

[*Then she turns and walks away toward the beach.* RANDY *looks after her. A long string of firecrackers. Then the lights fade on him. Song: sung this time by an individual male voice, preferably* RANDY'*s, with the others humming in the background:*

O Rose, climb up to her window,
  And into her casement reach . . .
And say what I may not utter,
  In your beautiful silent speech . . .

And then—who can tell?—she may whisper
  While the city sleeps below:
I was dreaming of him when you woke me,
  But, Rose, he must never know. . . .

The lights come up again, it is night. The terrace is bathed in moonlight. Light also spills onto it from the windows of the house, and for the first time, one can see the cozy rooms inside. The sound of the sea, offstage left, can be heard. MOTHER'*s suitcase is still where she left it.* RANDY *sits on the edge of a chair, still in his bloody foot-*

ball uniform, all huddled into himself. After a moment,
BARBARA *comes out of the house. She sees him.*]

BARBARA: Nice going.

RANDY: [*Looking up*] He's all right, isn't he?

BARBARA: Oh, fine. Fifteen stitches on his forehead.
Scarred for life. But fine.

RANDY: Can't he have it—fixed?

BARBARA: Oh, sure he can. But he won't. Not Pokey. He'll
wander around for the rest of his life, pointing out his
scar, saying, "This is what my brother did. My Wasp
brother. Who lost control."

RANDY: Is he leaving?

BARBARA: I have no idea. He's in his room. With the door
closed. With Miriam.

RANDY: Is Mother leaving?

BARBARA: I don't know. Last time I noticed, she was sitting
out in the car. Talking to Uncle Bill.

RANDY: Where's Jane?

BARBARA: Putting the kids to bed. Half of them plastered
with band-aids. They started throwing firecrackers at
each other.

RANDY: Oh, God.

BARBARA: It was a pretty explosive evening all around.
[*Pause; he holds his head in his hands. She watches him.*]
I assume *you're* leaving.

RANDY: I guess so.

BARBARA: Oh, you booted the ball, Mr. Yale Football
player. You really did. Any way you slice it, you lose but
good. I'll bet Mother gives Pokey the house all summer,
all by himself, and I'll bet he sells it in the fall.

RANDY: [*Shaking his head*] Oh, gee. . . .

BARBARA: Oh, you'll have a lot of money, my stone-
throwing friend. After a huge tax, why you'll still have
enough left to rent a cottage down here for a couple of
years. And after that, you can send your kids to a YMCA
camp. Or why not buy a tent, big enough for all of you?
You can all huddle together out of the rain and the mos-
quitoes in some trailer park in New Hampshire. I'm sure
if you drove for twenty miles, you might find a public
tennis court where you can wait in line to play.

RANDY: Quit it, please. Lay off.

BARBARA: At least I don't throw large rocks at people when their back is turned.

[*Pause*]

RANDY: You lose, too, Barbara.

BARBARA: Oh, I might be right here, after all.

RANDY: What do you mean?

BARBARA: Wait and see, kiddo. Just wait and see.

[MOTHER *comes on from upstage right. Both* RANDY *and* BARBARA *stand up instinctively when they see her.*]

MOTHER: Randy. Go upstairs, and knock on Pokey's door, and ask him if he'd please come down here. I want to talk to him alone.

[RANDY *moves toward the door.*]

And don't throw anything at him this time, dear.

[*He turns protestingly. She waves him out, smiling.*]

Go on. Shoo. I know you won't.

[*He exits into the house.* BARBARA *stands defiantly, facing her* MOTHER. *Pause.* MOTHER *speaks very coldly to her.*]

Your—truck seems to be parked out in the driveway.

BARBARA: [*Equally coldly*] Thank you.

[*She starts out upstage right.*]

MOTHER: Barbara.

[BARBARA *stops, her back to her mother.*]

Ask your friend out there whether he wants you or this house. Ask him that. Ask him what he'd do if he can't have the house. Just ask him.

[BARBARA *gives her a grim look and exits quickly stage right. A moment.* MOTHER *sighs, then adjusts the chairs. She sits and waits. Then a sound is heard within the house. She turns toward the door. A man appears, a shadowy figure behind the screen, a shadowed bandage on his head.*]

Pokey?

[*The shadow stands silently, she sighs.*]

Pokey. [*Pause*] Pokey, you lied to your brother and sister about me. What you said was not the truth. Do you hear me? I won't ask you to apologize, because I know you won't, but you told a lie, Pokey. [*Pause*] And now I'm going to tell you something. I'm going to tell you a story. I want you to listen very carefully. I don't want you to squirm and become impatient, as you used to, years ago, when I tried to hold you in my lap. [*Pause*] Once upon a

time there was a very naive young girl who decided to
marry a very upright young man. And at their wedding,
she danced with one of his ushers, who had just married
someone else. And for a moment, she was carried away.
For a moment, she thought, oh, dear, have I married the
wrong person? And for a moment, the usher thought the
same thing. [*Pause*] But that was that. She never mentioned it, and neither did the usher, but they knew it,
and her husband knew it, and his wife knew it, and they
all lived with it, all four of them, for thirty-five years.
All four were very good sports about it. They played by
the rules, and life went on. [*Pause*] Do you believe this
story, Pokey? I doubt if you do. You never believed the
fairy tales I used to tell you. But this one is true. [*Pause*]
Randy would believe it. And Barbara would too. Oh,
she'd say it was very dumb. Very dumb of these people to
live this way. And maybe it was dumb. Maybe that's
what made your father turn to himself so much, tinker-
ing with his notebook, puttering with the house,
swimming all alone. Maybe one day he said to himself,
Oh, the heck with it, and kept on swimming out to sea.
[*Pause*] Now this woman had three lovely children. And
the first two seemed very happy, at least for a while. But
the third, the youngest, was not. He seemed to sense
something wrong almost the day he was born. He'd look
at his mother with dark, suspicious eyes. And as soon as
he was old enough, he'd struggle out of her arms. But
he'd always crawl back. He'd come, and go. And it went
on that way for a long time. [*Pause*] Well finally, the
woman's husband died, and the usher's wife died, and
the two of them thought they might spend their golden
years together, sailing into a golden sunset, with a
golden nest-egg between them. But then, at the last minute, the woman—she was an old woman now—changed
her mind. It was difficult to do, but she did it. She saw
that her two older children had never grown up. And she
blamed herself. She said to herself, "I've made my bed,
and I must sleep in it. Alone," she said. "Alone." [*Pause*]
So you win, Pokey. I won't marry Uncle Bill. I'll hold
onto this house until the day I die. And the children can
come here every summer with their children, and I'll
pay for it, gladly. [*Pause*] But you can't come, dear. I

won't invite you again. I don't think our family is good for you anymore. I think all these years you've been at least trying to grow up, and now the best thing I can do is send you on your way. I'll try to be as fair as I can at Christmas, and when I die, but I think we should say good-bye to each other, once and for all. I wish you well, dear. I really do. I think you're an impossible person, but I love you dearly, and I hope this will help you settle on something you want to do. I think the best thing you've done is to marry Miriam and have those sweet children. I don't understand them, they're out of my league, but they seem to make you happy, which is more than I could ever do. So good-bye, Pokey. I'll get Randy to take you to the ferry in the morning, and I hope you make it up with him before you leave. He's a good boy, and he was trying to defend me. Good-bye, dear. [*She turns toward the screen, and rises as if to kiss him good-bye. But he has gone. She whispers to herself.*] Good-bye.

[BARBARA *comes in hurriedly from stage right.*]

BARBARA: [*Breathlessly*] Mother, what did you mean about the house? Artie wants to know.

MOTHER: [*Calmly*] I'm keeping the house.

BARBARA: Ex*plain* that, Mother.

[MOTHER *walks away from her.*]

Mother, he's *wai*ting!

MOTHER: Why don't you tell him you're just a little tired of talking about real estate?

[BARBARA *looks at her, looks around, sees her father's watch, picks it up, shakes it futilely, looks at her* MOTHER *again.*]

BARBARA: I'll tell him it's later than I thought.

MOTHER: Good idea, dear. Tell him that.

[BARBARA *goes offstage toward the driveway, shaking the watch.* RANDY *comes out, now wearing his father's bathrobe.*]

RANDY: Mother, I can't find Jane.

MOTHER: I think she's sitting on the beach, dear.

RANDY: [*Beaming*] I knew it! I knew that's where she was! [*He whips off his bathrobe, tosses it to* MOTHER.] Here. Hold this.

[*He runs offstage left, naked, calling.*]

Hey, Jane! Hey, Jane!

120

MOTHER: [*Calling after him*] Ssshh. You'll wake the children.

[*She stands in the moonlight. Then she picks up the bathrobe, holding it limp in her arms, and stands looking out to sea for a moment. Then she walks into the house as the lights fade on her and the screen-door slams behind.*]

THE END

THE MIDDLE AGES

THE MIDDLE AGES was first produced by Center Theatre Group of Los Angeles at the Mark Taper Forum Lab in January 1977, with the following cast:

BARNEY .... Cliff de Young
ELEANOR .... Kitty Winn
CHARLES .... Keene Curtis
MYRA .... Toni Lamonde

It was directed by Gordon Hunt.

It opened for a three week run at the Hartman Theatre in Stamford, Connecticut, in January 1978, with the following cast:

BARNEY .... Peter Coffield
ELEANOR .... Swoosie Kurtz
CHARLES .... Douglass Watson
MYRA .... Patricia O'Connell

It was directed by Melvin Bernhardt, designed by John Lee Beatty, and lit by Dennis Parichy.

It was first produced in New York City in a Showcase production at The Ark Theatre in March, 1982, and subsequently opened at The Theatre at St. Peter's Church in March 1983, with the following cast.

BARNEY	Jack Gilpin
ELEANOR	Ann McDonough
CHARLES	André Gregory
MYRA	Jo Henderson

It was directed by David Trainer, designed by John Lee Beatty, and lit by Francis Aronson. The production stage manager was M. A. Howard. The producers were Stephen Graham, Alison Clarkson, Joan Stein and The Shubert Organization.

CAST OF CHARACTERS

BARNEY
ELEANOR
CHARLES, *Barney's father.*
MYRA, *Eleanor's mother*

The action takes place in the trophy room of a men's club in a large city over a span of time from the mid-forties to the late seventies.

The trophy room: Victorian Gothic. Plenty of wood, plenty of leather, plenty of dusty old trophies on shelves. Upstage, a Gothic, mullioned window, with leaded glass, looking out over a gray cityscape. Branches of a tree or shrub intervene. On the walls, above the wainscotting, are a number of stuffed heads of animals: moose, bear, mountain goat, gazelle; also several racks of guns, fishing rods, along with cases of flies and reels, and mounted game fish. Along shelves, in addition to the trophies, are plaques indicating who killed or caught what, who beat whom, and when. Old wooden tennis racquets, squash racquets, and polo mallets are crossed heraldically and mounted on the wall.

There's a cracked old leather couch, several chairs, and a large oaken table, displaying more trophies and prizes. The effect should be baronial, cluttered, and unused. This is a place where members of the club put things that they've won, or inherited, things they don't know quite what to do with.

Stage left, a wooden door leads to an old, rarely used bathroom; stage right, larger wooden double doors lead to a paneled hall and the main rooms of the club.

ACT I

BEFORE CURTAIN: *The sound of a piano playing a hymn: "Now the Day Is Over."*

AT CURTAIN: BARNEY *stands at the window, back to the audience, looking out. Snow on the branches indicates winter, the light indicates late afternoon. He wears a gray flannel suit, and he looks forty-ish.*

After a long moment, the doors on the right open. The sound of the hymn is heard, louder, from offstage. ELEANOR *comes in, wearing a trim black dress, in the style of the late seventies.* BARNEY *turns at the noise.* ELEANOR *closes the doors behind her, shutting out the offstage sound. She is in her forties, lovely, well gotten up. They look at each other for a moment.*

ELEANOR: I knew you'd be in here.

BARNEY: Where else would I be?

ELEANOR: [*Indicating the door*] Out there. With the rest of us.

BARNEY: Doing what?

ELEANOR: Holding the fort, at least today.

BARNEY: I'll be out when they begin the service.

[*He turns back to look out the window. She moves into the room*]

ELEANOR: Mother sent me to track you down.

BARNEY: She did, did she?

ELEANOR: She wants you to join the family.

BARNEY: She's not *my* mother.

129

ELEANOR: Well she's mine, Barney, and she's your father's widow, and we should do what she wants on this particular day.

BARNEY: I'll be out when I'm ready, El.

[*Pause. She joins him by the window.*]

ELEANOR: She's worried about you, Barney. She thinks you're upset.

BARNEY: She's right, for once.

ELEANOR: She thinks you're going to make some kind of speech.

BARNEY: Right again.

ELEANOR: Well she's nervous about that, Barney.

BARNEY: So am I. That's why I'm in here, thinking it out.

ELEANOR: No, but look, the thing is, everyone's pretty exhausted from the church. The feeling is here, here at the club, we should probably boil things down to a bare minimum. Your father would have hated dragging things out. He would have been the first to complain.

BARNEY: So?

ELEANOR: So here, after people arrive, all mother wants to do is just sing his favorite hymn—

BARNEY: "A Mighty Fortress Is Our God."

ELEANOR: I guess so, Barney, I don't know. The point *is* Billy will play it on the piano, and we'll all *sing* it. And then a few members of the club will get up and make some very brief remarks, and then we'll have a moment of silence, and then—over and out and into the bar. OK?

BARNEY: OK. Got the picture.

ELEANOR: Good. Then I'll tell mother. . . . [*She starts for the door.*]

BARNEY: Tell her I'll be brief. [ELEANOR *stops, turns back, takes a deep breath.*]

ELEANOR: Please, Barney.

BARNEY: What's the matter?

ELEANOR: Mother doesn't want you to say anything at all.

BARNEY: Why?

ELEANOR: You know why.

BARNEY: Why can't I say a few words in memory of my own father?

ELEANOR: Because everybody's absolutely terrified, that's why.

BARNEY: Terrified? Of what?

ELEANOR: That you'll say something perfectly ghastly and ruin the whole goddam day!

BARNEY: You think I'd do that?

ELEANOR: Oh, Barney.

BARNEY: You really think I'd do that?

ELEANOR: I think you might. Yes.

BARNEY: You really think I'd fuck up my own father's funeral?

ELEANOR: [*Defiantly*] I really think you might. Yes.

BARNEY: Oh, Christ, El.

ELEANOR: Well you've done it before.

BARNEY: What do you mean? He never *died* before.

ELEANOR: You know what I mean, Barney. Whenever people have gotten together around here, you've done something awful.

BARNEY: All because of you, El.

ELEANOR: [*Coming down from the window*] That's a lie.

BARNEY: [*Following her*] All because of you.

ELEANOR: That's not true, Barney.

BARNEY: Everything I've done is because of you.

ELEANOR: That is a big, fat *lie,* Barney.

BARNEY: You should have chosen me, El.

ELEANOR: That's enough, please.

BARNEY: Me, instead of my nice, straight little brother.

ELEANOR: I said that's enough.

BARNEY: Of course you can still repair the damage.

ELEANOR: Please stop.

BARNEY: I'm still around. Still here. All you need to do is make your move.

ELEANOR: Barney, we are at a *funeral!* Honestly! [*Pause*] Whatever went on between you and me is over. [*Pause*] It was all back in the Middle Ages. [*Pause*] Now. Are you going to make a speech? Or not?

BARNEY: I have things to say. [*He returns to the window.*]

ELEANOR: Well you just plain can't.

BARNEY: Why not?

ELEANOR: Only members can speak.

BARNEY: I'm a member.

ELEANOR: You are not, Barney. You're from out of town.

BARNEY: I am a *permanent* member of this club! I've been trying for thirty years to resign, they've been trying for thirty years to kick me out. It can't be done. It's against

131

some fundamental rule. Once you're born into these things, you're doomed to lifetime membership.

ELEANOR: Not me. I'm not.

BARNEY: Well I am. And so was my father. Hell, this room— here's where we really live.

ELEANOR: Nobody ever comes in here, Barney.

BARNEY: Nobody dares. It's too much. It's the holy of holies, the inner sanctum, the castle keep.

ELEANOR: For you, maybe. . . .

BARNEY: For everyone, if they'd just admit it. [*Looks around*] Look. Here it all is. The weapons, the battle trophies, the sacred chronicles. Pick a book, any book. [*Takes a book from the shelf, blows off the dust, reads the title*] Ivanhoe, by Sir Walter Scott. That's us, in three volumes. Heavy armor, extravagant crusades, endless tournaments. And a hero in love with the wrong woman.

ELEANOR: Barney, mother's waiting.

BARNEY: So what? We're in the sanctuary, El. No one can touch us here. What's out there, anyway? The world, that's all. It doesn't mean much. Because wherever we go, whatever we do, we carry all this with us. On our backs. In our heads. In our blood. Till we die. [*He falls on his knees.*]

ELEANOR: Get up, Barney.

BARNEY: Can't. I'm a prisoner in here. Tried to escape. Couldn't. Here I am. Caught. Doomed. Dead. Hell, bury me in here. Bury the old man. Bury us all. Stack us all up, body on top of body, generation on generation, and let us moulder in here forever.

[*Pause*]

ELEANOR: Is that the speech you've been working on?

BARNEY: I've been working on it all my life. [*He gets up, brushes off his knees.*]

ELEANOR: Well now you've gotten it out of your system, suppose you just come and stand quietly next to mother, and greet people as they arrive from the cemetery.

BARNEY: Just . . . stand?

ELEANOR: Stand, and even hug people occasionally, and then take mother to her seat, and sit with her during the service.

BARNEY: Just . . . sit?

ELEANOR: Sit, and hold her hand for once in your life, and keep her from going to pieces.

BARNEY: And you and Billy?

ELEANOR: We'll be sitting on her other side.

BARNEY: Together?

ELEANOR: Together. For your father's sake, Barney. We can all close ranks for that.

BARNEY: Is Billy going to speak?

ELEANOR: Billy?

BARNEY: Billy. My younger brother. Is he going to speak?

ELEANOR: Now, Barney—

BARNEY: Yes or no. Is he?

ELEANOR: Mother asked Bill to just say a few words, Barney.

BARNEY: Knew it!

ELEANOR: Oh, dear.

BARNEY: Are you going back to him?

ELEANOR: Barney—

BARNEY: After the funeral, are you getting back together?

ELEANOR: Barney, people are beginning to *arrive!*

BARNEY: [*Calling offstage*] I don't give a SHIT! You're going back to him, aren't you?

ELEANOR: I'm not going back, Barney.

BARNEY: Sure you are.

ELEANOR: Here we go.

BARNEY: Damn right here we go! It's the story of my life! You get me all softened up and then you nail me with Billy!

ELEANOR: I think I'll scream!

BARNEY: OK, baby, here's the thing. [*Takes an envelope out of his pocket*] I've got something written down here, and I'm going to read it, *all* of it, out loud, out there, in front of the assembled multitude. You run and tell your mother that, OK? [*He sits defiantly on the couch.*]

ELEANOR: All *right*, Barney. I'll tell her that. [*She goes to the door, turns.*] But before I do, I want to tell you something. Just so you'll know. As soon as we get through this *day*, as soon as we put your father quietly to rest, I'm through, Barney! I'm through with this family, and this club, and this city! I've spent half my life running back and forth between you, and Billy, and mother, and your father, and my*self*, and this is the last day I'm going to do it! [*She opens the door, the sounds of a group gathering can be heard.*] All of you may be permanent members around here, Barney, but I'm not, and I can't wait to get the HELL out!

BARNEY: Oh, Christ. I love you, El.

ELEANOR: Nuts to you, Barney. Just—nuts to you.

[*She strides out, leaving the door open.* BARNEY *watches her, then goes to stand at the fireplace. The lights fade on the trophy room, except for on him and on the door. The funeral music comes up louder as* CHARLES, BARNEY'*s father, appears in the doorway, shadowy and ghostly at first, wearing a dark suit.* BARNEY *remains lost in thought.*]

CHARLES: Now, Barney: Once again, once again I am obliged to excuse myself from a pleasant occasion in order to cope with my elder son. How many times, Barney, I'm asking you, how many times have I been called out of the office, off the golf course, away from a congenial gathering simply to deal with you.

[*He closes the doors behind him. The music can no longer be heard. The lights begin to dim on* BARNEY.]

It seems to me, Barney, that your only interest in this world is to interrupt those few rare moments of social intercourse which men and women have managed to create for themselves in this city. What is the difficulty, Barney? I'd appreciate an answer.

[BARNEY *can no longer be seen.* CHARLES *addresses the audience, isolated in light.*] I'd appreciate advice from any quarter. Everything he's done has been disruptive. And it's been that way from the beginning. Why he was even born in the middle of a dinner party. His poor mother had to leave before the dessert. What's more, Doctor Russell tells me the first thing he showed the world was his rear end. And he's continued to show us very little else. When I think of Barney, I think of a whole history of unpleasant incidents. I think of nursemaids in tears because he refused to submit to the ducky chair. I think of cooks packing their bags because he peeked at them in the bathtub. I think of cleaning women huddled in corners while he covered them with a B-B gun. I've tried to civilize him. I send him to kindergarten: The first thing he finds is the fire alarm. The first thing he writes is a four-letter word. The first thing he draws is the male member. On Winnie-the-Pooh. I send him to birthday parties: He pins the tail on the hostess. I send him to summer camp. They send him back. Apparently the only thing he learned was to break wind. At will. And put a match to it. I'm at a loss, my friends. He's a good dancer, but he was expelled from dancing school. For goosing people in the conga line. He's a good hockey player, but he spent half a game in the penalty box. For hiding the puck. In his athletic supporter. He's a good student, but he continually fails history. Why? Because he only will learn about riots, revolutions, and Franklin D. Roosevelt. I am at a loss, my friends.

[CHARLES *goes to the door, opens it; we hear the sound of people singing around the piano, amateurishly but joyously, "O Little Town of Bethlehem."* CHARLES *listens for a moment as the lights come up on the room.* BARNEY *is standing in the same place, now in a sweater and saddle shoes, and with the slicked-back hair of the mid-forties.* CHARLES *closes the doors and turns to him.*] And now this. This completely outrageous behavior at our first Christmas party since World War Two! How old are you, Barney? [*No response*] I am asking you a question! How old are you?

BARNEY: [*Quickly joining him downstage*] You know how old I am, Dad.

CHARLES: I want to hear it from you.

BARNEY: Sixteen.

CHARLES: Six-teen. Sixteen years old.

BARNEY: You knew that, Dad.

CHARLES: Never mind what I know and what I don't know. Do you consider yourself a man or a boy?

BARNEY: I consider myself—in the middle.

CHARLES: I see. And which do you want to be for the rest of your life?

BARNEY: A man.

CHARLES: And which do you think you were, out there, just now, during the Christmas party?

BARNEY: We were just hacking around, Dad.

CHARLES: Were you a man or a boy out there this afternoon?

BARNEY: All right, I was a boy.

CHARLES: You were a boy, all right. You were a baby. Your little brother, your brother Billy, who is only fourteen, is playing the piano out there, and acting twice your age. Now there are families out there who haven't been together since the war. All they wanted to do was come down to this club and gather around the piano and sing some fine old Christmas music. That's all they wanted to do. But would you let them do that? Apparently not.

[BARNEY *shrugs*.]

My friends have suggested you miss your mother.

BARNEY: I hardly remember her, Dad.

CHARLES: I miss her.

BARNEY: I know you do, Dad.

CHARLES: Sometimes I miss her so much I almost—lose control.

BARNEY: I know, Dad.

CHARLES: But I hold on. I don't run around rooms causing trouble.

BARNEY: I know, Dad.

CHARLES: Then why do you?

BARNEY: Maybe I'm just—bad.

CHARLES: Nonsense.

BARNEY: You don't know me, Dad.

CHARLES: I know you perfectly well. And I know it's not too late to repair the damage.

BARNEY: How?

CHARLES: You can apologize.

[*Pause*]

BARNEY: All right. I apologize.

CHARLES: Out there.

BARNEY: Out—?

CHARLES: There.

BARNEY: You mean, make a speech?

CHARLES: That's exactly what I mean.

BARNEY: What about the other boys?

CHARLES: You were the ringleader.

BARNEY: You mean I have to make a speech all by my*self*?

CHARLES: That's what I had to do when I spilled a cocktail on old Mr. Sidway.

BARNEY: But I'm not you, Dad.

CHARLES: You're my older son. And you've got to answer for it. [*He starts for the door.*]

BARNEY: Hey, Dad. Tell you what. Let's have a compromise. OK? You go back out there, and I'll go to the movies, OK?

CHARLES: I told you this morning. No.

BARNEY: But it's Errol Flynn in *Robin Hood,* Dad. They've brought it back.

CHARLES: Then you've already seen it.

BARNEY: I want to see it *again,* Dad. I could see it a thousand times! I love that movie.

CHARLES: No. I'm sorry. I'm not going to allow my elder son to go to a Hollywood movie in place of a Christmas party. Whose name is on these walls more than any other name?

BARNEY: [*With a sigh*] Yours.

CHARLES: *Ours.* Who was the first president of this club?

BARNEY: My grandfather.

CHARLES: Your *great*-grandfather. Who—

BARNEY: I *know,* Dad. I know who shot that moose in Wyoming, and who dragged that poor fish out of some lake in the Adirondacks, and whose name is on that cup. [*He indicates cup, downstage left.*]

CHARLES: You scoff because you like to be fresh, but someday your name will be on it.

BARNEY: *Why?* Why will it?

CHARLES: Because you're my son. And you can't get away from it. [CHARLES *opens the door partway. The singing can be heard: "God Rest Ye Merry, Gentlemen."*] All right. Everything seems to have settled down. Now we will go out there, you and I, and I'll announce that you'd like to say a few words.

BARNEY: But what would I say, Dad?

CHARLES: Why you'd simply say you were sorry. For galloping through the halls. For sneaking into the pool when it was closed. For snapping towels in the locker room when someone could lose an eye or a testicle. For going off in the corner when the singing started, and whooping and giggling and cat-calling like a bunch of hoodlums from the South Side.

BARNEY: Do I have to say all that?

CHARLES: You should find your own words, of course.

BARNEY: Can I say balls instead of testicles?

CHARLES: Now watch it.

BARNEY: But I can't *do* it, Dad.

CHARLES: Well you've got to.

BARNEY: [*Setting his jaw, carefully*] Well I won't.

[*Pause. Charles turns to face him.*]

CHARLES: What did you say?

BARNEY: I said I won't.

[*Another pause.* CHARLES *stares at him.* BARNEY *holds his ground defiantly.*]

CHARLES: Then you'll stay in here until you do. Merry Christmas!

[*He strides out of the room, slamming the doors behind him.*]

BARNEY: [*Calling after him*] I still won't! [*Then louder*] I'll never apologize! [*Even louder*] NEVER! [*Pause, then tentatively*] Screw you, Dad! [*Pause. More confidently*] Go frig a pig, Dad! Go fuck a duck! [*He gives the door the finger, he gives the door his whole arm. He grabs a long polo mallet and gives that to the door. Then he gives it to the stuffed heads, one by one. Then he tosses it away and looks around for an escape. He sees the door at stage left, goes to it, opens it, goes in, comes out in a moment.*] Cripes!

[*He slams the door, looks around, goes to the window, gets it open, climbs out on the sill, looks down, gets ready to jump as the door to the hall opens, slowly, and* ELEANOR *comes in. We hear singing behind her: "Bring the Torch, Jeanette, Isabella: Bring the Torch to the Stable Run." * ELEANOR *looks about fourteen: She wears a dark velvet dress with a lace collar, long hair with a velvet ribbon in it, and black shoes. She comes in hesitantly as if looking for someone. Then suddenly she sees* BARNEY *poised on the window ledge. She screams.*]

ELEANOR: Don't JUMP!

[*Her scream startles him so that he loses his balance and almost falls. But he grabs onto a mullion and saves himself. He sees her, remains on the windowsill, halfway in, halfway out.*]

BARNEY: Close the door!

ELEANOR: What?

[*It's hard for her to hear since he's half outside and the music is behind her*].

BARNEY: Close the goddamn door!

ELEANOR: Oh. [*She closes the door.*]

BARNEY: [*Standing on the sill*] Otherwise, he'd try to prevent my escape.

ELEANOR: Who?

BARNEY: My father.

ELEANOR: Why?

BARNEY: He hates my guts.

ELEANOR: But why?

BARNEY: Because I'm not like him.

ELEANOR: Were you really going to jump?

BARNEY: Sure.

ELEANOR: Really?

BARNEY: [*Posing*] Sometimes a man's got to risk his life for freedom.

ELEANOR: Gosh.

BARNEY: [*Standing at the railing*] Who are you?

ELEANOR: Eleanor.

BARNEY: Eleanor who?

ELEANOR: [*Awkwardly holding out her hand*] Eleanor Gilbert.

BARNEY: Never heard of you.

ELEANOR: [*Awkwardly letting her hand fall*] We're visiting here.

BARNEY: Oh.

ELEANOR: We're guests of the Robbinses.

BARNEY: Never heard of them.

ELEANOR: Well I've never heard of you either.

BARNEY: That's because I haven't told you my name.

ELEANOR: Well what is it, then?

BARNEY: Barney Rusher.

ELEANOR: Never heard of you.

BARNEY: Well you better start, kid. My ancestors are plastered all over these walls.

ELEANOR: [*Indicating stuffed head*] Is that one of them?

BARNEY: [*Laughing*] Yeah, well, my father's president of this club. I can bowl here whenever I want, and play billiards even on weekends.

ELEANOR: Then why do you want to jump out the window? [*Pause*]

BARNEY: Maybe I won't. [*He closes the window.*]

ELEANOR: [*Crossing to steps*] Were you one of those noisy boys out there, during the singing?

BARNEY: Maybe.

ELEANOR: Yes, you were. You were one of those rowdy boys off in the corner.

BARNEY: Maybe I was, maybe I wasn't.

ELEANOR: I was watching the whole thing. You were the ringleader.

BARNEY: All right. I was.

ELEANOR: You stood out like a sore thumb.

BARNEY: You were watching, huh?

ELEANOR: I watched your father throw you in here, too.

BARNEY: He didn't throw me in here.

ELEANOR: I saw him grab your arm.

BARNEY: I *walked* in here. He followed. [*Pause*] Anyway he's not my real father. [*Pause*] I'm an adopted child.

ELEANOR: A what?

BARNEY: An adopted child. It's obvious. My mother had an affair with someone else. I'm not sure who, exactly, but I think it might have been Errol Flynn.

ELEANOR: Oh, sure.

BARNEY: Really. Oh, my father forgave her. He probably got her to make a speech, and apologize.

ELEANOR: Oh, sure. Any day.

BARNEY: It's *true*. And then they went on and had my brother Billy and my mother got so bored she died. [*He falls onto couch, downstage right.*]

ELEANOR: I just don't believe that.

BARNEY: [*Sitting up*] Do you believe I'm adopted?

ELEANOR: I—don't know.

BARNEY: [*Jumping onto table*] I must be. I'm so different. But I know that somewhere else in this world I have a twin, who's adopted too. And someday we'll meet, and recognize each other, and—click.
[*Pause*]

ELEANOR: Would you do me a big favor?

BARNEY: Depends on what it is.

ELEANOR: Would you continue this conversation out there?

BARNEY: Why out there?

ELEANOR: Because I've got this mother. I'm supposed to meet people my own age, and I want her to see that I've done it.

BARNEY: Was that your mother standing by the piano?

ELEANOR: Yes.

BARNEY: That fussy lady?

ELEANOR: That was her—she—her. Do you want to meet her?

BARNEY: No thanks.

ELEANOR: Well you don't even have to. All you have to do is talk to me out there. If we run out of steam, you could introduce me to one of your friends.

BARNEY: [*Shaking his head*] Uh-uh. Can't do it.

ELEANOR: Oh, please. You don't know what it's like to be new someplace. Everyone stares at you.

BARNEY: I like that.

ELEANOR: I just hate it. I could sink through the floor.

BARNEY: Maybe that's why I hack around all the time. So people will notice me.

ELEANOR: I noticed you, all right.

BARNEY: I saw you noticing. That made me do it all the more.

ELEANOR: I *thought* so. That's why I followed you in here. I thought you were the most exciting person there. [*Pause, they look at each other.*]

BARNEY: What was your name again? I might give you a call and take you to the movies.

ELEANOR: Eleanor Goldberg.

BARNEY: *Goldberg?*

ELEANOR: [*Quickly*] I mean, Gilbert.

BARNEY: Which is it?

ELEANOR: Gilbert.

BARNEY: Why'd you say Goldberg?

ELEANOR: We changed it to Gilbert.

BARNEY: Are you Jewish?

ELEANOR: [*Quickly*] No.

BARNEY: My father says anything ending with berg is Jewish.

ELEANOR: My father is Jewish. My mother made him change his name.

BARNEY: Where's your father?

ELEANOR: Back in Harrisburg.

BARNEY: Harrisburg's Jewish.

ELEANOR: Well my mother comes from here, and she's High Episcopalian.

BARNEY: What's so hot about that?

ELEANOR: Nothing. It doesn't make any difference what you are, anyway.

BARNEY: Come on. We'll go to the movies.

ELEANOR: [*Backing away, stage left*] I don't like prejudiced people.

BARNEY: I'm not prejudiced. *They're* prejudiced out there. That's why we should go to the movies.

ELEANOR: What do you mean?

BARNEY: If they find out you're a Jew, they'll kick you right out.

ELEANOR: I don't believe you.

BARNEY: They will. They don't allow Jews in here. I've heard them say it. [*Mimicking them*] If you let one Jew in, they bring all their friends, and pretty soon, they're all over the place. In the squash courts, in the pool, in the bar . . . and you can't say anything without getting into an argument.

ELEANOR: You're prejudiced!

BARNEY: No I'm not.

ELEANOR: You most certainly *are!*

BARNEY: See? Argument!

ELEANOR: [*Walking away*] Oh, honestly.

BARNEY: [*Grabbing the polo mallet*] Come on. Let's go the movies. It's *Robin Hood.* I'll lead you down the back way, and if anyone tries to persecute you, I'll run him through.

[*He protects her with his "sword."*] Come on. Got any money?

ELEANOR: Won't you please come out there with me?

BARNEY: Can't. If I did, I'd just end up one of them.

ELEANOR: What's so bad about that?

BARNEY: It'd kill me, that's all. I'd die.

[*He falls melodramatically on his sword. The door bursts open.* CHARLES *puts his head in angrily.*]

CHARLES: [*To* BARNEY] I'll give you five more minutes! [*He sees* ELEANOR.] Excuse me, young lady, but this boy has five more minutes!

[*He turns, goes out, slamming the door.*]

ELEANOR: That was your father, wan't it?

BARNEY: No. That was just someone I pay to tell me the time.

[ELEANOR *laughs in spite of herself.*]

ELEANOR: You *are* kind of funny.

BARNEY: I got that joke from a movie.

ELEANOR: What did he mean, five more minutes?

BARNEY: [*Climbing the book ladder*] Oh, well, he just meant that in five more minutes, he's going to drag me out into that public square, and tie me to the piano, and light a fire under me, and burn me alive for being a heretic. And before I can surrender my soul to heaven, while my flesh is crackling like a leg of lamb, he's going to reach into the flames and grope around in my chest cavity, and hold up to the hooting multitude my warm, red, palpitating, human heart! And so . . . [*He reaches the top.*] to prevent that from happening . . . [*He jumps to the railing.*] to rob him of that obscene pleasure . . . [*He grabs an old bellpull.*] I have no choice but to bid you farewell!

[*He swings to windowsill, jumps off, disappears.* ELEANOR *screams and runs up to the window. Before she gets there,* BARNEY*'s head pops up casually.*] It's OK. There's a roof here.

ELEANOR: [*Embarrassed for showing concern*] You *are* a showoff, aren't you?

BARNEY: I sure am.

ELEANOR: Is that *all* you do? Just show off for people?

BARNEY: [*Looking at her*] Oh, no. I'm a very deep guy. Ug-glug-glug.

[*He holds his nose and disappears as if he were going under water. She rushes to the window, stands half-waving, romantically, looking after him, then closes the window. The door opens. Singing can be heard: "O Come, All Ye Faithful."* MYRA, ELEANOR*'s mother, stylishly dressed, fortyish, and fussy, comes in. She stands looking at* ELEANOR *for a long moment. Then she shakes her head and closes the doors.*]

MYRA: Eleanor, dear love, what are you doing in this musty old room?

ELEANOR: I was just . . .

MYRA: I've been combing the woods for you. Are we playing Hide-and-Seek at the age of fourteen?

ELEANOR: Oh, no. [*Proudly*] I was talking to a boy, Mother.

MYRA: [*Looking around*] Boy? What boy? I don't see any boy.

ELEANOR: [*Indicating window*] He just . . . he . . . [*She looks at bell-cord, looks at window, looks at* MYRA, *gives up with a sigh.*] Oh, golly.

MYRA: [*Patiently*] The boys are out *there*, Eleanor. Boys and parties happen to occur around pianos and people.

ELEANOR: I get so shy, Mother.

MYRA: That's part of your charm. You just don't realize. How could you, sitting around Harrisburg, playing chess with your father? Now go have fun!

ELEANOR: I'll try. [*She starts glumly for the door.*]

MYRA: Chin up, shoulders back, smile.

[ELEANOR *stiffens her shoulders, turns at the door with a ghastly fake smile.*]

That's it. The boys will gather like flies.

ELEANOR: What if they run away? [*Glances at window*]

MYRA: Don't let them. Pretend you're having a perfectly marvelous time.

ELEANOR: [*Losing heart*] I can't pretend. . . .

MYRA: Of course you can. That's what growing up is. Pretend that party is for you.

ELEANOR: Oh, not for me. . . .

MYRA: As far as I'm concerned, that is your party. [*Leads her to the couch*] My sweet lamb, you have only five more years, at the most, before everyone goes to college, and gets married, and scatters to the four winds. You've got to stake your claim, sweetie pie.

ELEANOR: Oh, Mother. . . .

MYRA: You do. This is the time and this is the place. In fact, I've decided to stay, dear.

ELEANOR: You mean, for supper?

MYRA: I mean . . . for supper. Now go find some *salle de bain* and comb your hair. And then you and I together will rejoin the human race.

[ELEANOR *gets up.*]

Go on. Shoo. There's still the shank of the evening to go. [ELEANOR *goes to the door, opens it, turns, squares her shoulders, gives the ghastly forced smile, and goes out. The music is heard softly from the hall: "Deck the Halls with Boughs of Holly."* MYRA *watches* ELEANOR *go, then turns to the audience, leaving the door open.*]

Well I almost spilled the beans, didn't I? Couldn't help it. This place, this party. I was riding the crest of the wave. [*Comes downstage*] Because I've finally decided to do it. I've decided to divorce Myron Gilbert. We have been at each other's throats since square one. This visit was a trial separation. I've tried. I'm separating. [*Glancing toward the party offstage*] Eleanor will be fine. She can see her father any time she wants. But she won't want to. Not after she's lived here. Oh, she'll be right in the swim of things before she knows it. She's lucky, actually. [*She takes a compact out of her purse, snaps it open, powders her nose, looks at herself in the compact mirror.*] When I was her age, my father changed his job, yanked us out of town, and dragged us around the country, not knowing a soul. Naturally I married the first man to look in my direction. What a life, wandering the face of the earth, chained to a stranger, frantically seeking out every second-rate bridge group and garden club and church supper, looking for some sense of connection. Never again! Not for me, not for her! We have come home. This is it. This club. This is the real thing. My mother told me about it, and it's true. Everything happens here; parties, dances, weddings. The whole life of this great city congeals right in this building. And that is why I paid sixty-three dollars for that velvet dress, and why I got Mimi Robbins to take us on, and why I want Eleanor out by that piano with everyone else. We'll stay here, and I'll launch her here, and she'll pick and choose and marry a man here, and she'll know what it means to be happy for the rest of her life!

[CHARLES *comes in, looks around.*]

CHARLES: Oh, excuse me. I was looking for my son.

MYRA: I'm afraid there's nobody here but us chickens.

CHARLES: I'm sorry. Have you lost your way?

MYRA: *Au contraire.* I've found it, after fifteen long years. [*She holds out her hand.*] Myra Gilbert. We're with the Robbins.

CHARLES: [*Taking her hand, bowing*] Charles Rusher.

MYRA: I know. You're the man we should thank for this spectacular *soirée.*

CHARLES: You're most welcome.

MYRA: I believe your son is out there, playing the piano.

CHARLES: That's my younger son, Bill. I was looking for Barney, the older.

MYRA: Well I don't know about him, but I do know the pianoplayer is an absolute dream-boat. I have a daughter who's dying to meet him.

CHARLES: [*Offering her his arm*] Then let's get them together.

MYRA: All right, let's. And maybe, after we've all struggled through a few more Christmas carols, we can talk people into some dancing!

CHARLES: Why not!

[*They go out as the singing comes up loud: "O come ye, O come ye to Bethlehem." Then the music immediately modulates to a loud Lester Lanin–like dance tune from the early fifties, played by a party orchestra: something like "Green-Up Time." The lights from the hall spill into the trophy room. Through the window outside, we see the city lit at night. The branches in the foreground might have blossoms on them. BARNEY and ELEANOR swirl into the room from the hall, dancing well together. BARNEY is in a black tuxedo, ELEANOR in a long evening dress with white gloves. They do a couple of elegant spins to the music which wafts in, and then BARNEY, in a particularly deft turn, slyly kicks the doors closed as they spin by. The music becomes very faint, the only light is from the moon through the window.*]

ELEANOR: Hey!

BARNEY: [*Sexily, still dancing*] Hmmm?

ELEANOR: [*Breaking away from him*] Open that door.

BARNEY: What's the matter?

ELEANOR: I said open that door, please.

BARNEY: Aw, El.

ELEANOR: I want that door open, please. Right now, Barney.

[BARNEY *looks at her, goes to the door, turns the key, locks the door, takes the key out, tosses it into the air, then puts it in his pocket.*]

Very funny, Barney. Ha, ha. Big joke.

BARNEY: [*Imitating Brando*] You and I have had this date from the beginning, Blanche.

ELEANOR: I want to *dance*, Barney.

BARNEY: OK. [*He opens an old air vent or the transom over the door, the music wafts in, faintly.*] See? [*He bows to her.*] Let's dance.

[*They dance briefly, more passionately, then she breaks away.*]

ELEANOR: No, seriously, Barney. Really. I don't like this. I was out there dancing with Billy, and you just grabbed me.

BARNEY: That's called cutting in.

ELEANOR: That was not cutting in. Cutting in is reasonably polite. You just grabbed. [*She goes to the door, tries it, turns.*] Give me the key, please.

BARNEY: Nope.

ELEANOR: Barney, I want the key to this door, please.

BARNEY: Nope.

ELEANOR: [*Turning on the lights, returning to him*] Well what do we do then? Stand here, eyeing each other?

BARNEY: I've got a bone to pick with you, El.

ELEANOR: About what?

BARNEY: I've got a gripe with you.

ELEANOR: About WHAT?

BARNEY: How come you're going to Bermuda tomorrow with Billy for the rest of the spring vacation?
[*Pause*]

ELEANOR: Who told you?

BARNEY: The word got out.

ELEANOR: Who told you?

BARNEY: [*Angrily*] THE WORD GOT OUT, EL!

ELEANOR: You see? That's why it was a secret. Because you always yell bloody murder.

BARNEY: Damn right.

ELEANOR: Whoever told you was a big fat stinker.

BARNEY: You said it. It was your mother.

ELEANOR: Oh.

BARNEY: She told me I could just stop telephoning you after today.

ELEANOR: I'm going to Bermuda, Barney. A whole bunch of us are going.

BARNEY: She said you organized the whole goddamn thing! You didn't even ask me.

ELEANOR: Because I knew you wouldn't go.

BARNEY: [*Crossing downstage right*] Damn right I wouldn't go. Frolicking around that crumby island with a bunch of superficial preppies!

ELEANOR: See? See the way you are? Well I want to go, and

147

I'm going. I've had to baby-sit on the Cape for two summers to pay for it, and I can't stand it around here during the slush season and I've seen all the movies with you, and I want to go to Bermuda.

BARNEY: Who's paying for Billy?

ELEANOR: I don't know and I don't care.

BARNEY: I know. My father's paying for him.

ELEANOR: Maybe he is.

BARNEY: He'd never pay for me.

ELEANOR: Well he's mad because you flunked out of college.

BARNEY: I didn't flunk. I left. Because they wouldn't let me on the fencing team.

ELEANOR: I don't blame them. You wanted to do it like Robin Hood.

BARNEY: Well Jesus. Who wants to just stand there?

ELEANOR: [*Sitting in chair*] I don't know, Barney, but I want to go to Bermuda and have some fun.

BARNEY: You'll have fun, all right.

ELEANOR: I'm certainly going to try.

BARNEY: You'll get *laid* down there, El!

ELEANOR: Oh, Barney.

BARNEY: You will! You'll get laid! I know that scene, El. All those blonde Ivy-League pricks running around in Madras shorts. They'll play volleyball with you, and then take you out on a motorbike, and get you all hotted up, and then you'll get *laid!*

ELEANOR: Barney, I promise. . . .

BARNEY: You will! And then it'll be all over. [*He sinks onto the couch.*]

ELEANOR: Barney, trust me, for God's sake.

BARNEY: I don't trust *them*. They'll drag you into the poison ivy. They'll spill beer all over you. They'll get you all sandy. They'll barf! And then they'll go back to their grubby, sweaty Greek-letter fraternities and stand around in the showers and scratch themselves and brag about you.

ELEANOR: I'll be with Billy.

BARNEY: [*Getting up*] Then Billy will lay you, the sneaky little son-of-a-bitch! Oh, gosh, El! Stay here with me.

ELEANOR: There's nothing to do here, Barney. The snow's gone. The skiing's over.

BARNEY: We could do it right, El.

ELEANOR: Do what?

BARNEY: It. *IT.* We could make it, El. Right here. Right now. You and me. We could—bang.
[*Pause*]

ELEANOR: I could bang on that door, Barney, unless you give me that key.

BARNEY: No listen, El, really. Tonight's the night. And this is the place. You know we can't get into a hotel, and everyone says it's no fun in a car, and if we go to your place, your mother starts farting around, and if we go to mine, that son-of-a-bitch Billy hangs in there, so this is it, El, here, right here, where we first met.
[ELEANOR *looks at him, then runs to the door.*]

ELEANOR: [*Pounding*] Help!
[BARNEY *grabs her arm, brings her back to couch.*]

BARNEY: No, listen, El, *please.* Will you just *listen?* I've got it all figured out. Just give me two minutes, just *two,* and then if you don't like the idea, I'll open the door and take you back to Billy. OK?
[*Pause*]

ELEANOR: OK. [*She sits down on the edge of the couch, suspiciously.*]

BARNEY: OK. Now. Here's what we do. [*He looks at his watch.*] It's late. Billy will think you were tired, I took you home.

ELEANOR: Hey, just a—

BARNEY: [*Sitting at her feet*] Will you *wait?* Meanwhile, I've already moved my car around the corner, and I've called your mother and told her it broke down so you're sleeping over at Lucy Dunbar's. OK?

ELEANOR: [*Standing up*] *Not* OK!

BARNEY: [*Forcing her to sit*] Will you let me *finish?* Now Lucy's parents are in Florida, so her grandmother's there, who doesn't know diddly-squat, and I've told my father I'm staying over at a friend's, so everyone thinks we're somewhere else! We're covered, El! All the way! All the way down the line! We can stay here tonight, and bang, right on this couch, we can bang all we want, we can bang two or three times if we feel like it, El. What do you say? What do you say, El?
[*Long pause. She looks at him, then gets up and starts pounding on the door.*]

A. R. GURNEY, JR.

ELEANOR: Help! Somebody! Help!

BARNEY: [*Leaping over couch, grabbing her*] Aw hell.
[*He carries her downstage right.*]

ELEANOR: [*Shrieking*] Help! Rape!

BARNEY: [*Kneeling at her feet, arms around her waist*] Jesus, El. We're not kids anymore. You'll be in college next year, and I'll be drafted and sent to Korea to *die!* Oh, this is it, El! I know it! If I don't get you tonight, I'll lose you forever!
[ELEANOR *looks down at him affectionately. Knocks are heard on the other side of the door.*]

VOICES: Anybody in there? [*The handle is turned, the door rattled.*] Anybody there?
[ELEANOR *continues to look at* BARNEY.]
It's locked. Guess no one's there. Maybe it was someone downstairs. [*Voices fade away.*]

ELEANOR: [*Quietly*] Barney, sweetie, I love you dearly, but Bermuda is all planned.

BARNEY: [*Bouncing up*] So's this. This is planned. Look. [*He hurriedly drags a large suitcase out from the couch by the fireplace.*] Look what I smuggled in this afternoon!

ELEANOR: What's that?

BARNEY: Just wait. [*With a sweep, he clears the large oaken table downstage left of its sporting magazines.*] I'm going to make Bermuda look silly.

ELEANOR: [*Skeptical*] Oh, Barney.

BARNEY: [*Opening the suitcase*] Just give me a CHANCE, El! At least let me get into the *game!* [*He spreads an elaborate tablecloth on the table, quoting:*]

Then by the bed-side, where the faded moon
Made a dim silver twilight, soft he set
A table, and, half-anguished, threw thereon
A cloth of woven crimson, gold, and jet . . .

[*To* ELEANOR] That's from "The Eve of Saint Agnes." Did you read that in school?

ELEANOR: Yes.

BARNEY: [*Setting out silver candlesticks*] I doubt it. It's a little raunchy for Miss Muff's in the Mountains or wherever it is you go. We had to memorize it. It's about this great love affair in the Middle Ages.

150

ELEANOR: I know what it's about.

BARNEY: Then you'll know that . . . [*He continues to set the table with silver dishes quoting:*]

He, from forth a suitcase brought a heap . . .
Of candied apple, quince, and plum, and gourd
With jellies soother than the creamy curd . . .

ELEANOR: [*Taking up the poem*]

. . . And lucent syrups, tinct with cinnamon;
Manna and dates, in argosy transferred . . .

BARNEY: [*Looking at her*] Hey!

ELEANOR: We had to learn it, too . . . "From Fez"—

BARNEY: [*Joining her*]

From Fez, and spiced dainties, every one,
From silken Samarcand to cedared Lebanon.

[*He has finished setting the table with goodies. From the air vent, music wafts in: a romantic song from the early fifties.*]

ELEANOR: Did you steal all that?

BARNEY: No.

ELEANOR: [*Eating a cookie*] Mmmm. Toll House cookies. And the chocolate's still soft inside.

BARNEY: Made 'em myself. And there's banana ice cream, unless it's melted.

ELEANOR: Oh, it's my favorite!

BARNEY: I know. And smoked oysters, which are supposed to be terrific for sex. [*He produces the oysters and ice cream side by side.*]

ELEANOR: Barney— [*She crosses downstage left.*]

BARNEY: The only thing I stole was this. [*Brings out a bottle of wine*] From my father. [*Reads the label*] Chateauneuf du Pape. [*Looks at her*] Unless you prefer Mogen David.

ELEANOR: Just cut that out.

BARNEY: [*Going to table, taking the silver cup*] We'll drink it from this. The Holy Grail. The city-wide mixed doubles invitational tennis cup. Which my mother and father won in 1933.

[*He kneels in front of her again.*]

ELEANOR: The only reason I'm going along with this, Barney, is to see what you'll do next.

BARNEY: [*Handing her matches and a corkscrew*] Here. Light the candles. Open the wine. [*He looks at her, then turns.*] I've got to go pee.

[*He goes into the bathroom.*]

ELEANOR: [*Calling after him*] You're absolutely crazy, Barney! You know that, of course. [*She eats another cookie.*] Mmmm. These cookies are divine. I'll have a bite with you, Barney, because I can see you've worked hard over this. But that's that. [*She lights the candles.*] And if someone comes in, I'm going to sink through the floor.

BARNEY: [*From the bathroom*] No one can come in. There's only one key.

ELEANOR: And I'm going to Bermuda, Barney. I'll have one glass of wine with you, for old time's sake, but if you try anything else, I'm going to scream my head off.

[BARNEY *comes out of the bathroom wearing an exotic bathrobe.*]

BARNEY: Hi.

ELEANOR: Oh, my God.

BARNEY: It's my father's. What do you think?

ELEANOR: Oh, Lord. What next?

BARNEY: This. [*From behind his back, he produces a black lacy negligée.*] Like it? I got it on sale.

ELEANOR: Help.

BARNEY: Put it on and we'll have a midnight supper.

ELEANOR: I'll stay as I am, thank you.

BARNEY: [*Hanging it by the fireplace*] Suit yourself. I'll put it here for when you change your mind.

ELEANOR: I'll never change my mind, Barney.

[*He goes back into the bathroom.*]

BARNEY: [*From within*] Sure you will.

ELEANOR: Never.

BARNEY: Wait till you see this.

[*He comes back out with a huge protuberance in the front of his bathrobe.*]

Stick 'em up.

ELEANOR: [*Shrieking*] Oh, HEAVENS!

BARNEY: That's just a preview of coming attractions!
[*He pulls a toilet brush out from under his bathrobe, tosses it back into the bathroom.*]

ELEANOR: [*Bursting into laughter*] Oh, Barney, you absolute imbecile!
[*She collapses onto the couch in laughter. He rushes to join her, sits down beside her, begins to kiss her. The music through the vent changes to "Goodnight, Sweetheart."* ELEANOR, *sitting up.*]
The party's ending.

BARNEY: I know. . . .

ELEANOR: Oh, Barney, let's go out there.

BARNEY: [*Indicating his bathrobe*] Like this?

ELEANOR: Let me go out there then.

BARNEY: [*Indicating the spread table*] What about that?

ELEANOR: I don't know what to do.

BARNEY: When in doubt, dance.
[*He pulls her up from the couch, they dance to the music very slowly, very affectionately.*]
I love this push music.

ELEANOR: Barney, just shut up, please. Just shut your trap for once, OK?
[*They rock together. Suddenly* BARNEY *shudders and freezes.*]

BARNEY: Uh-oh.

ELEANOR: What?

BARNEY: Never mind.

ELEANOR: What's the trouble?

BARNEY: I said never MIND.

ELEANOR: Well I mean—

BARNEY: I just had a little accident.

ELEANOR: You what?

BARNEY: [*Turning away*] I had a little ACCIDENT!
[*Pause*]

ELEANOR: [*Getting it*] Oh.
[*She carefully extricates herself. Pause*]
Well. That does it, doesn't it.

BARNEY: Not at all. I'll be right back.
[*He goes into the bathroom, slams the door. The music ends. Through the vent, we hear the sounds of conversation. The party is breaking up.*]

ELEANOR: [*Calling offstage to* BARNEY] The party's over,

A. R. GURNEY, JR.

Barney. Everyone's leaving. I want to leave too. I don't want to stay here tonight, sweetie. Really. I don't. [*She picks up a cookie, takes a bite, shakes her head, puts it down.*] I want my eight hours sleep. I want to go to Bermuda, Barney. I want to lie around in the sun with Billy and the whole gang. I want to play tennis and hear the Whiffenpoofs at the Elbow Beach Club. What's wrong with that, Barney? What's wrong with people having fun? I love all that, Barney. I love all those people. They're good-looking, and they play games, and they know all the lyrics to all the songs. [*Pause*] You don't, Barney. You can't sing and your tennis is terrible. You're bad for me, Barney. Mother says so, and it's true. Every time I get with you, I get all mixed up. That's why I arranged Bermuda. You're too much for me, Barney. [*She blows out the candles.*] I don't love you, Barney. I love Billy. He was editor of the year book and he's going to Princeton in the fall, and he wants to be a lawyer. You? You couldn't even stay in Franklin and Marshall. What kind of a future would I have with you? I want a home. I want a family. I've never had them. I'll never get them with you, Barney. Barney? Did you hear me, Barney?

[*Silence. Then the sound of a shot from within the bathroom.* BARNEY *staggers out, stark naked except for a bloody towel clutched to his gut. He falls face down onto the couch by the fireplace.* ELEANOR *screams, then sees the gun dangling from his hand. It is obviously a cap gun.* ELEANOR *takes his hand, lets it fall.*]

Oh, Barney! It's that same fake gun you used last summer. And probably the same ketchup. Jesus, Barney. Now you're even *repeating* yourself. Grow up!

[*There is banging on the door.*]

VOICES: [*From outside*] What happened? Who's in there? Open the door.

ELEANOR: [*Whispering*] Barney, get up! Please!

VOICES: Who's hurt? Somebody hurt in there?

[ELEANOR *frantically starts to clear the table, dumping the stuff back into the suitcase.*]

ELEANOR: Barney, help! For God's sake!

BARNEY: [*Lifting his head*] Only if you don't go to Bermuda.

ELEANOR: [*Defiantly*] Never!

154

[BARNEY *falls melodramatically back onto the couch.*]

MYRA'S VOICE: [*From outside*] Eleanor! It's your mother! Are you in there, dear?

ELEANOR: [*Frantically clearing*] Barney, I'll never forgive you for this. Never!

CHARLES'S VOICE. [*From outside*] Barney? I'm coming in there, Barney. [*To others outside*] Wait. I think I've got a master key.

ELEANOR: [*Closing the suitcase, shoving it behind the couch*] This is it, Barney. This is the END!

[*A key is heard rattling in the door.* ELEANOR *tosses the tablecloth to* BARNEY, *who covers himself. She turns bravely to face the door. The door bursts open.* MYRA *and* CHARLES *come in, both in overcoats over their night clothes; they take one look and turn back to the hall.*]

CHARLES: [*As if to crowd in hallway*] It's all right, everybody. Go home. I'll handle this.

[ELEANOR *has noticed the black nightie, still hanging by the fireplace. She quickly grabs it, shoves it under her dress.* CHARLES *and* MYRA *close the doors behind them, enter the room.*]

MYRA: [*Indicating the prone* BARNEY, *the defiant* ELEANOR] You see? You see why I telephoned you! Car breaking down, my eye!

CHARLES: [*Infinitely patient*] What's the story, Barney?

MYRA: I might ask you the same question, Eleanor. With the door locked.

CHARLES: Barney, I am waiting for an answer.

BARNEY: [*Carefully*] I got drunk. Took a shower. Passed out. She found me here and locked the door so I wouldn't be embarrassed.

CHARLES: [*Skeptically*] They heard a shot. A scream.

BARNEY: I was goofing around with that old starter gun. [*To* ELEANOR] Sorry, El.

[*Pause*]

MYRA: Eleanor, Billy is out there, and I'm sure he'd be delighted to take you home.

[ELEANOR *looks at her, looks at* BARNEY, *and then walks out slowly and stiffly, the black nightie dragging behind her.*]

CHARLES: Barney, get up, and go into that bathroom, and put your clothes on. You're coming home with me.

A. R. GURNEY, JR.

[BARNEY *gets up, wrapping the tablecloth around him.*
MYRA *turns discreetly away.* BARNEY *goes into the bathroom and closes the door.* MYRA *draws her overcoat
around her ample bosom.*]

MYRA: I don't think we heard the whole story, Charles.
There was obviously some hanky-panky going on. But I
think it's safe to say we nipped it in the bud.

CHARLES: You were right to telephone, Myra.

MYRA: I hope I didn't wake you up.

CHARLES: [*Covering up his pajamas*] Not at all. I was reading in bed.

MYRA: Oh. So was I.

CHARLES: Really? What book?

MYRA: You'll laugh.

CHARLES: Not at all. Tell me.

MYRA: *The Black Rose.* By Thomas B. Costain. Am I hopelessly middle-brow?

CHARLES: No, no.

MYRA: Actually, it's quite risqué.

CHARLES: Is it?

MYRA: Yes. It tries to give an accurate picture of what went
on in the Middle Ages.

CHARLES: What did?

MYRA: [*Looks at him, laughs flirtatiously*] Won't tell.

CHARLES: [*Carefully*] Well I imagine whatever went on then
. . . still does.

MYRA: Oh, yes. Oh, yes. Absolutely.
[*Pause. He notices her bosom.*]

CHARLES: [*Quickly calling offstage*] Hurry up there, Barney.

MYRA: Of course, now, with all this confusion, I doubt if
even a good book will do it.

CHARLES: Do it?

MYRA: Put me to sleep.

CHARLES: You might try an aspirin.

MYRA: Does that do it?

CHARLES: Sometimes. [*Pause. He glances again at her
bosom, then calls offstage.*] We're waiting, Barney.

MYRA: I must confess, sometimes I resort to a nightcap.

CHARLES: So do I.

MYRA: I always feel very sheepish; dipping into the Scotch,
all by myself.

CHARLES: I know the feeling.

156

MYRA: Perhaps you'd like to stop by and join me?
[*Pause*]

CHARLES: But we'll have Barney.

MYRA: [*With a sigh*] Oh. Yes.

CHARLES: And Eleanor will be there. With Bill.

MYRA: Yes. [*Pause*] Of course, I intend to send her right to bed. She has to get up at the crack of dawn for Bermuda.

CHARLES: Yes. Bill should go to bed, too.

MYRA: Eleanor will go out like a light, of course. She sleeps like a top.
[*Pause. Her overcoat has unaccountably fallen open again, to reveal some magnificent cleavage.*]

CHARLES: I see. [*Suddenly calling offstage*] Barney, we can't wait any longer! You'll have to get home by yourself. And don't wait up! I am having a nightcap with Mrs. Gilbert!
[*He takes* MYRA's *arm and quickly escorts her offstage taking a good sidelong look at her bosom. They leave the door to the trophy room open. As they leave, crowd sounds and music come up from offstage right; a piano, accordion and bass playing a bouncy version of "For Me and My Gal." The lights come up on the trophy room. It is a bright late afternoon in early summer. The curtains are open and through the windows we see blossoms on the branches.* ELEANOR *comes in from the hall. She wears a white bridal gown in the style of the mid-fifties, carrying her train over one arm.*]

ELEANOR: [*Softly, furtively*] Barney? Are you in here, Barney? [*She looks behind the couch.*] Barney, where are you? [*She knocks on the bathroom door.*] Barney? [*She opens the bathroom door, looks in. Then she climbs to the balcony, goes to the window, opens that; looks out.*] Barney? [*She leaves the window open, sighs, speaks to herself.*] Well I've done it, anyway, Barney. I've married Billy, and we're going to be happy, and there's nothing you can do about it now.
[CHARLES *comes in, now dressed in a cutaway. The sounds of the wedding party come up loud behind him.*]

CHARLES: When do I get a chance to dance with the bride?

ELEANOR: [*Brightly*] Oh, any time. Any time at all.

CHARLES: What brings you in here, of all places?

ELEANOR: I—I thought I might find Barney.

CHARLES: Barney?

ELEANOR: I thought he might be hiding.

CHARLES: Eleanor, sweetheart, he's in San Francisco.

ELEANOR: But he might just *arrive*.

CHARLES: How can he? The Navy wouldn't let him. His ship sails today for the Far East.

ELEANOR: I know, I know.

CHARLES: That's why we set this date!

ELEANOR: I just have this awful feeling. . . . [CHARLES *looks at her, then closes the door behind him, shutting out the music.*]

CHARLES: Let me show you something. [*He crosses to the cup, downstage left.*] You see this cup? My wife and I won this in 1933. Our names are right here.

ELEANOR: I know.

CHARLES: You've seen it?

ELEANOR: Someone showed it to me once.

CHARLES: It's been here forever. Look. Here's the dent from 1912 when old Mrs. Stevens grabbed it from the winning couple and threw it at her husband.

ELEANOR: Why did she do that?

CHARLES: She hated to lose. Everyone wanted to win in those days. My wife Helen and I tried every year after we were married. And never came close. Until 1933. When we won hands down.

ELEANOR: What made you win?

CHARLES: We found our rhythm. There wasn't a point we played that we weren't in tune. It was absolutely exhilarating.

ELEANOR: It sounds ideal.

CHARLES: It was. It was so ideal that I've never married again. I don't think I could ever find that rhythm with anyone else.

ELEANOR: Oh, that's sad.

CHARLES: No, because we had a good thing going. And good things go. But I can remember it. And reflect on it. And recognize it in others. I see it in you and Bill.

ELEANOR: Our game has its problems.

CHARLES: That's what I'm saying. You have to practice, you have to play. And some day you and Bill will have your names on this cup.

ELEANOR: I hope so.

[CHARLES *puts the cup back.*]

Do you think Barney will ever be on it?

CHARLES: I used to hope so.

ELEANOR: But not anymore?

CHARLES: He doesn't have any staying power. He gets all wound up, but it doesn't last.

ELEANOR: [*Reminiscently*] I know. . . .

CHARLES: He leaves himself wide open. That's why Bill always beats him.

ELEANOR: Maybe he doesn't want to win.

CHARLES: Not at mixed doubles, anyway. But you wait. He'll come back from the Navy and turn into a champion—what? Bowler. He loves knocking things down. Now come on. Let me trot you around that dance floor.

ELEANOR: All right.

[*The door bursts open.* MYRA *comes in, all gussied up in a flowered dress, with hat and gloves.*]

MYRA: *Here* you are. Eleanor, poor Billy is out there surrounded by old ladies.

ELEANOR: Oh, poor guy!

[*She rushes out.* MYRA *watches her go, then closes the door and turns to* CHARLES.]

MYRA: Oh, Charles, guess what just arrived.

CHARLES: What?

MYRA: A wedding present. Special delivery to the club.

CHARLES: From Barney?

MYRA: From your elder son.

CHARLES: I'm delighted he finally sent one.

MYRA: You won't say that when you hear what it was. I took the liberty of opening it.

CHARLES: Go on.

MYRA: It was a picture frame.

CHARLES: What's wrong with that?

MYRA: A silver picture frame. From Gump's.

CHARLES: What's wrong with Gump's?

MYRA: Nothing's wrong with Gump's. Gump's is one of the finest stores in San Francisco. It's what was *in* the frame that's wrong.

CHARLES: Well what was, Myra?

MYRA: His picture.

CHARLES: Barney's picture?

MYRA: Barney's picture was in that frame.

CHARLES: Well I think that's rather touching. I should have a picture of Barney in his sailor suit. I'll put it on the piano.

MYRA: He wasn't in his sailor suit.

CHARLES: Oh?

MYRA: He was in his birthday suit.

CHARLES: [*Exploding*] Barney sent, as a wedding present, a picture of himself in the NUDE?

MYRA: Full front. Eleven by thirteen. In Kodacolor.

CHARLES: Oh, good Lord!

[*He sits on couch, downstage right.* MYRA *follows him.*]

MYRA: And. . . .

CHARLES: *And?*

MYRA: How do I say this?

CHARLES: How do you say WHAT?

MYRA: He had this great big white bow tied around his—dingy.

[*She sits beside him on the couch.*]

CHARLES: [*Striking his head*] Oh, oh, oh.

MYRA: And. . . .

CHARLES: [*Anguished*] AND? AND?

MYRA: There was a note.

CHARLES: SAYING WHAT?

MYRA: Saying "wish we could be there."

CHARLES: Oh, God; oh, God; oh, God.

MYRA: Thank heavens he's a million miles away, Charles.

CHARLES: That's what I told Eleanor.

MYRA: Absolutely. And that's what I told those two sailors downstairs.

CHARLES: [*Looking at her*] Sailors?

MYRA: Yes. Sailors. I think they were sailors. Except they wore leggings and armbands and carried nightsticks, like policemen.

CHARLES: [*Jumping up, grabbing her*] Shore Patrol! What the hell did they want?

MYRA: They wanted Barney. So I said he was on his ship for the Far East. They asked if they could wait outside. I said there was no point, but they could. And I sent them each down a glass of champagne. Because they're defending us all against communism.

CHARLES: I'd better talk to them.

MYRA: All right, Charles. [*Indicates bathroom*] I'm going to powder my nose. The downstairs ladies room has been occupée all afternoon with tipsy bridesmaids. I'll see you on the dance floor.

[CHARLES *hurries out as* MYRA *crosses to the bathroom. After a moment* BARNEY *appears at the window in a white sailor suit. He climbs in stealthily, looks around. The party sounds waft in, the music might be "The Girl That I Marry." He watches the party for a moment. From the bathroom comes the sound of flushing. He starts, turns, hides.* MYRA *begins to sing again, from within: "Ding, dong, the bells are gonna chime!"* BARNEY *gets an idea: He grabs an old gun from the gun racks on the wall. He hides behind the couch, stage right. The bathroom door opens, and* MYRA *backs out, primping as if at a mirror, clucking, singing, "Get me to the church on time." She stops, adjusts her girdle, stops again, straightens a seam, stops again to brush off some lint. When she is at center stage—*]

BARNEY: [*Suddenly popping out with the gun.*] OK, baby, reach!

MYRA: [*Jumps, gasps*] Barney!

BARNEY: [*Waving the gun*] One peep out of you, I'll plug you from your guzzle to your snatch!

MYRA: Oh, Barney, no. . . .

[BARNEY *threatens her with the gun.*]

BARNEY: Now. Go to the door, open it, and call your daughter in here.

MYRA: [*Pleading*] Barney. . . .

BARNEY: DO IT!

[*She jumps. They sidle together to the door.*]

Open it slowly.

[*She does.*]

Not too far.

[*She has it open a crack. The sounds of the party come up.* BARNEY *stands behind her so he can't be seen.*]

Can you see her?

MYRA: [*Weakly*] She's dancing with Billy.

BARNEY: Call her.

MYRA: [*Weakly waving*] Yoo-hoo. [*Turning to him*] There's too much going on.

BARNEY: Get somebody to get her.

MYRA: [*Hastily, as if to someone in the hall*] Oh, Roger? Roger Bliss, would you ask Eleanor to come in here. I . . . I . . .

[*She looks hopelessly over her shoulder at* BARNEY.]

BARNEY: You're drunk. You're sick. You've got the whirlies!

MYRA: [*To hallway*] I'm—having trouble with my slip. . . . Thank you, Roger.

BARNEY: Good. [*He closes door.*]

MYRA: [*Desperately backing toward center stage*] Oh, Barney, please, please, PLEASE leave her alone! Let her be happy, Barney, please!

BARNEY: She'll be happy with me.

MYRA: She's married, Barney. They've got furniture. They've got *lamps!*

BARNEY: She can return that crap.

MYRA: But she doesn't *want* to, Barney.

BARNEY: She can return Billy.

MYRA: She *loves* Billy.

BARNEY: Wrong! She loves *me!*

[*The door opens.* ELEANOR *comes in, sees* BARNEY, *quickly closes the door behind her.*]

ELEANOR: Goddamn it, Barney. I knew it.

MYRA: He's got a gun, Eleanor.

[BARNEY *goes through an elaborate gun drill.*]

ELEANOR: [*Walking up to* BARNEY] Give it to me, Barney. [*He hands it to her.*] He's always playing with fake guns, Mother.

[*Tosses the gun onto the couch*]

BARNEY: [*To* ELEANOR] I have to see you.

ELEANOR: Let me talk to him, Mother.

MYRA: Eleanor, I'm not going to—

ELEANOR: I can handle it, Mother.

MYRA: Eleanor, I won't allow—

ELEANOR: [*Forcefully*] Get out of here, Mother!

MYRA: [*Backing out*] Yes. All right. Yes. [*She opens the door.*]

ELEANOR: And close the door after you, please. Tell Billy I'm fixing my dress. Period.

MYRA: Yes. Oh, yes. Oh, dear.

[MYRA *goes out, closing the door behind her.* ELEANOR *faces* BARNEY.]

BARNEY: [*Saluting her*] Hi.

ELEANOR: Oh, Barney. How'd you get here?

BARNEY: I went AWOL and grabbed a plane . . . let's go. [*Indicating window*] I've got a Hertz-U-Drive-It hidden in back.

ELEANOR: Barney, I'm married to Bill!

BARNEY: Fair enough. He gets the wedding. I get the honeymoon. . . . Come *on!*

ELEANOR: [*Backing away*] You're on some ship.

BARNEY: Hell, that's halfway to Hawaii.

ELEANOR: Then you're a deserter!

BARNEY: No, no. I'm a conscientious objector. I object to Billy. You do the same!

ELEANOR: Oh, I don't know where I am!

BARNEY: It doesn't matter, as long as you're not here. Come on. Out the window. We'll drive all night. We'll change clothes, change cars, change lives. We'll cross borders, El. Name your border, and we'll cross it. Skiing in Canada, swimming in Mexico, which do you want?

ELEANOR: It's like some movie. . . .

BARNEY: [*Moving toward her*] What's wrong with that? Here's what they do in the movies.

ELEANOR: [*Backing away.*] Stay away from me.

BARNEY: I just want to kiss the bride.

ELEANOR: You just stay away.

BARNEY: Movies are better than ever. [*He corners her. They kiss. She responds. The door bursts open.* CHARLES *rushes in, followed by* MYRA, *who shrieks.*]

CHARLES: [*To* MYRA] Close the door. Quickly.

[MYRA *does,* CHARLES *surveys* BARNEY.]

Young Lochinvar out of the west, eh? About to sweep the bride off her feet, Barney?

BARNEY: We were just leaving, Dad.

CHARLES: Oh, no you're not.

BARNEY: We are, aren't we, El?

ELEANOR: [*Anguished, going to window*] I don't know!

MYRA: Eleanor!

CHARLES: Nobody's leaving except you, Barney. And you

are leaving quietly, down the backstairs, where the Shore Patrol is waiting to fly you back west.

ELEANOR: [*Turning from window*] Shore Patrol?

MYRA: Two of the nicest boys. One's even a Negro.

CHARLES: Will you go, boy, or will you cause trouble?

BARNEY: I'm going out the window, and she's coming with me. Now stand back.

[*He leaps to the windowsill, holding* ELEANOR *behind him, as if she were Maid Marion.*]

ELEANOR: [*To* BARNEY, *breaking away*] How'd the Shore Patrol know?

CHARLES: [*Going to door*] All right, Barney. I'll bring them up here, and we'll have a very messy scene.

MYRA: Oh, Charles, how ghastly!

ELEANOR: Wait! Please wait.

[CHARLES *stops. She turns to* BARNEY.]

How'd they know you were here, Barney?

BARNEY: I don't know.

ELEANOR: What made them come here? Right to this club? Right in time for the reception?

BARNEY: I don't know.

ELEANOR: Did you tell someone you were coming here?

BARNEY: No. I—

ELEANOR: You told people, didn't you?

BARNEY: I just told—

ELEANOR: You told *every*one! You told your buddies, you told your captain. . . .

BARNEY: I didn't tell the captain!

ELEANOR: You probably sent a wire to President Eisenhower, saying "Help, bring in the cavalry at the last minute!"

BARNEY: I might have told—

ELEANOR: Oh, Barney, you left a trail a mile wide!

BARNEY: [*Looking at her, scratching his head*] Maybe I did.

ELEANOR: You were just playing games, weren't you? You didn't even want to win.

BARNEY: Maybe I didn't.

ELEANOR: [*To* CHARLES *and* MYRA] He never wanted to. Ever.

BARNEY: Oh, El. . . .

ELEANOR: [*Squaring her shoulders*] OK, Barney. You can keep on playing. You can play Robin Hood right now. You can have your Merry Men rush in here, and ruin my

164

wedding. You can do that, Barney. Or you can grow up, and get the hell out of here, quietly, down the back way. Which is it, Barney?

[*Pause*]

BARNEY: I'll go quietly.

MYRA: Then there is a God.

CHARLES: They said you could meet your ship in Hawaii, Barney.

[BARNEY *goes to* CHARLES, *holds out his hand.*]

BARNEY: Good-bye, Dad.

[*They shake hands.*]

CHARLES: And I'll call someone in Washington. We'll get you off with a light punishment.

[BARNEY *goes to* MYRA, *holds out his hand.*]

BARNEY: Good-bye, Mrs. Gilbert.

MYRA: [*Coldly, refusing to shake hands*] Frankly, Barney, I think it will do you a lot of good if they put you in the clink or the jug or the mess or whatever it is they put you in.

[BARNEY *shrugs, crosses to* ELEANOR, *who is still on the balcony by the window.*]

BARNEY: Good-bye, El.

[ELEANOR *holds out her hand for him to shake.*]

ELEANOR: Good-bye, Barney.

[*He takes her hand, then suddenly kisses it passionately.*]

BARNEY: I still love you, El.

[ELEANOR *quickly withdraws her hand.*]

CHARLES: [*Threateningly*] Get going, Barney!

[MYRA *opens the door. Out he goes.*]

MYRA: Eleanor, I think you and Bill should be changing for your wedding trip.

[ELEANOR *nods and starts for the door.*]

CHARLES: And don't look so sad, Eleanor. The next time you see Barney, he'll be just another member of the family.

MYRA: Exactly. This sort of thing will never, never happen again.

ELEANOR: [*Turning in the doorway*] Oh, I know. That's what's so sad.

[*She goes offstage.*]

MYRA: [*Crossing downstage center*] How can she say a thing like that?

CHARLES: Because she'll miss him. So will I.

MYRA: He pointed a GUN at me, Charles!

CHARLES: Oh, Myra, he's harmless. Look, it's just one of those old things off the wall. Here. I'll put it back.

[*He picks it up. It goes off with a bang, knocking down one of the stuffed heads.* MYRA *screams, stands aghast.* CHARLES *looks at the gun, looks at* MYRA, *looks at the door. The lights fade quickly.*]

END OF ACT ONE

ACT II

The early sixties. Afternoon. The greenery outside the window indicates mid-summer. The window is open; the door is open. Through the door, we hear sounds of a baby crying and other children's voices, and the murmurs and laughter of a small gathering. Someone on the piano might be playing musical comedy selections. After a moment, BARNEY *and* ELEANOR *come in together from the hall, arm in arm.* ELEANOR *wears a summer dress and carries a knitting bag, and* BARNEY *wears conventionally collegiate summer clothes: seersucker jacket, khakis, shirt and tie. He carries a gin-and-tonic.*

ELEANOR: [*As they enter, indicating the room*] See? Nothing's changed.
BARNEY: [*Remaining at door*] Except us.
ELEANOR: Mmmm. Well come on *in*. We haven't had a chance to catch up.
BARNEY: [*Indicating door*] Shall I?. . .
ELEANOR: Um. No. Better leave it open. Just in case.
BARNEY: In case what?
ELEANOR: In case the baby needs me. [*She sits on the couch downstage left.*]
BARNEY: Oh.
ELEANOR: You look marvelous. That California sun.
BARNEY: You look fine, too.
ELEANOR: Me? Oh, I'm a cow. Since the baby. Since three babies. I'm two sizes larger. Upstairs.

167

BARNEY: Lucky baby.

ELEANOR: Now, now.

BARNEY: Lucky Billy.

ELEANOR: I said, now, now.

[*Pause, she pats the couch. He sits beside her.*]

Barney, I want you to know how much I appreciate your coming all the way for the christening.

BARNEY: I wanted to. For my own godson, after all.

ELEANOR: But from San Francisco!

BARNEY: Oh, I hitched a ride. With friends. It was OK.

ELEANOR: Where'd you go after the church? We all got worried.

BARNEY: I just came right here.

ELEANOR: Here?

BARNEY: I was hot. I took a quick swim.

ELEANOR: You still like it here, then?

BARNEY: Can't stay away.

[*Pause*]

ELEANOR: Thank you for the christening present, by the way.

BARNEY: That's all right.

ELEANOR: A silver spoon. It was lovely.

BARNEY: Well, you know. Born with it in his mouth. Might as well face up to these things.

ELEANOR: Mmm. Frankly, when I was opening it, I was a little nervous.

BARNEY: Really?

ELEANOR: Yes. I thought you might come up with something ghastly which would shock the pants off everybody.

BARNEY: Were you disappointed?

ELEANOR: [*Too insistently*] No. Of course not. No. [*Pause*] But I wanted you to be his godfather, Barney. I stuck to my guns on that.

BARNEY: Why?

ELEANOR: Oh . . . I don't know. My third child. Probably my last. I thought *some*body in my family should have some connection with something outside these . . . walls.

BARNEY: That's why I came.

ELEANOR: What do you mean?

BARNEY: I needed some connection *inside*. [*Pause. They look at each other. From through the door, the sound of a baby crying]* Don't you want to?. . .

ELEANOR: He just needs changing. Billy will do it. He's terribly helpful. [*The piano stops. The crying subsides.*] See? [*Pause.* ELEANOR *takes out her knitting.*] Now I want to hear all about you. It's been so long, Barney.

BARNEY: I took a second hitch in the Navy, I finished college on the G.I. Bill. . . .

ELEANOR: Oh, I know *that,* Barney. I want to hear the gory details. In the Navy, for example. Did you sow your wild oats?

BARNEY: I tried.

ELEANOR: I'll bet you did. Did you have any romantic adventures?

BARNEY: Sure.

ELEANOR: Can you talk about them?

BARNEY: Sure. Do you want to hear what happened one June, in Rangoon, during a monsoon, with a baboon?

ELEANOR: No thank you . . . so you won't talk about your adventures.

BARNEY: I'll talk about one.

ELEANOR: Go ahead.

BARNEY: I got married.

ELEANOR: [*Shocked*] Barney!

BARNEY: Oh, not legally. But married. She was Japanese.

ELEANOR: [*Flippantly*] Oh, gosh. *Madame Butterfly. Sayonara.* All that.

BARNEY: It was serious, El. I lived with her whenever we were in port. We had a little house. Made a little nest. I even mowed a little lawn.

ELEANOR: Just like me and Bill.

BARNEY: [*Looking at her*] Right.

ELEANOR: Well what *hap*pened?

BARNEY: I wanted to bring her home. I went to the embassy, filled out the papers, everything . . . and then suddenly, I chickened out.

ELEANOR: Because of the club?

BARNEY: Because of you.

[Pause]

ELEANOR: Oh.

BARNEY: I was still playing *games!* That was just a Japanese imitation of you and Bill. I was still competing with my brother, halfway around the world!

ELEANOR: Poor girl.

BARNEY: Poor *me*. I'll never love anyone, El.

ELEANOR: Oh, phooey.

BARNEY: Never. I know that now. I'm doomed to live alone.

ELEANOR: You'll find someone.

BARNEY: Nope. It wouldn't be fair. I'd always be comparing her to you.

[*Pause*]

ELEANOR: Barney, tell you what: Now you're back, why not stay? Bill and I have this marvellous house out in Fairview. We've fixed it all up. You could come out to dinner. Once a week, even. A regular thing. I'm a marvellous cook, Barney. We'll have these marvellous meals. And there's a guest room. You could spend the night. Any time. You'd be a breath of spring, out there, actually. Bill works his tail off, and I don't seem to get beyond the washer and the dryer, and the kids see nothing but green grass. You'll open us up, Barney. You'll be like one of those fabulous uncles in children's books— Uncle Wiggly, Doctor Doolittle. You'll take us where the wild things are.

[*She sits on the edge of his chair, ruffles his hair.*]

BARNEY: Um, no thanks, El. [*He gets up, moves downstage left.*]

ELEANOR: Why not? We need you out there.

BARNEY: No. I'm going back to Berkeley.

ELEANOR: That's silly. You've finished school.

BARNEY: No. I've just started. I'm going to get my Ph.D.

ELEANOR: On what, for God's sake?

BARNEY: I want to work on the Middle Ages!

ELEANOR: The Middle *Ages?*

BARNEY: That's my area. I know it cold. [*He moves to the raised area by the window.*] The Middle Ages are very much like this.

ELEANOR: [*Following him up*] This?

BARNEY: A quiet, dull life, punctuated by ceremony. . . .

ELEANOR: Oh. . . .

BARNEY: A closed universe, halfway between the last Roman emperor . . . [*Indicates a portrait on the wall*] . . . and a new way of life. . . . [*He looks out the window.*]

ELEANOR: I see.

BARNEY: I know that world. I'm half in, half out. I can study it, write about it, teach it.

ELEANOR: Will you teach "The Eve of Saint Agnes"?

BARNEY: Hell no. That was just an adolescent version.

ELEANOR: [*Leaning against a pillar*] I suppose . . . well. That's fine, Barney. Very sensible. Very mature.

BARNEY: [*Looking at her, carefully*] I'm going to focus in on the idea of courtly love.

ELEANOR: Courtly love?

BARNEY: There was a whole movement. Of guys who were in love with married women. Courtiers, jesters, fools. . . .

ELEANOR: And what did they do?

BARNEY: They wrote these fantastic love poems. They worshipped from afar.

ELEANOR: Is that all they did? Just—write poems?

BARNEY: They wrote, they went on quests—they sublimated.

ELEANOR: Didn't they ever just—come around?

BARNEY: Not much.

ELEANOR: Why not?

BARNEY: It was too dangerous.

[*Long pause*]

ELEANOR: Well. I think we should be joining the others, don't you?

BARNEY: [*Getting up*] Yes I do.

[CHARLES *comes in hurriedly, closing the door behind him. He looks older, is dressed in a summer suit.*]

CHARLES: I'm sorry to interrupt, but I've just had to call the police.

ELEANOR: The *police?*

CHARLES: There's trouble. Old Mr. Sidway went down to take his afternoon dip, and what did he find but three naked Negroes and a woman, all splashing around in the pool! They've obviously broken in, and the police will have to get them out.

BARNEY: They're my guests, Dad.

CHARLES: They're your WHAT?

BARNEY: I rode with them from Berkeley. They were hot.

[CHARLES *stands looking at him, dumbfounded.*]

ELEANOR: [*Quietly, exultantly*] Welcome home, Barney.

171

[*Pause.* CHARLES *looks from one to the other, then speaks with great restraint.*]

CHARLES: Eleanor, I wonder if you'd tell the police we were mistaken.

ELEANOR: Yes. All right.

[*She goes out quickly.*]

CHARLES: And, Barney, I want you to go down to the pool, and ask your friends to put on their clothes, and come up to the main room, and raise a glass to my new grandson. Go on, Barney. Do it.

[BARNEY *looks at him, then goes out. The lights begin to dim on the trophy room.* CHARLES *continues to speak, as if to himself.*]

I will greet them, I will shake their hands, I will see that they are made comfortable, because they're guests, and the cardinal rule of this club is hospitality. And if I hear one rude remark from anyone in the room about these—guests, then whoever makes it will feel my full fury. And then, when the party's over, when these guests have decided to depart, I am going to do something which I should have done ten years ago. [*Turning to audience*] I am hereby blackballing my elder son! He is no longer welcome here, now or in the future. I will speak to Alice in the coatroom, and Fred in the bar, and John in the locker room, and if they see hide or hair of him, ever again, they should call me, or the police, or the National Guard! I want him OUT! Permanently and forever! [*He paces.*] We have always prided ourselves on our openness here. I like to think we are a democratic institution. In recent years, we have admitted many fine Jewish members, and there's talk that Walter Fay is partly Chinese. Fine. Good. But we are not ready for the invasion of naked barbarians. Poor old Mr. Sidway was profoundly disturbed by what he saw. He seems to have had a slight stroke. Fortunately, Doctor Russell was here. I shall tell him to send Barney the bill. [*He sighs.*] Now I wish him well in Berkeley. I hope he works hard. I even hope he comes home, now and then, to visit. He's my son, after all, and I love him. But when he returns, he may not—repeat not—come to this club. If he wants to swim or play a game, let him seek out some public facility. If he wants to have a drink with old friends, let them meet

in some gloomy saloon. If he wants to cash a check, let
him stand in line at the bank. Oh, we'll still break bread
together, he and I. We'll still do that. But not here. Oh,
no. We will go out. To a restaurant. We will be shown to
a dirty table in a dark corner by a cheap woman who
chews gum. After an endless wait, she will bring us two
watery cocktails, crackers wrapped in cellophane, call
us "honey," and serve us lukewarm coffee with the main
course. That's what democracy is these days. That's
what Barney wants apparently. And I'm sorry.

[*He crosses the stage to read a magazine, getting older by
the step. The lights come up as* MYRA *comes on in a pant-
suit, also looking older. Her costume suggests the late sixties.*]

MYRA: [*Hesitantly*] Charlie . . .

[*He turns to her.*]

There was a telephone message at the desk. I told them
I'd give it to you.

CHARLES: Yes?

MYRA: Long distance. From California. From you-know-
who.

CHARLES: Go on.

MYRA: He needs money again.

CHARLES: Why?

MYRA: For bail. Again.

CHARLES: What did he do this time?

MYRA: What difference does it make? It's all the same.
Marching without a permit, lying down in front of troop
trains, picketing against poor Mr. Nixon.

CHARLES: How much does he need?

MYRA: It's higher this time.

CHARLES: How much?

MYRA: A thousand.

[*Pause*]

CHARLES: What time do the banks close these days?

MYRA: Oh, Charlie, you're not going to keep *doing* this.

CHARLES: He hasn't got a dime.

MYRA: Whose fault is that? He lost a perfectly good teaching job. Because he *stole*, Charles.

CHARLES: He didn't *steal*, Myra.

MYRA: He stole private *pro*perty, Charles.

CHARLES: It was public property.

MYRA: He stole the university president's *car.* And drove it *around.*

CHARLES: He didn't keep it. He gave it to the poor.

MYRA: He gave it to Angela *Davis.*

CHARLES: Well Angela Davis is poor, Myra. Quite poor. I don't believe Angela Davis has a net worth of more than—

MYRA: Charlie, *honestly!*

CHARLES: [*With a sigh*] Oh, Myra, I'm suddenly very tired.

MYRA: So am I, Charlie. So am I. Tired of seeing you tear yourself apart over that boy. Charlie, he is simply *de trop.* Now you've got a wonderful, hard-working son and a lovely daughter-in-law, and three marvelous grandchildren—

CHARLES: They tire me too.

MYRA: Charlie!

CHARLES: They do. I don't like it out there. Those noisy meals, the television blaring away, the endless chatter about schools. I don't like it out there much.

MYRA: Why, Charlie: You're getting old.

CHARLES: That's it. Old. And I want to be with people my own age. [*He looks at her.*] Let's get married, Myra.

MYRA: Charlie!

CHARLES: Why not?

MYRA: I thought you were tired.

CHARLES: I am. Let's lean on each other in our autumn years.

MYRA: But, Charlie. . . .

CHARLES: Think about it. Take your time. I'll go see about that boy.

[*He goes off.* MYRA *looks after him, looks at audience, ponders very briefly, clears her throat.*]

MYRA: After long and careful thought, I have decided to marry Mr. Charles Rusher, of this city. It will be a small, sober ceremony, family only, I probably won't even wear a hat. Then a few friends back here afterward for a quiet drink. A glass of champagne, maybe, French champagne, and I hope someone will get on his feet and make a toast. There might be music. I could bring in that accordian player from the Park Plaza who plays nothing but Fred Astaire. Which means someone might want to dance. . . . [*She begins to sing; dance.*] "Heaven . . . I'm

174

in Heaven . . ." [*Stops*] And let there be food. Chicken in patties and peas. Oh hell, let's have a party! Let's have a biggie! Let's have the most spectacular get-together since the Cerebral Palsy Ball!

[CHARLES *appears at the door.*]

CHARLES: Myra. . . .

MYRA: [*Swirling to him*] Oh, Charlie, yes, yes, YES!

CHARLES: [*Patting her hand*] That's fine, dear. You make the arrangements. I've got to rush to the bank before they close.

[*He goes out. She stands looking after him, then comes slowly downstage.*]

MYRA: Make the arrangements, make the arrangements, Myra. . . . Strange . . . my first husband used to say the same thing. Wouldn't drive, wouldn't carve, wouldn't . . . never mind what he wouldn't do. Oh, why do I seem to attract such exhausted men? Or are they only exhausted when they get to me? [*She sits down.*] Why can't I be exhausted once in a while? What if I said No. I refuse. I am hereby *hors de combat.* [*She leans back, closes her eyes.*] Oh, this is marvellous. [*She opens her eyes; sits up.*] But then who will move him out of that great barn of a house and into a nice apartment? And who will remind him to take his pills? And who will get him to think about his will, and the college education of three grandchildren? [*She stands up, squares her shoulders.*] Me! I'll do it! Myra Rusher will make the arrangements! I'll plan the trips and manage the meals and send out the Christmas cards year after year! And when things fall apart, I'll hold them together with Scotch tape and Elmer's glue and Gilbey's gin! Somebody has to do these things! On my head be it! *Après moi, le déluge!* I'll arrange things until the day I die! Then I'll arrange my own funeral! Nobody else will bother, that's for sure!

[*The lights come up on the trophy room. She defiantly takes a tape measure out of her pocket and begins to measure a chair, getting older with each move. Through the open doors we now hear the sounds of women's voices. After a moment,* ELEANOR *comes in, in a trim shirt and pants, suggesting the early seventies. Through the window, the red and brown shrubbery now suggests early autumn, late afternoon.*]

ELEANOR: [*Stands for a moment, watching* MYRA] Mother. What are you doing?

MYRA: I am measuring this ratty old furniture. I plan to put slipcovers on everything I can get my hands on.

ELEANOR: Why?

MYRA: Because no one else will.

ELEANOR: Not this room, Mother. Please. Leave it just the way it is.

MYRA: [*Huffily*] All right. You're the boss, after all. This is your day.

ELEANOR: Oh, not just mine, Mother. [*She goes to the window, looks out.*]

MYRA: Well I mean, you fought for it. You won. It's primarily because of you that women now have the run of the club every Thursday.

ELEANOR: [*At the window, vaguely*] We all fought.

MYRA: Well you were the leader. [*Looks at her*] Why aren't you out there, enjoying it?

ELEANOR: I got a little bored, Mother.

MYRA: Well go bowl or play bridge or something! Go meet the new members. You can't just walk out on the whole she*bang!* I mean, if Charlie knew you were hiding in here after you fought tooth and nail for women to be out there, my God, he'd have *another* heart attack.

ELEANOR: [*Suddenly*] He didn't even call me, Mother.

MYRA: Who?

ELEANOR: Barney.

MYRA: Oh, Eleanor.

ELEANOR: I sat by the telephone all morning. He didn't even call.

MYRA: He was at the hospital, seeing his father.

ELEANOR: He still could have called.

MYRA: Eleanor, he's a busy man now. Or says he is. At least he seems to come and go every other minute.

ELEANOR: But he always calls.

MYRA: Well I can't stand here and sympathize with someone who doesn't receive a *tele*phone call from a crazy brother-in-law. I've been sitting around hospitals for weeks. I'm going to try my hand at paddle tennis. [*She goes to the door, then turns.*] One thing sure. He can't come here!

[MYRA *goes out.* ELEANOR *sighs, and turns back to look out*

176

the window. After a moment, a tall blonde woman backs into the room, wearing a raincoat and slacks. She closes the door stealthily behind her. ELEANOR *turns at the sound, faces her back.*]

ELEANOR: Yes? May I help you?

[*The woman doesn't turn around.*]

I don't believe we've met. Are you a new member?

[*The woman turns to face* ELEANOR. *A long moment. It's* BARNEY, *of course, in a wig.*]

BARNEY: No. I'm a guest. [*He tosses off the wig.*]

ELEANOR: [*With a shriek of joy*] Barney!

BARNEY: Dad said it was women's day, but faint heart ne'er won fair lady. [*He tosses off his raincoat, revealing a mod, mid-seventies outfit.*] So I bought a disguise. [*He puts the wig on a post.*]

ELEANOR: Well it worked.

BARNEY: Oh, boy, did it! One of the waiters tried to make a pass at me.

ELEANOR: [*Looks at wig*] Wow. That must be a fifty-dollar wig.

BARNEY: That's OK. I'm rich now.

ELEANOR: Doing what, Barney? Nobody can figure out what you do.

BARNEY: Oh, I sell things, buy things.

ELEANOR: In San Francisco?

BARNEY: There, and New York. I've got apartments in both places.

ELEANOR: But what's your product?

BARNEY: Let's say I'm a middle man. As usual. As always. [*Looks at watch*] And I'm in between planes. So fill me in on yourself.

ELEANOR: Oh. Me.

BARNEY: You. Dad says you're the high priestess around here now.

ELEANOR: Oh, I do my bit. I also have a part-time job. [*She comes down from the balcony.*]

BARNEY: Hey! Doing what?

ELEANOR: I'm a family counselor. I went back to school, like everyone else. Now I'm an expert in keeping families together on Mondays, Wednesdays, and Fridays.

BARNEY: Are you any good?

ELEANOR: Oh, I'm terrific. We all get together in this hot,

177

white room. And then we gripe, like mad. [*Pause*] I gripe, too. [*Pause, she turns to him, hugs him.*] Oh, Barney, it's so good to see you. If you hadn't come, I would have telephoned you, wherever you were.

BARNEY: Why?

ELEANOR: I've got a vacation coming up. And I want to visit you.

BARNEY: Good God! With the whole gang?

ELEANOR: No, just me.

BARNEY: What about—Bill?

ELEANOR: Separate vacations are good occasionally, Barney. I've learned that much. He went duck-hunting with the boys last fall. The year before I visited my father. Now it's my turn again.

BARNEY: What about the kids?

ELEANOR: Oh. [*She laughs.*] They're big, Barney. They're huge. Bill can spoon out their spaghetti. Or they can do it themselves. No, I want *out* for a couple of weeks, Barney. I want to visit you.

BARNEY: Where?

ELEANOR: New York. I love New York. I'll come the next time you're there.

BARNEY: That might be a little tricky, El.

ELEANOR: Why? You could take me in tow. You probably have all these weird, wonderful New Yorky friends.

BARNEY: [*Mock-sophisticated*] Oh, I do; I do.

ELEANOR: Then— [*Looks at him*] Ah-hah. [*Pause*] You've got a girl there.

BARNEY: Right. [*He sits on the arm of the couch.*]

ELEANOR: She lives in your apartment.

BARNEY: Right.

ELEANOR: Do you love her?

BARNEY: No.

ELEANOR: But you *like* her.

BARNEY: When I'm there.

ELEANOR: And I might mess that up.

BARNEY: You might mess *me* up.

[*Pause*]

ELEANOR: Then I'll come to San Francisco.

BARNEY: El. . . .

ELEANOR: You've got a girl there too.

BARNEY: Yes.

ELEANOR: Do you love *her?*

BARNEY: God, no . . . she's married.

ELEANOR: Then let me *visit* you. Send her back to her husband.

BARNEY: No.

ELEANOR: Why the hell not?

BARNEY: I'm also involved with the husband.
 [*Pause*]

ELEANOR: What?

BARNEY: I like the husband, too.
 [*Pause*]

ELEANOR: Oh, God.

BARNEY: You asked.

ELEANOR: Oh, Jesus, Barney. [*She turns away, comes downstage. Pause, then she turns back to him, brightly.*] Who do you like the best?

BARNEY: I don't know. I like them all.

ELEANOR: I can't *stand* this. Do they know about each other?

BARNEY: Sure.

ELEANOR: They do?

BARNEY: Sure.

ELEANOR: Aren't they jealous of each other?

BARNEY: Not at all.

ELEANOR: Have they all *met* each other?

BARNEY: Sure.

ELEANOR: They *have?*

BARNEY: They've made it with each other.

ELEANOR: Oh, no.

BARNEY: We've all made it together.

ELEANOR: Barney!

BARNEY: I told you I was a middle man.

ELEANOR: Yes. You told me.

BARNEY: And you might as well know what I do for a living.

ELEANOR: [*Walking downstage left*] I don't want to hear.

BARNEY: [*Following her*] I'm in the film business.

ELEANOR: Oh, well, at least that's half-decent.
 [*Pause*]

BARNEY: Decent's not quite the word.

ELEANOR: You make *pornographic* movies.

BARNEY: I don't like that word, either.

ELEANOR: What are they then?

BARNEY: They are films about physical love.

ELEANOR: Are you *in* these things?

BARNEY: Hell no. I'm not good enough. [*Quickly*] I mean, I'm good, but not that good. . . . You should go to one.

ELEANOR: No thank you.

BARNEY: Billy goes.

ELEANOR: He does not.

BARNEY: He does. He told me. And Jackie Onassis goes. And the Unitarian church shows them on retreats.

ELEANOR: Well I won't go.

[*She moves away from him, he pursues her.*]

BARNEY: There's one you ought to see.

ELEANOR: I doubt it.

BARNEY: You ought to. It was my idea. We based it on *Robin Hood*. It's called *The Arrow and the Quiver*.

ELEANOR: Christ, Barney.

BARNEY: It's good. It's very artistic. We won a special prize at Cannes.

ELEANOR: [*Suddenly reeling on him*] I think it's disgusting.

BARNEY: Oh, yeah?

ELEANOR: I think your whole life sounds cheap and sad and disgusting.

BARNEY: Oh, yeah? And what about you? What do you do now, in the swinging suburbs? Don't you all throw your car keys in the center of the rumpus room, and go home with whoever picks them up?

ELEANOR: No.

BARNEY: I'll bet.

ELEANOR: You think I'd do that?

BARNEY: How do I know? I've kind of lost touch with the middle class. Maybe you've got something different going with those dykes out in the main room.

[ELEANOR *looks at him, hauls off and slaps him, hard. He looks at her, then slaps her back.*]

Equality of the sexes, friend. [*He strides upstage toward the door.*]

ELEANOR: Bastard!

[*She hurls herself at him, begins to pummel him. He grabs her arms. They struggle. He holds her, then gives her a hard, passionate kiss. She struggles, then responds. Finally she breaks away.*

BARNEY: The thing is . . . you don't realize this, but . . . by showing these films, we liberate people. There's a big connection between sex and politics. . . . Open things up, spell things out, people will learn to be free. . . . Hell, it's still Robin Hood, El. . . . I'm still fighting the good fight.

ELEANOR: Do you really believe that?

[*Pause*]

BARNEY: No.

ELEANOR: I didn't think so.

BARNEY: [*Indicating window*] Out there, I believe it. [*Looks at her*] In here, with you, it seems like a pile of crap.

ELEANOR: Glad to hear it.

BARNEY: Forget your vacation, El. Stick around here. It's a decent place.

[*Pause*]

ELEANOR: Too decent for me, I'm afraid.

BARNEY: [*Coming down to her*] That'll be the day.

ELEANOR: No, I mean it. Last summer, I almost had an affair.

BARNEY: Hey. Truth telling time. Who with? [*He sits on the arm of her chair.*]

ELEANOR: You don't know him. Neither do I, really. He stopped by one time before supper, collecting for the Heart Fund. Bill wasn't home yet, the kids were hanging around some game, I was slapping a meal together before I went to a meeting. So in he came. I offered him a sherry. We got along. We decided to meet in town for lunch, and all that. So I got down my Sierra Club calendar and he got out his Mutual of Omaha appointment book, and we tried to arrange a day, but we never could get our schedules together. Finally I gave him a check. For twenty-five dollars. For the Heart Fund. And he left.

BARNEY: Just as well.

ELEANOR: I guess. But the family's not enough anymore, Barney. At least, not for me. I thought I could make this club into a place where different people could get together.

BARNEY: Well it worked, didn't it? Ladies Day, open membership, all that?

ELEANOR: Oh, I don't know. I wanted to turn it into a kind of camp, every summer, when people were away. You know: ghetto kids playing games, learning to swim. I mean it just *sits* here. But they voted me down.

BARNEY: What did you expect?

ELEANOR: I guess half the fun of clubs is keeping people out.

BARNEY: Mmm.

ELEANOR: Well. I got what I asked for, anyway, Barney. I got in.

BARNEY: And I got out. And now where are we?

ELEANOR: Nowhere.

BARNEY: [*Arm around her*] I'll always count on you, El. You keep me honest.

ELEANOR: Yes. Between New York and San Francisco.

BARNEY: You're different, and you know it. I happen to love you.

ELEANOR: Whatever that means.

BARNEY: It means a lot, these days. [*Pause. He looks at her, looks at his watch.*] Oh, my gosh. My plane leaves in forty-five minutes. [*Looks at her again.*] Want to come along?

ELEANOR: With you?

BARNEY: Sure.

[*Long pause*]

ELEANOR: No.

[*Pause*]

BARNEY: Thank God. I couldn't deal with you out there.

ELEANOR: Well I can't deal with you in here, Barney. [*Pause*] So maybe you'd better go.

BARNEY: Uh . . . huh. [*He gets up.*] It's good-bye, then. [*He puts on his raincoat.*]

ELEANOR: [*Not looking at him*] Yes it really is.

BARNEY: [*Brightly*] I mean, so long.

ELEANOR: I mean good-bye.

[*Pause*]

BARNEY: Christ. . . . [*No response. He gets the wig and puts it on.*] Hey. I better wear this. Maybe I can still get it on with that waiter. [*No response. He goes to the door, turns.*] Someday something will happen, El. Right here in this room, where we first met. And you'll know it, and I'll know it, and it'll be absolutely fantastic.

[*He opens the doors and minces out exaggeratedly as we hear the women's voices come up.* ELEANOR *gets up, looks out window as* MYRA *bustles in.*]

MYRA: [*Looking back down the hall*] What a large woman that was. Do you suppose she's interested in bowling?

ELEANOR: She's from out of town.

MYRA: Oh. Well. Billy's on the phone, and he wants to know when he's supposed to put the pizza in the oven.

ELEANOR: Tell him I'll . . . [*Pause*] Tell him . . . [*She starts to cry.*] Oh, Mother, I don't want to go home.

MYRA: [*Rushing to hold her*] Eleanor! Dear love!

[ELEANOR *sobs in her arms as the lights dim on the room. The lights come up on* BARNEY, *who is wheeling* CHARLES *into the room in a wheelchair.* CHARLES *looks old and weak, and is covered with a lap robe.* BARNEY *now wears a dark blue blazer.*]

CHARLES: [*As he is being wheeled downstage center*] Put me over there. Away from the draught. . . . [*Looking around*] I have the feeling I'm in this room for the last time.

BARNEY: Oh, no, Dad. You're just having a bad day.

CHARLES: I'm all right. [*Pause*] What brings you to town this time?

BARNEY: I just wanted to see you, Dad.

CHARLES: You need money?

BARNEY: No, Dad.

CHARLES: You won't get any more money from me.

BARNEY: I don't want money, Dad.

CHARLES: [*Indicating couch*] Sit there.

BARNEY: [*Sitting on edge of chair*] That's all right, Dad.

CHARLES: I said sit there.

BARNEY: [*Quickly*] All right.

[*He sits on the edge of the couch.*]

CHARLES: Will you see Eleanor this time?

BARNEY: No.

CHARLES: You sure?

BARNEY: I'm sure.

CHARLES: Thou shalt not covet thy brother's wife!

BARNEY: Neighbor's.

CHARLES: What?

BARNEY: It's "thy *neigh*bor's wife."

CHARLES: Doesn't matter. Nobody reads the Bible these days. [*Pause*] They're separated now. You must know that. She's living in some miserable apartment. Can't make up her mind. Bursts into tears at parties. The chil-

183

dren come and go. Billy sees another woman. It's very bad.

BARNEY: I'm sorry, Dad.

CHARLES: You damn well ought to be. You've been badgering the poor girl for thirty years!

BARNEY: Not anymore, Dad.

CHARLES: She chose Bill.

BARNEY: I know, Dad.

CHARLES: You lost, Barney! You lost the game! Now get off the damn court! Do it! Promise me you'll leave her alone. We're not fooling around now. Promise.
[*Pause*]

BARNEY: I promise I'll stay away, Dad.

CHARLES: Thank you.

BARNEY: Unless she comes to me.

CHARLES: Fair enough. [*Pause*] I hear you've got a lot of money.

BARNEY: A little.

CHARLES: A lot. Myra told me how you made it. Peddling smut. [*Shakes his head*] I can't discuss it.

BARNEY: I've sold out, Dad. I'm through.

CHARLES: What does it matter, anyway? There are only a few more apples in the barrel for me.

BARNEY: Oh, no, Dad.

CHARLES: Oh, yes. I'm going, it's all going. The club is going, did you know that?

BARNEY: I heard.

CHARLES: Oh, yes. It's on the market. Nobody wants to keep it up anymore. The waiters steal, the pool leaks. The men don't have time to stop by after work. The women don't bother with lunch. So it's up for sale. They plan to build some bubble in the suburbs. Held up by thin air.

BARNEY: It won't be the same, Dad.

CHARLES: I don't know who will buy this damn thing. Even the Catholics can't afford it anymore. Probably some developer will break it up into doctors' offices. People will be getting rectal examinations right here in this room. [*Pause, looks at him*] Not that you care. You never liked the club anyway.

BARNEY: I did, Dad. I always came back.

CHARLES: Just to cause trouble.

BARNEY: Not always.

CHARLES: Always.

BARNEY: Not this time, Dad. I want— [*Pause*] I want your blessing, Dad.

[*Pause*]

CHARLES: Do you know the story of the prodigal son? No, of course you don't. Nobody reads the—

BARNEY: I know it, Dad.

CHARLES: A man has two sons, one good, one bad. The bad son comes home, the father kills the fatted calf for him, even after all the trouble he's caused.

BARNEY: I remember, Dad.

CHARLES: That father was a fool.

BARNEY: [*With a sigh*] Yes, Dad.

CHARLES: Bill gets the fatted calf.

[*Pause*]

BARNEY: Fair enough.

CHARLES: Well, he needs it, he has three children, he's stayed at the wheel all these years.

BARNEY: OK. Fine, Dad. I'm with you.

CHARLES: And all you've ever done is break up the party. Am I right? Am I right, Barney?

[*Pause.* MYRA *appears at the door, in an older-looking dress.*]

MYRA: Barney, your taxi's here.

BARNEY: Thanks.

[MYRA *goes off.* BARNEY *gets up.*]

I'd better go.

[*He gives his father a quick kiss on his head and starts for the door.*]

Good-bye, Dad.

CHARLES: Barney! [BARNEY *stops.*] Barney, there's a psychiatrist at the club, Jewish fella, I've forgotten his name, who told me once that the trouble with the world is that everyone wants to kill his father. Do you agree with that?

BARNEY: No.

CHARLES: And he said, if I understood him correctly, that's what you've been trying to do all your life. Trying to kill me.

BARNEY: [*With a groan*] Oh, no, Dad!

CHARLES: Because if that's true, you've succeeded.

BARNEY: Oh, Dad, PLEASE! [*He kneels by the wheelchair.*]

CHARLES: [*Looking at him tenderly*] Did you really come to town just to see me?

BARNEY: To see you, Dad, I swear.

CHARLES: Oh, Barney, why have you been so difficult all these years?

BARNEY: Maybe I wanted *you* to see *me*.

[CHARLES *stares at him for a long moment, touches him tenderly, then closes his eyes.*]

CHARLES: I'm very tired.

BARNEY: [*Getting up*] Good-bye, Dad. [*Bends over, kisses him again and starts out.*]

CHARLES: Good-bye, Barney . . . thank you for stopping by. [BARNEY *goes off as* MYRA *comes in.*]

MYRA: Good-bye, Barney. [*To* CHARLES] Now I think it's time for our nap. [*She begins to wheel him out.*] And then we'll have our blue pills, and one cocktail, and two poached eggs with Walter Cronkite.

CHARLES: I want to change my will, Myra.

MYRA: Oh, Charles, not again.

CHARLES: I want to make things fair and square.

MYRA: We'll discuss it later, Charles.

CHARLES: He's a good boy.

MYRA: Billy's a good boy.

CHARLES: They're both good boys. We didn't do so badly after all, Helen.

MYRA: Helen? Charlie, I'm Myra. Really I must ask you to stop confusing me with your first wife.

[*She wheels him out as the lights darken. When they come up again,* BARNEY *is standing at the fireplace, holding his speech, dressed in his gray suit, as he was at the beginning.* ELEANOR *comes in, in black again. A funeral prelude is heard.*]

ELEANOR: Now we really *are* ready to begin, Barney. [*No answer*] I spoke to mother, and she said yes, all right, read your speech. But please be brief. And respectful. [*No answer*] Did you hear me, Barney?

BARNEY: [*Turning, passionately*] I can't do it, El. I'd stand up there and cry like a goddamn baby.

ELEANOR: [*Moving toward him*] Oh, Barney. . . .

BARNEY: [*Tossing the speech onto the couch*] You do it.

ELEANOR: Me?

BARNEY: [*Moving away from her*] Go on. I'm staying in here.

[ELEANOR *picks up envelope, opens it, looks at speech.*]

ELEANOR: This isn't a speech, Barney. This is some . . . document.

BARNEY: [*His back to her*] It's a deed.

ELEANOR: It's a what?

BARNEY: It's a deed, it's a DEED. I went and bought the place.

ELEANOR: Bought it?

BARNEY: Bought the whole frigging CLUB! With the proceeds of my pornography business.

ELEANOR: But what for?

BARNEY: I don't know. I don't even know. I wanted to give it to the old man.

ELEANOR: I think that's wonderful.

BARNEY: It was dumb.

ELEANOR: I think it's fabulous.

BARNEY: It was just dumb. I'm a dumb clown. All my life making faces in front of the mirror. Still doing it, and the mirror isn't even here anymore!

ELEANOR: I think it's the most fantastic thing. Oh, Barney, I want to go out there and tell them.

BARNEY: Fine. Do that. And tell them to clear their smellies out of the locker room so I can have the place torn down.

[*He crosses to chair, sinks into it.*]

ELEANOR: Tear it *down?* You wouldn't do that!

BARNEY: What else can I do with the damn thing?

ELEANOR: I don't know. . . . [*Reaching for it*] What would Robin Hood do?

BARNEY: Oh, El, come off it.

ELEANOR: No really. What does he do, at the end of the movie?

BARNEY: I don't remember.

ELEANOR: *I* remember. He wins this great contest and gets his castle back.

BARNEY: That does not happen.

ELEANOR: It does. I know it does.

BARNEY: What does he do when he gets it? Sit around? And pay huge property taxes to the Sheriff of Nottingham?

ELEANOR: Um. No. What he does is . . . lower the drawbridge. And open the gates. Everyone rushes in. There's singing and dancing all over the place.

BARNEY: Oh, sure.

ELEANOR: It's true! And you have the feeling he'll turn it into a wonderful place. [*Pause*] And Maid Marion helps him.

BARNEY: Take a look at the latest version. Robin dies in battle. Maid Marion is a nun.

ELEANOR: That's not my version. In mine, they get together and start the Renaissance.

[MYRA *comes in, in black.*]

MYRA: [*Looking from one to the other*] Just what do you two think you're doing?

BARNEY: Dreaming.

ELEANOR: No. Planning.

MYRA: There happens to be a funeral going on. Eleanor, come with me. Billy's waiting.

ELEANOR: I'll come with Barney, Mother.

MYRA: Eleanor. . . .

ELEANOR: And sit with him, too. In front of everyone. That's that.

MYRA: [*Taking a deep breath*] This has been a long and difficult day. I have lost a husband. Now apparently I am losing a daughter. What can I say? *Tant pis.*

BARNEY: Watch your language.

[MYRA *turns and starts out huffily.* BARNEY *calls to her.*] Hey.

[MYRA *stops, looks at him stonily. He gets up, goes to her, touches her hand.*]

I'm sorry.

MYRA: Thank you, Barney.

[*She goes out.* BARNEY *goes to look out the window.*]

ELEANOR: [*Carefully*] I'll tell you something else Maid Marion does. When the service is over, she rides out to the supermarket, where she gets a box of Toll House cookies, a quart of banana ice cream, and some smoked oysters. Then she stops at the liquor store for some Chateauneuf du Pape. Then she returns to the castle, and opens the bottle, and pours it into this cup. [*She gets the cup from downstage left, places it on the table, center stage.*] Then she just waits to see who walks through that door.

[*Pause*]

BARNEY: Do you think . . . after all these years . . . I could walk through that door?

ELEANOR: [*Eyes closed, anguished*] Couldn't you?

BARNEY: Hell no! I'd come through the window!

[*He opens the windows wide and then comes downstage to join her.* ELEANOR *puts the deed in the cup, faces him. The funeral music begins offstage. People begin to sing: "A Mighty Fortress Is Our God."* BARNEY *bows to* ELEANOR, *offers her his arm. She takes it. They stride off joyfully, as if to their own wedding. The cup on the table catches the last of the light.*]

THE END

THE DINING ROOM

THE DINING ROOM was first produced in the Studio Theatre at Playwrights Horizons in New York City in January 1982 with the following cast:

1st ACTOR .... Remak Ramsay
2nd ACTOR .... John Shea
3rd ACTOR .... W. H. Macy

1st ACTRESS .... Lois de Banzie
2nd ACTRESS .... Ann McDonough
3rd ACTRESS .... Pippa Pearthree

It was directed by David Trainer. Loren Sherman designed the set, Deborah Shaw the costumes, and Frances Aronson the lighting. M. A. Howard was the production stage manager.

The play takes place in a dining room—or, rather, many dining rooms. The same dining room furniture serves for all: a lovely, burnished, shining dining room table; two chairs, with arms, at either end; two more, armless, along each side; several additional matching chairs, placed so as to define the walls of the room. Upstage somewhere, a sideboard, possibly with a mirror over it. There should be a good hardwood floor, possibly parquet, covered with a good, warm oriental rug.

Upstage left, a swinging door leads to the pantry and kitchen. Upstage right, an archway leads to the front hall and the rest of the house. But we should see no details of these other rooms. Both entrances should be masked in such a way as to suggest a limbo outside the dining room.

A sense of the void surrounds the room. It might almost seem to be surrounded by a velvet-covered low-slung chain, on brass stanchions, as if it were on display in some museum many years from now.

Since there are no walls to the dining room, windows should be suggested through lighting. The implication should be that there are large French doors downstage, and maybe windows along another wall. The place-mats, glassware, china, and silverware used during the course of the play should be bright, clean, and tasteful. We should only see used what is absolutely necessary for a particular scene. Actual food, of course, should not be served. The thing to remember is that this is not a play about dishes, or food, or costume changes, but rather a play about people in a dining room.

Since the play takes place during the course of a day, the light should change accordingly.

For costumes, it is suggested that the men wear simple, conservative suits, or jackets and slacks, which can be modified as required. For more informal scenes, for example, an actor might appear in shirt-sleeves, or a sweater. Women's costumes might seem to pose a more complicated problem, but again the best solution turns out to be the simplest: the actresses may wear the same simple, classically styled dress—or skirt and blouse—throughout, with perhaps an occasional apron when playing a maid. There is hardly enough time between scenes for actors to fuss with changes or accessories, and there is an advantage in being as simple and straightforward as possible.

The blending and overlapping of scenes have been carefully worked out to give a sense of contrast and flow. When there is no blending of scenes, one should follow another as quickly as possible. The play should never degenerate into a series of blackouts.

CAST

The play requires a cast of six—three men, three women—and seems to work best with this number. It is conceivable that it could be done with more, but it would be impossible to do with fewer. The various roles should be assigned democratically; there should be no emphasis on one particular actor, and no actor should repeat one particular type of role. It might be good to cast the play with people of different ages, sizes, and shapes, as long as they are all good actors. It would seem to make more sense to end the play with the same actors playing RUTH, ANNIE, *and the* HOST *as played* MOTHER, ANNIE, *and* FATHER *in the breakfast scene in Act I. If a cast of six is used, and there are strong arguments for using this number, the following casting of the roles has proved to be workable and successful:*

First Actor:	FATHER, MICHAEL, BREWSTER, GRANDFATHER, STUART, GORDON, DAVID, HARVEY, and HOST
Second Actor:	CLIENT, HOWARD, PSYCHIATRIST, TED, PAUL, BEN, CHRIS, JIM, DICK, and GUEST
Third Actor:	ARTHUR, BOY, ARCHITECT, BILLY, NICK, FRED, TONY, STANDISH, and GUEST
First Actress:	AGENT, MOTHER, CAROLYN, SANDRA, DORA, MARGERY, BETH, KATE, CLAIRE, and RUTH
Second Actress:	ANNIE, GRACE, PEGGY, NANCY, SARAH, AUNT HARRIET, EMILY, ANNIE and GUEST
Third Actress:	SALLY, GIRL, ELLIE, AGGIE, WINKIE, OLD LADY, HELEN, MEG, BERTHA, and GUEST

196

ACT I

No one onstage. The dining room furniture sparkles in the early morning light. Voices from offstage right. Then a woman real estate AGENT *and her male* CLIENT *appear in the doorway. Both wear raincoats.*

AGENT: . . . and the dining room.

CLIENT: Oh, boy.

AGENT: You see how these rooms were designed to catch the early morning light?

CLIENT: I'll say.

AGENT: French doors, lovely garden, flowering crabs. Do you like gardening?

CLIENT: Used to.

AGENT: Imagine, imagine having a long, leisurely breakfast in here.

CLIENT: As opposed to instant coffee on Eastern Airlines.

AGENT: Exactly. You know this is a room after my own heart. I grew up in a dining room like this. Same sort of furniture. Everything.

CLIENT: So did I.

AGENT: Then here we are. Welcome home.
   [*Pause*]

CLIENT: What are they asking again?

AGENT: Make an offer. I think they'll come down.
   [*Another pause*]

CLIENT: Trouble is, we'll never use this room.

AGENT: Oh, now.

CLIENT: We won't. The last two houses we lived in, my wife used the dining room table to sort the laundry.

AGENT: Oh, dear.

CLIENT: Maybe you'd better show me something more contemporary.

AGENT: That means something farther out. How long have we got to find you a home?

CLIENT: One day.

AGENT: And how long will the corporation keep you here, after you've found it?

CLIENT: Six months to a year.

AGENT: Oh, then definitely we should look farther out. [*She opens the kitchen door.*] You can look at the kitchen as we leave.

CLIENT: You shouldn't have shown me this first.

AGENT: I thought it was something to go by.

CLIENT: You've spoiled everything else.

AGENT: Oh, no. We'll find you something if we've got all day. But wasn't it a lovely room?

CLIENT: Let's go, or I'll buy it!

[*They both exit through the kitchen door as* ARTHUR *comes in from the hall, followed by his sister,* SALLY. *Both are middle-aged.*]

ARTHUR: The dining room.

SALLY: Yes. . . .

ARTHUR: Notice how we gravitate right to this room.

SALLY: I know it.

ARTHUR: You sure mother doesn't want this stuff in Florida?

SALLY: She hardly has room for what she's got. She wants us to take turns. Without fighting.

ARTHUR: We'll just have to draw lots then.

SALLY: Unless one of us wants something, and one of us doesn't.

ARTHUR: We have to do it today.

SALLY: Do you think that's enough time to divide up a whole house?

ARTHUR: I have to get back, Sal. [*He looks in the sideboard.*] We'll draw lots and then go through the rooms taking turns. [*He brings out a silver spoon.*] Here. We'll use this salt spoon. [*He shifts it from hand to hand behind his back, then holds out two fists.*] Take your pick. You get the spoon, you get the dining room.

SALLY: You mean you want to start here?

ARTHUR: Got to start somewhere.

[SALLY *looks at his fists.* ANNIE, *a maid, comes out from the kitchen to set the table for breakfast. She sets place-mats and coffee cups with saucers at either end.* SALLY *and* ARTHUR *take no notice of her.* ANNIE *then leaves.*]

SALLY: [*Not choosing*] You mean you want the dining room?

ARTHUR: Yeah.

SALLY: What happened to the stuff you had?

ARTHUR: Jane took it. It was part of the settlement.

SALLY: If you win, where will you put it?

ARTHUR: That's my problem, Sal.

SALLY: I thought you had a tiny apartment.

ARTHUR: I'll find a place.

SALLY: I mean your children won't want it.

ARTHUR: Probably not.

SALLY: Then where on earth? . . .

ARTHUR: Come on, Sal. Choose.

[*He holds out his fists again. She starts to choose.* ANNIE *comes in from the kitchen, bringing the morning paper. She puts it at the head of the table, as* ARTHUR *lowers his hands.*]

You don't want it.

SALLY: Of course I want it.

ARTHUR: I mean you already have a perfectly good dining room.

SALLY: Not as good as this.

ARTHUR: You mean you want two dining rooms?

SALLY: I'd give our old stuff to Debbie.

ARTHUR: To Debbie?

SALLY: She's our oldest child.

ARTHUR: Does Debbie want a dining room?

SALLY: She might.

ARTHUR: In a condominium?

SALLY: She might.

ARTHUR: In Denver?

SALLY: She just might, Arthur.

[*A* FATHER *comes in from the right. He settles comfortably at the head of the table, unfolds his newspaper importantly.*]

ARTHUR: [*Shuffling the spoon behind his back again; then holding out his fists*] I don't want to fight. Which hand? [SALLY *starts to choose, then stops.*]

SALLY: Are you planning to put it in storage?

ARTHUR: I might.

SALLY: I checked on that. That costs an arm and a leg.

ARTHUR: So does shipping it to Denver. [*He holds out his fists.*]

FATHER: [*Calling to kitchen*] Good morning, Annie.

SALLY: [*Almost picking a hand, then stopping*] I know what will happen if you win.

ARTHUR: What?

SALLY: You'll end up selling it.

ARTHUR: Selling it?

SALLY: That's what will happen. It will kick around for a while, and you'll end up calling a furniture dealer. [ANNIE *comes out with a small juice glass on a tray.*]

ARTHUR: I am absolutely amazed you'd say that.

SALLY: I don't want to fight, Arthur.

ARTHUR: Neither do I. Maybe we should defer the dining room. [*He starts for door, stage right.*]

SALLY: [*Following him*] Maybe we should.

ANNIE: Good morning, sir.

FATHER: Good morning, Annie.

ARTHUR: Selling the dining room? Is that what you told mother I'd do?

SALLY: [*Following him out*] I told her I'd give you the piano if I can have the dining room. . . .

ARTHUR: I'll be lucky if I keep this spoon.

SALLY: I'll give you the piano and the coffee table if I can have the dining room.
[ARTHUR *and* SALLY *exit into the hall.*]

FATHER: Annie. . . .
[ANNIE *is almost to the kitchen door.*]

ANNIE: Yes, sir. . . .

FATHER: Did I find a seed in my orange juice yesterday morning?

ANNIE: I strained it, sir.

FATHER: I'm sure you did, Annie. Nonetheless I think I may have detected a small seed.

ANNIE: I'll strain it twice, sir.

FATHER: Seeds can wreak havoc with the digestion, Annie.

ANNIE: Yes, sir.

FATHER: They can take root. And grow.

ANNIE: Yes, sir. I'm sorry, sir.

[ANNIE *goes out.* FATHER *drinks his orange juice carefully, and reads his newspaper. A little* GIRL *sticks her head out through the dining room door.*]

GIRL: Daddy. . . .

FATHER: Yes, good morning, Lizzie Boo.

GIRL: Daddy, could Charlie and me—

FATHER: Charlie and I. . . .

GIRL: . . . Charlie and I come out and sit with you while you have breakfast?

FATHER: You certainly may, Lizzikins. I'd be delighted to have the pleasure of your company, provided—

GIRL: Yippee!

FATHER: I said, PROVIDED you sit quietly, without leaning back in your chairs, and don't fight or argue.

GIRL: [*Calling into kitchen*] He says we *can!*

FATHER: I said you *may*, sweetheart.

[*The* GIRL *comes out adoringly, followed by a little* BOY.]

GIRL: [*Kissing her* FATHER] Good morning, Daddy.

BOY: [*Kissing him too*] Morning, Dad.

[*They settle into their seats.* ANNIE *brings out the* FATHER's *"breakfast."*]

ANNIE: Here's your cream, sir.

FATHER: Thank you, Annie.

ANNIE: You're welcome, sir.

[ANNIE *goes out. The children watch their* FATHER.]

BOY: Dad. . . .

FATHER: Hmmm?

BOY: When do we get to have fresh cream on our shredded wheat?

GIRL: When you grow up, that's when.

FATHER: I'll tell you one thing. If there's a war, no one gets cream. If there's a war, we'll all have to settle for top of the bottle.

GIRL: Mother said she was thinking about having us eat dinner in here with you every night.

FATHER: Yes. Your mother and I are both thinking about that. And we're both looking forward to it. As soon as you children learn to sit up straight . . .

[*They quickly do.*]

A. R. GURNEY, JR.

... then I see no reason why we shouldn't all have a pleasant meal together every evening.

BOY: Could we try it tonight, Dad? Could you give us a test?

FATHER: No, Charlie. Not tonight. Because tonight we're giving a small dinner party. But I hope very much you and Liz will come down and shake hands.

GIRL: I get so shy, Dad.

FATHER: Well you'll just have to learn, sweetie pie. Half of life is learning to meet people.

BOY: What's the other half, Dad?

[*Pause. The* FATHER *fixes him with a steely gaze.*]

FATHER: Was that a crack?

BOY: No, Dad. . . .

FATHER: That was a crack, wasn't it?

BOY: No, Dad. Really. . . .

FATHER: That sounded very much like a smart-guy wisecrack to me. And people who make cracks like that don't normally eat in dining rooms.

BOY: I didn't mean it as a crack, Dad.

FATHER: Then we'll ignore it. We'll go on with our breakfast.

[ANNIE *comes in.*]

ANNIE: [*To* GIRL] Your car's here, Lizzie. For school.

GIRL: [*Jumping up*] OK.

FATHER: [*To* GIRL] Thank you, Annie.

GIRL: Thank you, Annie. . . .

[*Kisses* FATHER]

Good-bye, Daddy.

FATHER: Good-bye, darling. Don't be late. Say good morning to the driver. Sit quietly in the car. Work hard. Run. Run. Good-bye.

[GIRL *goes off.* FATHER *returns to his paper. Pause.* BOY *sits watching his* FATHER.]

BOY: Dad, can I read the funnies?

FATHER: Certainly. Certainly you may.

[*He carefully extracts the second section and hands it to his son. Both read, the* BOY *trying to imitate the* FATHER *in how he does it. Finally—*]

FATHER: This won't mean much to you, but the government is systematically ruining this country.

BOY: Miss Kelly told us about the government.

FATHER: Oh, really. And who is Miss Kelly, pray tell?

BOY: She's my teacher.

FATHER: I don't remember any Miss Kelly.

BOY: She's new, Dad.

FATHER: I see. And what has she been telling you?

BOY: She said there's a depression going on.

FATHER: I see.

BOY: People all over the country are standing in line for bread.

FATHER: I see.

BOY: So the government has to step in and do something.

[*Long pause. Then—*]

FATHER: Annie!

ANNIE: [*Coming out of kitchen*] Yes, sir.

FATHER: I'd very much like some more coffee, please.

ANNIE: Yes, sir.

[ANNIE *goes out.*]

FATHER: You tell Miss Kelly she's wrong.

BOY: Why?

FATHER: I'll tell you exactly why. If the government keeps on handing out money, no one will want to work. And if no one wants to work, there won't be anyone around to support such things as private schools. And if no one is supporting private schools, then Miss Kelly will be standing on the bread lines along with everyone else. You tell Miss Kelly that, if you please. Thank you, Annie.

[ANNIE *comes in and pours coffee.* FATHER *returns to his paper.* ANNIE *has retreated to the kitchen.* BOY *reads his funnies for a moment. Then—*]

BOY: Dad. . . .

FATHER: [*Reading.*] Hmmm?

BOY: Could we leave a little earlier today?

FATHER: We'll leave when we always leave.

BOY: But I'm always late, Dad.

FATHER: Nonsense.

BOY: I am, Dad. Yesterday I had to walk into assembly while they were still singing the hymn.

FATHER: A minute or two late. . . .

BOY: Everyone looked at me, Dad.

FATHER: You tell everyone to concentrate on that hymn.

BOY: I can't, Dad. . . .

FATHER: It's that new stoplight on Richmond Avenue. It affects our timing.

BOY: It's not just the new stoplight, Dad. Sometimes I come in when they're already doing arithmetic. Miss Kelly says I should learn to be punctual.

FATHER: [*Putting down paper*] Miss Kelly again, eh?

BOY: She said if everyone is late, no one would learn any mathematics.

FATHER: Now you listen to me, Charlie. Miss Kelly may be an excellent teacher. Her factoring may be flawless, her geography beyond question. But Miss Kelly does not teach us politics. Nor does she teach us how to run our lives. She is not going to tell you, or me, to leave in the middle of a pleasant breakfast, and get caught in the bulk of the morning traffic, just so that you can arrive in time for a silly hymn. Long after you've forgotten that hymn, long after you've forgotten how to factor, long after you've forgotten Miss Kelly, you will remember these pleasant breakfasts around this dining room table.

[MOTHER *glides into the room from the right.*]

And here is your mother to prove it.

MOTHER: [*Kissing* FATHER] Good morning, dear.

[*Kissing* CHARLIE]

Good morning, Charlie.

FATHER: [*Remaining seated*] I know people who leap to their feet when a beautiful woman enters the room.

[CHARLIE *jumps up.*]

MOTHER: Oh, that's all right, dear.

FATHER: I also know people who rush to push in their mother's chair.

[CHARLIE *does so.*]

MOTHER: Thank you, dear.

FATHER: And finally, I know people who are quick to give their mother the second section of the morning paper.

CHARLIE: Oh! Here, Mum.

MOTHER: Thank you, dear.

FATHER: Now, Charlie: Take a moment, if you would, just to look at your lovely mother, bathed in the morning sunlight, and reflected in the dining room table.

MOTHER: Oh, Russell.

[CHARLIE *looks at his* MOTHER.]

FATHER: Look at her, Charlie, and then ask yourself carefully: Which is worth our ultimate attention? Your mother? Or Miss Kelly?

MOTHER: Who is Miss Kelly?

FATHER: Never mind, dear. Which, Charlie?

CHARLIE: My mother.

FATHER: Good, Charlie. Fine. [*He gets up; taking his section of the paper.*] And now, I think you and I should make a trip upstairs before we say good-bye and are on our way. [MOTHER *smiles sweetly.* FATHER *and* CHARLIE *leave the room.* ANNIE *enters, carrying coffee server.*]

MOTHER: Good morning, Annie.

ANNIE: Good morning, Mrs.

MOTHER: Tell Irma I'll have poached eggs this morning, please, Annie.

ANNIE: Yes, Mrs.

[ANNIE *goes out.* MOTHER *sits sipping coffee, reading her section of the paper. A youngish woman—call her* ELLIE— *comes out of the kitchen. Her arms are stacked with a small portable typewriter, papers, several books and notebooks. She finds a place at the table and begins to spread things out around her.* MOTHER *pays no attention to her. A man called* HOWARD, *carrying a briefcase, appears at right.*]

HOWARD: Hey!

ELLIE: Oooops. I thought you had gone.

HOWARD: I forgot my briefcase. . . . What's going on?

ELLIE: I have to get this term paper done.

HOWARD: In here?

ELLIE: Where else.

HOWARD: You're going to *type?*

ELLIE: Of course I'm going to type.

HOWARD: In here? At that table?

ELLIE: Why not?

HOWARD: You're going to sit there, banging a typewriter on my family's dining room *table?*

ELLIE: Why not?

HOWARD: Because it wasn't designed for it, that's why!

ELLIE: [*Sighing*] Oh, Howard. . . .

HOWARD: Lucky I came back. Next thing you know, you'll be feeding the dog off our Lowestoft china.

ELLIE: It's got rubber pads under it. I checked. [*Gets up, goes to sideboard]* And I'll get something else, if you want. [*She takes out a couple of place-mats.*]

HOWARD: You're not going to use those place-mats?

ELLIE: I thought I would. Yes.

HOWARD: Those are good place-mats.

ELLIE: We haven't used them in ten years.

HOWARD: Those are extremely good place-mats, Ellie. Mother got those in Italy.

ELLIE: All *right.*

[*She puts the same mats back in the sideboard, rummages around, finds a couple of hot pads. He watches her carefully.*]

I'll use these, then. Mind if I use these? We put pots on them. We can certainly put a typewriter. . . .

[*She carries them to the table, puts them under the typewriter, continues to get things set up.* HOWARD *watches her. Meanwhile,* MOTHER, *impatient for her poached eggs, puts down her paper and rings a little silver bell on the table in front of her.* ANNIE *comes out of the kitchen.*]

ANNIE: Yes, Mrs?

MOTHER: I wonder if anything might have happened to my poached eggs, Annie.

ANNIE: Irma's cooking two more, Mrs.

MOTHER: Two more?

ANNIE: The first ones slid off the plate while she was buttering the toast.

MOTHER: [*Standing up*] Is she drinking again, Annie?

ANNIE: No, Mrs.

MOTHER: Tell me the truth.

ANNIE: I don't think so, Mrs.

MOTHER: I'd better go see. . . . A simple question of two poached eggs. [*She starts for the kitchen.*] Honestly, Annie, sometimes I think it's almost better if we just do things our*selves.*

ANNIE: Yes, Mrs.

[MOTHER *goes out into the kitchen;* ANNIE *clears the* MOTHER's *and* FATHER's *places, leaving a glass and plate for the next scene.* ANNIE *exits.*]

ELLIE: [*To* HOWARD, *who is standing at the doorway, still watching*] Don't you have a plane to catch? It's kind of hard to work when your husband is hovering over you, like a helicopter.

HOWARD: Well it's kind of hard to leave when your wife is systematically mutilating the dining room table.

ELLIE: I'll be careful, Howard. I swear. Now good-bye. [*She begins to hunt and peck on the typewriter.* HOWARD *starts out, then stops.*]

HOWARD: Couldn't you *please* work somewhere else?

ELLIE: I'd like to know where, please.

HOWARD: What's wrong with the kitchen table?

ELLIE: It doesn't work, Howard. Last time the kids got peanut butter all over my footnotes.

HOWARD: I'll set up the bridge table in the living room.

ELLIE: I'd just have to move whenever you and the boys wanted to watch a football game.

HOWARD: You mean, you're going to leave all that stuff *there?*

ELLIE: I thought I would. Yes.

HOWARD: All that shit? All over the dining room?

ELLIE: It's a term paper, Howard. It's crucial for my degree.

HOWARD: You mean you're going to commandeer the *din*ing room for the rest of the *term?*

ELLIE: It sits here, Howard. It's never used.

HOWARD: What if we want to give a dinner party?

ELLIE: Since when have we given a dinner party?

HOWARD: What if we want to have a few people *over,* for Chrissake?

ELLIE: We can eat in the kitchen.

HOWARD: Oh, Jesus.

ELLIE: Everybody does these days.

HOWARD: That doesn't make it right.

ELLIE: Let me get this done, Howard! Let me get a good grade, and my master's degree, and a good job, so I can be *out* of here every day!

HOWARD: Fine! What the hell! Then why don't I turn it into a *tool* room, every night?

[*He storms out.* ELLIE *doggedly returns to her work angrily hunting and pecking on the typewriter.* GRACE *enters from stage right; she sits downstage left and begins to work on her grocery list.* CAROLINE, *a girl of fourteen, enters sleepily a moment later.*]

CAROLYN: Why did you tell Mildred to wake me up, Mother?

GRACE: Let me just finish this grocery list.

CAROLYN: I mean it's Saturday, Mother.

GRACE: [*Finishing the list with a flourish*] Sh. . . . There. [*Puts down the list*] I know it's Saturday, darling, and I apologize. But something has come up, and I want you to make a little decision.

CAROLYN: What decision?

GRACE: Start your breakfast, dear. No one can think on an empty stomach.

[CAROLYN *sits at the table.*]

Now. Guess who telephoned this morning?

CAROLYN: Who?

GRACE: Your Aunt Martha.

CAROLYN: Oh, I love her.

GRACE: So do I. But the poor thing hasn't got enough to do, so she was on the telephone at the crack of dawn.

CAROLYN: What did she want?

GRACE: Well now here's the thing: She's got an extra ticket for the theatre tonight, and she wants you to join her.

CAROLYN: Sure!

GRACE: Now wait till I've finished, dear. I told her it was your decision, of course, but I thought you had other plans.

CAROLYN: What other plans?

GRACE: Now think, darling. Isn't there something rather special going on in your life this evening?

[*Pause*]

CAROLYN: Oh.

GRACE: Am I right, or am I right?

CAROLYN: [*Grimly*] Dancing school.

ELLIE: Shit. [*She begins to gather up her materials.*]

GRACE: Not dancing school, sweetheart. The first session of the Junior Assemblies. Which are a big step beyond dancing school.

ELLIE: I can't work in this place! It's like a tomb!

[*She goes out into the kitchen.*]

GRACE: I told Aunt Martha you'd call her right back, so she could drum up someone else.

CAROLYN: I thought it was my decision.

GRACE: It is, sweetheart. Of course.

CAROLYN: Then I'd like to see a play with Aunt Martha.

[*Pause*]

GRACE: Carolyn, I wonder if you're being just a little impulsive this morning. You don't even know what the play is.

CAROLYN: What is it, then?

GRACE: Well it happens to be a very talky play called *Saint Joan*.

CAROLYN: Oh, we read that in school! I want to go all the more!

GRACE: It's the road company, sweetheart. It doesn't even have Katharine Cornell.

CAROLYN: I'd still like to go.

GRACE: To some endless play? With your maiden aunt?

CAROLYN: She's my favorite person.

GRACE: Well then go, if it's that important to you.

CAROLYN: [*Getting up*] I'll call her right now.
[*She starts for the door.*]

GRACE: Carolyn. . . .
[CAROLYN *stops.*] You realize, of course, that on the first Junior Assembly, everyone gets acquainted.

CAROLYN: Really?

GRACE: Oh, heavens yes. It starts the whole thing off on the right foot.

CAROLYN: I didn't know that.

GRACE: Oh, yes. It's like the first day of school. Once you miss, you never catch up.

CAROLYN: Oh, gosh.

GRACE: You see? You see why we shouldn't make hasty decisions. [*Pause*]

CAROLYN: Then maybe I won't go at all.

GRACE: What do you mean?

CAROLYN: Maybe I'll skip all the Junior Assemblies.

GRACE: Oh, Carolyn.

CAROLYN: I don't like dancing school anyway.

GRACE: Don't be silly.

CAROLYN: I don't. I've never liked it. I'm bigger than half the boys, and I never know what to say, and I'm a terrible dancer. Last year I spent half the time in the ladies' room.

GRACE: That's nonsense.

CAROLYN: It's true, Mother. I hate dancing school. I don't know why I have to go. Saint Joan wouldn't go to dancing school in a million years!

GRACE: Yes, and look what happened to Saint Joan!

CAROLYN: I don't care. I've made up my mind.

[*Pause*]

GRACE: Your Aunt Martha seems to have caused a little trouble around here this morning.

CAROLYN: Maybe.

GRACE: Your Aunt Martha seems to have opened up a whole can of worms.

CAROLYN: I'm glad she did.

GRACE: All right. And how do you propose to spend your other Saturday nights? I mean, when there's no Aunt Martha. And no Saint Joan? And all your friends are having the time of their life at Junior Assemblies?

CAROLYN: I'll do something.

GRACE: Such as what? Hanging around here? Listening to that stupid Hit Parade? Bothering the maids when we're planning to have a party?

[AGGIE, *a maid, comes out of the kitchen, sits at the table, begins to polish some flat silver with a silver cloth.*]

CAROLYN: I'll do *something*, Mother.

GRACE: [*Picking up* CAROLYN's *breakfast dishes*] Well you're obviously not old enough to make an intelligent decision.

CAROLYN: I knew you wouldn't let me decide.

GRACE: [*Wheeling on her*] All right, then! Decide!

CAROLYN: I'd like to—

GRACE: But let me tell you a very short story before you do. About your dear Aunt Martha. Who also made a little decision when she was about your age. She decided—if you breathe a word of this, I'll strangle you—she decided she was in love with her riding master. And so she threw everything up, and ran off with him. To Taos, New Mexico. Where your father had to track her down and drag her back. But it was too late, Carolyn! She had been . . . overstimulated. And from then on in, she refused to join the workaday world. Now there it is. In a nutshell. So think about it, while I'm ordering the groceries. And decide.

[*She goes out, carrying* CAROLYN's *glass and plate.* AGGIE *polishes the silver.* CAROLYN *sits and thinks. She decides.*]

CAROLYN: I've decided, Mother.

GRACE'S VOICE: [*From the kitchen*] Good. I hope you've come to your senses.

CAROLYN: [*Getting up*] I've decided to talk to Aunt Martha.
[*She goes out.*]

GRACE: [*Bursting through the kitchen door*] You've got a
dentist appointment, Carolyn! You've got riding lessons
at noon—no, no, we'll skip the riding lessons, but—
Carolyn! Carolyn!
[*She rushes out through the hall as* MICHAEL *comes in
through the kitchen. He is about twelve.*]

MICHAEL: [*Suddenly*] Boo!

AGGIE: Michael! You scared me out of my skin!

MICHAEL: I wanted to.
[*Pause. He comes further into the room.* AGGIE *returns to
her polishing.*]

AGGIE: Your mother said you was sick this morning.

MICHAEL: I was. I am.

AGGIE: So sick you couldn't go to school.

MICHAEL: I *am*, Aggie! I upchucked! Twice!

AGGIE: Then you get right straight back to bed.
[*He doesn't.*]

MICHAEL: How come you didn't do my room yet?

AGGIE: Because I thought you was sleeping.

MICHAEL: I've just been *lying* there, Ag. Waiting.

AGGIE: Well I got more to do now, since Ida left. I got the
silver, and the downstairs lavatory, and all the beds besides.
[*He comes farther in.*]

MICHAEL: My mother says you want to leave us.
[*Pause. She polishes.*]

AGGIE: When did she say that?

MICHAEL: Last Thursday. On your day off. When she was
cooking dinner. She said now there's a war, you're looking for a job with more money.
[*Pause.* AGGIE *polishes.*]

MICHAEL: Is that true, Ag?

AGGIE: Maybe.

MICHAEL: [*Coming farther in*] Money isn't everything, Aggie.

AGGIE: Listen to him now.

MICHAEL: You can be rich as a king and still be miserable.
Look at my Uncle Paul. He's rich as Croesus and yet he's
drinking himself into oblivion.

AGGIE: What do you know about all that?

MICHAEL: I know a lot. I eat dinner here in the dining room

211

now. I listen. And I know that my Uncle Paul is drinking himself into oblivion. And Mrs. Williams has a tipped uterus.

AGGIE: Here now. You stop that talk.

MICHAEL: Well it's *true*, Ag. And it proves that money isn't everything. So you don't have to leave us.

[*Pause. She works. He drifts around the table.*]

AGGIE: It's not just the money, darlin'.

MICHAEL: Then *what*, Ag?

[*No answer*] Don't you like us any more?

AGGIE: Oh, Michael. . . .

MICHAEL: Don't you like our family?

AGGIE: Oh, Mikey. . . .

MICHAEL: Are you still mad at me for peeking at you in the bathtub?

AGGIE: That's enough now.

MICHAEL: Then what *is* it, Ag? How come you're just leaving?

[*Pause*]

AGGIE: Because I don't . . . [*Pause*] I don't want to do domestic service no more.

[*Pause*]

MICHAEL: Why?

AGGIE: Because I don't like it no more, Mike.

[*Pause. He thinks.*]

MICHAEL: That's because Ida left and you have too much to do, Ag.

AGGIE: No, darlin'. . . .

MICHAEL: [*Sitting down near her*] I'll help you, Ag. I swear! I'll make my own bed, and pick up my towel. I'll try to be much more careful when I pee!

AGGIE: [*Laughing*] Lord love you, lad.

MICHAEL: No, no, really. I will. And I'll tell my parents not to have so many dinner parties, Ag. I'll tell them to give you more time off. I'll tell them to give you all day Sunday.

AGGIE: No, darlin'. No.

MICHAEL: I'm *serious*, Ag.

AGGIE: I know, darlin'! I know.

[*Two men come in from stage right; an* ARCHITECT *and a new owner who is a* PSYCHIATRIST.]

ARCHITECT: OK. Let's measure it out then.

[*The* ARCHITECT *has a large-reel tape measure and a roll of blueprints. They begin to measure the room systematically, the* ARCHITECT *reading the figures and recording them in a small notebook, the* BUYER *holding the end of the tape.*]

MICHAEL: When will you be going then, Ag?

AGGIE: As soon as your mother finds someone else.

MICHAEL: She can't *find* anyone, Aggie.

AGGIE: She will, she will.

MICHAEL: She says she *can't.* They keep showing up with dirty fingernails and dyed hair!

ARCHITECT: [*Reading measurements, writing them down*] Twenty-two feet, six inches.

PSYCHIATRIST: Fine room.

ARCHITECT: Big room.

MICHAEL: So you *got* to stay, Ag. You can't just leave people in the *lurch.*

PSYCHIATRIST: Look at these French doors.

ARCHITECT: I'm looking. I'm also thinking. About heat loss. [*They measure more.*]

AGGIE: I'll stay till you go away for the summer.

ARCHITECT: [*Measuring width of "French doors"*] Eight feet, two inches.

[MICHAEL *gets up and comes downstage, looks out through the French doors, as the* ARCHITECT *goes upstage, to record his notes on the sideboard.*]

MICHAEL: You gonna get married, aren't you, Ag?

AGGIE: Maybe.

MICHAEL: That guy you told me about from church?

AGGIE: Maybe.

MICHAEL: You gonna have children?

[AGGIE *laughs.*] You will. I know you will. You'll have a boy of your own.

ARCHITECT: Hold it tight now.

MICHAEL: Will you come back to see us?

AGGIE: Oh my, yes.

MICHAEL: You won't, Ag.

AGGIE: I will surely.

MICHAEL: You'll never come back, Ag. I'll never see you again! Ever!

ARCHITECT: [*Now measuring the width*] Twelve feet, four inches. . . .

AGGIE: [*Holding out her arms*] Come here, Mike.

MICHAEL: No.

AGGIE: Come here and give Aggie a big hug!

MICHAEL: No. Why should I? No.

AGGIE: Just a squeeze, for old time's sake!

MICHAEL: No! [*Squaring his shoulders*] Go hug your own kids, Agnes. I've got work to do. I've got a whole stack of homework to do. I'm missing a whole day of school. [*He runs out of the room.*]

AGGIE: Michael! [*She resumes polishing the last few pieces of silver.*]

ARCHITECT: [*Reeling in his tape with professional zeal*] OK. There's your dining room, doctor.

PSYCHIATRIST: There it is.

ARCHITECT: Big room . . . light room . . . commodious room . . .

PSYCHIATRIST: One of the reasons we bought the house.

ARCHITECT: And one of the reasons we should consider breaking it up.

PSYCHIATRIST: Breaking it up?

ARCHITECT: Now bear with me: What say we turn this room into an office for you, and a waiting room for your patients?

PSYCHIATRIST: I thought we planned to open up those maids' rooms on the third floor.

ARCHITECT: Hold on. Relax. [*He begins to spread a large blueprint out on the table, anchoring its corners with his tape measure and the centerpiece.* AGGIE *has finished polishing by now. She gathers up her silver and polishing stuff and leaves.*]

The patient trusts the psychiatrist, doesn't he? Why can't the psychiatrist trust the architect? [*He begins to sketch on the blueprint with a grease pencil.*] Now here's the ground plan of your house. Here's what you're stuck with, for the moment, and here, with these approximate dimensions, is your dining room.

PSYCHIATRIST: I see.

ARCHITECT: [*Drawing with his grease pencil*] Now suppose . . . just suppose . . . we started with a clean slate. Suppose we open this up here, slam a beam in here, break through here and here, blast out this, throw out that, and what do we have?

PSYCHIATRIST: I'm not quite sure.

ARCHITECT: Well we don't have a dining room anymore. That's what we don't have.

PSYCHIATRIST: But where would we eat?

ARCHITECT: Here. Right here. Look. I'm putting in an eating area. Here's the fridge, the cooking units, Cuisinart, Butcher Block table, chrome chairs. See? Look at the space. The flow. Wife cooks, kids set the table, you stack the dishes. All right here. Democracy at work. In your own home.

PSYCHIATRIST: Hmm.

ARCHITECT: Now, let's review your day. You come down to breakfast, everybody's fixing his or her own thing. [*He goes out through the hall, reappears through the kitchen door.*] Eggs, corn flakes, pop-tarts, whatever. You eat, chat, read the paper, say good-bye, come in here to go to work. Do you have a nurse or a receptionist?

PSYCHIATRIST: No, no. I'm just a humble shrink.

ARCHITECT: [*Beginning to move around the room*] Well, you come in here to the reception room, maybe adjust the magazines on a table, here, maybe add your newspaper to the pile, then you go through a soundproof door into your office. You turn on your stereo console here, maybe select a book from a wall unit here, and then settle behind your desk module here. You read, you listen to music. Soon—buzz—a patient arrives. You turn off the music, put aside your book, and buzz him in through the soundproof doors. He flops on the couch here [*He creates the couch with two upstage chairs.*], tells you his dream, you look out the window here, he leaves, you write him up, buzz in the next. Soon it's time for lunch. You go in here, have lunch with the wife, or one of the kids, and maybe stroll back in here for a nap. More buzzes, more patients, and soon it's time to go in for a good, easy cooperative supper with your family.

PSYCHIATRIST: But not in the dining room.

ARCHITECT: No. Not in the dining room.

PSYCHIATRIST: This room has such resonance.

ARCHITECT: So does a church. That doesn't mean we have to live in it.

PSYCHIATRIST: Mmm.

215

A. R. GURNEY, JR.

ARCHITECT: Look, I know whereof I speak: I grew up in a room like this.

PSYCHIATRIST: Oh, yes?

ARCHITECT: Oh, sure. This is home turf to me.

PSYCHIATRIST: Really.

ARCHITECT: Oh, God yes. My father sat in a chair just like that. . . .

PSYCHIATRIST: [*Beginning to look out the window*] Mmmmm.

ARCHITECT: And my mother sat here. And my sister here. And I sat right here. [*He sits.*] Oh, it all comes back. . . .

PSYCHIATRIST: [*With a sigh.*] Do you want to tell me about it?

ARCHITECT: It was torture, that's all. Those endless meals, waiting to begin, waiting for the dessert, waiting to be excused so they couldn't lean on you anymore.

PSYCHIATRIST: [*Almost by rote*] Was it that bad?

ARCHITECT: Man, it was brutal. I remember one time I came to the table without washing my hands, and my father— [*He stops.*]

PSYCHIATRIST: Go on.

ARCHITECT: [*Snapping out of it, getting up*] Never mind. The point is, doctor, it's time to get rid of this room. [*He begins to roll up his plans.*] Tell you frankly, I'm not interested in screwing around with any more maids' rooms. I can do that in my sleep.

[PEGGY *comes out of the kitchen, carrying a large tray, loaded with paper plates, napkins, hats, and favors for a children's birthday party. She begins to set the table.*]

What I want is the chance to get in here, so I can open up your whole ground floor! Now what do you say?

PSYCHIATRIST: I'll have to think about it.

ARCHITECT: OK. Fine. Take your time. [*He starts out.*] Tell you what. I'll send you my bill for the work I've done so far.

PSYCHIATRIST: Good. And I'll send you mine.

[*They exit out.* PEGGY, *meanwhile, is finishing setting the birthday table. She surveys it, then goes to the doorway, stage right, and calls offstage.*]

PEGGY: All right, Children! We're ready!

[*She is almost bowled over by a moiling, shrieking mob of* CHILDREN *coming in to celebrate the birthday party. They*

216

scream, yell, scramble over chairs, grab for favors, wrestle, whatever. PEGGY *claps her hands frantically.*]

Children, children, CHILDREN!

[*They subside a little.*]

This is a *dining* room! This is *not* the monkey house at the zoo!

[*They all start imitating monkeys.* PEGGY *shouts them down.*]

All right then. I'll just have to tell Roberta in the kitchen to put away all the ice cream and cake.

[*The noise subsides. There is silence.*]

Good. That's much better. Now I want everyone to leave the table . . . quiet, QUIETLY. . . .

[*The* CHILDREN *begin to leave.*]

And go into the hall, and then come back in here in the right way. That's it. Go out. Turn around. And come in. Come in as if you were your mummies and daddies coming in to a lovely dinner party.

[CHILDREN *come back in much more decorously, unconsciously parodying their parents.*]

No, no. Let Winkie go first, since it's her birthday and she's the hostess. . . . That's it. Good. Good. You sit at the head of the table, Winkie. . . . Good. . . . No, no, Billy, you sit next to Winkie. . . . It should be boy-girl, boy-girl. . . . That's it. Yes. Very good.

[CHILDREN *are making a concerted effort to be genteel, though there are occasional subversive pokings, hittings, and gigglings.*]

Now what do we do with our napkins?. . . Yes. Exactly. We unfold them and tuck them under our chins. . . . And then we put on our party hats. . . .

BREWSTER: [*One of the children*] Can the boys wear their hats in the house?

PEGGY: Yes they can, Brewster, because this is a special occasion. Sometimes on special occasions, the rules can change.

CHILDREN: [*Exploding*] Ray! Yippee!

PEGGY: [*Shouting them down*] I said *some*times. And I meant *some* of the rules.

BILLY: [*Another of the children, pointing toward the hall*] There's my daddy.

PEGGY: [*Quickly*] Where, Billy?

A. R. GURNEY, JR.

[TED *enters from the hall;* PEGGY *tries to be casual.*]
Oh. Hi.

TED: Hi. [*Waves to* BILLY] Hi, Bill.

[*Party activity continues, the* CHILDREN *opening favors.* PEGGY *and* TED *move downstage to get away from the noise.*]

PEGGY: What brings you here?

TED: Have to pick up Bill.

PEGGY: I thought Judy was picking him up.

TED: She asked me to.

PEGGY: You're a little early. We haven't even had our cake.

TED: She told me to be early.

SANDRA: [*Another one of the children, fussing with a favor, calls from the table.*] I can't get mine to work.

PEGGY: Help her. Brewster. Little boys are supposed to help little girls.

TED: Where's Frank?

PEGGY: Playing golf. Where else?

TED: On Winkie's birthday?

PEGGY: Don't get me started. Please.

[WINKIE *calls from the head of the table.*]

WINKIE: Can we have the ice cream now, please.

PEGGY: In a minute, dear. Be patient. Then you'll have something to look forward to.

[*The* CHILDREN *whisperingly begin to count to sixty.*]

TED: Judy must have known he'd be playing golf.

PEGGY: Judy knows everything.

TED: She knows about us, at least.

PEGGY: About us? How?

TED: She said she could tell by the way we behaved.

PEGGY: Behaved? Where?

TED: At the Bramwell's dinner party.

PEGGY: We hardly spoke to each other.

TED: That's how she could tell.

CHILDREN: [*Whose counting has turned into a chant*] We want ice cream! We want ice cream!

PEGGY: They want ice cream. [*She starts for the kitchen.*]

TED: [*Holding her arm*] She says she'll fight it, tooth and nail.

PEGGY: Fight *what?* We haven't done anything.

TED: She says she wants to nip it in the bud.

CHILDREN: Ice cream, ice cream!

PEGGY: All right, children. You win.

[*Cheers from* CHILDREN]

Now Roberta is very busy in the kitchen because she also has a dinner party tonight. So who would like to help bring things out?

CHILDREN: [*Hands up; squeals*] Me! Me!

PEGGY: All right. Tell you what. Billy, you get the ice cream, and Sandra, you bring out the cake!

CHILDREN: Ray! Yippee!

PEGGY: Careful, careful! Walk, don't run! And be polite to Roberta because she's working very hard. And Brewster and Winkie, you'll have other responsibilities!

[SANDRA *and* BILLY *go out into the kitchen.*]

For instance, Brewster: When Billy and Sandra reappear through that door, what will you do?

[*Long pause*]

BREWSTER: Sing the song.

PEGGY: Good, Brewster. Now be very quiet, and watch that door, and as soon as they come out, start singing.

[*The* CHILDREN *watch the door.* PEGGY *hurries back to* TED.]

So what do we do?

TED: She says she's thinking of telling her father.

PEGGY: Her *father?*

TED: He'll fire me. Immediately.

PEGGY: What if he did?

TED: I'd be out of a job, Peggy.

PEGGY: You could get another.

TED: Where? Doing what?

[*The dining room door opens.* BILLY *and* SANDRA *come out carefully, carrying a cake platter and an ice cream bowl. Everyone starts singing a birthday song, probably out of tune.* PEGGY *helps them along.* BILLY *puts the cake down in front of* WINKIE, *who takes a deep breath to blow out the candles.*]

PEGGY: No, no, sweetheart. Wait. Always wait. Before you blow out the candles, you have to make a wish. And mummy has to make a wish. See? Mummy is putting her wedding ring around one of the candles. Now we both close our eyes and make a wish.

WINKIE: I wish I could have—

PEGGY: No, no. Don't tell. Never tell a wish. If you do, it won't come true. All right. Now blow.

[WINKIE *blows out "the candles." The* CHILDREN *cheer.*]
Now, Winkie, would you cut the cake and give everyone
a piece, please. And, Brewster, you pass the ice cream.
[*The* CHILDREN *organize their food as* PEGGY *joins* TED
downstage. There is a kind of cooing hum of CHILDREN
eating which punctuates their dialogue.]

TED: What did you wish for?

PEGGY: Won't tell.

TED: Do you think it will come true?

PEGGY: No.

[*Pause*]

TED: She'd make it so messy. For everyone.

PEGGY: Judy.

TED: She'd make it impossible.

PEGGY: So would Frank.

TED: I thought he didn't care.

PEGGY: He'd care if it were messy.

[*Pause*]

TED: We could leave town.

PEGGY: And go where?

TED: Wherever I find another job.

PEGGY: Yes. . . .

TED: I've got an uncle in Syracuse.

PEGGY: Syracuse?

TED: We could live there.

PEGGY: Is it nice? Syracuse?

TED: I think it's on some lake.

PEGGY: Syracuse. . . .

TED: You'd have Winkie. I'd get Bill in the summer.

PEGGY: In Syracuse.

TED: At least we'd be free.

[*They look at their children.*]

PEGGY: Winkie, wipe your mouth, please.

[*She goes to* WINKIE.]

TED: Billy.

BILLY: What?

TED: Would you come here a minute, please?

[BILLY *does.* TED *takes him aside.*]
Do you have to go the bathroom?

BILLY: No.

TED: Then don't do that, please.

BILLY: Don't do what?

TED: You know what. Now go back and enjoy the party.

[BILLY *returns to his seat.* TED *rejoins* PEGGY.]

TED: Sorry.

PEGGY: I grew up here.

TED: Who didn't?

PEGGY: To just pick up stakes . . .

TED: I know.

PEGGY: I mean, this is where I *live.*

TED: Me, too. [*Touching her*] We'll just have to behave ourselves, then.

PEGGY: Oh, Ted. . . .

TED: Be good little children.

PEGGY: Oh, I can't stand it.

[*She takes his hand and presses it furtively to her lips.*]

TED: And if we're seated next to each other, we'll have to make a conscious effort.

PEGGY: Oh, we won't be seated next to each other. Judy will see to that.

TED: For a while anyway.

PEGGY: For quite a while.

[*The* CHILDREN *are getting noisy.* WINKIE *comes up.*]

WINKIE: Everyone's finished, Mummy.

PEGGY: Thank you, sweetheart.

WINKIE: And here's your ring. From the cake.

PEGGY: Good for you, darling! I forgot all about it! [*She puts the ring back on.*]

TED: Time to go, then?

PEGGY: I've planned some games.

TED: Want me to stay?

PEGGY: It would help.

TED: Then I'll stay.

PEGGY: [*To* CHILDREN] Into the living room now, children. For some games.

BREWSTER: What games?

PEGGY: Oh, all kinds of games! Blind Man's Bluff. Pin the Tail on the Donkey. . . .

CHILDREN: Yippee! Yay!

[*The* CHILDREN *run noisily offstage.* PEGGY *begins putting the mess back onto the tray.*]

TED: I'll get them started.

PEGGY: Would you. While I propitiate Roberta.

TED: I'll be the donkey.

221

A. R. GURNEY, JR.

PEGGY: Oh, stop.

TED: I'll be the ass.

PEGGY: Stop or I'll scream.

[*He is about to kiss her, over the tray, when* WINKIE *appears at the door. They break away.*]

WINKIE: Come *on*, Mummy! We're waiting!

PEGGY: We're coming, dear.

[WINKIE *disappears into the hall.* TED *and* PEGGY *go off different ways as a* GRANDFATHER *enters from the hall. He is about eighty. He sits at the head of the table and begins to read the paper as* DORA, *a maid, comes out of the kitchen and begins to set a place in front of him. After a moment, his grandson* NICK *appears, breathlessly, in the doorway from the hall. He is about thirteen or fourteen.*]

NICK: [*Panting, frightened*] Grampa?

GRANDFATHER: [*Looking up, over his paper*] Which one are you?

NICK: I'm Nick, Gramp.

GRANDFATHER: And what do you want?

NICK: To have lunch with you, Gramp.

GRANDFATHER: Then you're late.

NICK: I went down to the club.

GRANDFATHER: Who said I'd be at the club?

NICK: My parents. My parents said you always eat there.

GRANDFATHER: Lately I've been coming home.

NICK: Yes, sir.

GRANDFATHER: Don't know half the people at the club anymore. Rather be here. At my own table. Dora takes care of me, don't you, Dora?

DORA: Yes, sir.

GRANDFATHER: [*To* NICK] Well you tracked me down, anyway. That shows some enterprise. [*Indicates a place*] Bring him some lunch, Dora.

DORA: Yes, sir.

[*She goes out.*]

NICK: [*Sitting opposite him at the other end of the table*] Thank you, Gramp.

GRANDFATHER: And you're Nick, eh?

NICK: Yes. I am.

GRANDFATHER: You the one who wants to go to Europe this summer?

NICK: No, that's Mary. That's my cousin.

GRANDFATHER: You the one who wants the automobile? Says he can't go to college without an automobile?

NICK: No, that's my brother Tony, Gramp.

GRANDFATHER: What do you want then?

NICK: Oh, I don't really want . . .

GRANDFATHER: Everyone who sits down with me wants something. Usually it's money. Do you want money?

NICK: Yes, sir.

GRANDFATHER: For what?

NICK: My education, Gramp.

GRANDFATHER: Education, eh? That's a good thing. Or can be. Doesn't have to be. Can be a bad thing. Where do you want to be educated?

NICK: Saint Luke's School, in Litchfield, Connecticut.

GRANDFATHER: Never heard of it.

NICK: It's an excellent boarding school for boys.

GRANDFATHER: Is it Catholic?

NICK: I don't think so, Gramp.

GRANDFATHER: Sounds Catholic to me.

NICK: I think it's High Episcopalian, Gramp.

GRANDFATHER: Then it's expensive.

NICK: My parents think it's a first-rate school, Gramp.

GRANDFATHER: Ah. Your parents think. . . .

NICK: They've discussed all the boarding schools, and decided that this is the best.

GRANDFATHER: They decided, eh?

NICK: Yes, sir.

GRANDFATHER: And then they decided you should get your grandfather to pay for it.

NICK: Yes, sir.

[DORA *has returned, and set a place mat and a plate for* NICK.]

GRANDFATHER: Another one leaving the nest, Dora.

DORA: Yes, sir. [*She waits by the sideboard.*]

GRANDFATHER: And taking a piece of the nest egg.

DORA: Yes, sir.

[*Pause*]

GRANDFATHER: Why don't you stay home?

NICK: Me?

GRANDFATHER: You.

NICK: Oh. Because I want to broaden myself.

GRANDFATHER: You want to what?

NICK: I want to broaden my horizons. My horizons need broadening.

GRANDFATHER: I see.

NICK: And I'll meet interesting new friends.

GRANDFATHER: Don't you have any interesting friends here?

NICK: Oh, sure, Gramp.

GRANDFATHER: I do. I have interesting friends right here. I know a man who makes boats in his basement.

NICK: But . . .

GRANDFATHER: I know a man who plays golf with his wife.

NICK: But I'll meet different types, Gramp. From all over the country. New York . . . California . . .

GRANDFATHER: Why would you want to meet anyone from New York?

NICK: Well they're more sophisticated, Gramp. They'll buff me up.

GRANDFATHER: They'll what?

NICK: My mother says I need buffing up.

GRANDFATHER: Do you think he needs buffing up, Dora?

DORA: No, sir.

GRANDFATHER: [*To* NICK] Dora doesn't think you need buffing up. I don't think you need buffing up. You'll have to give us better reasons.

NICK: Um. Well. They have advanced Latin there. . . .

GRANDFATHER: I see. And?

NICK: And an indoor hockey rink.

GRANDFATHER: Yes. And?

NICK: And beautiful grounds and surroundings.

GRANDFATHER: Don't we? Don't we have beautiful surroundings? Why do we have to go away to have beautiful surroundings?

NICK: I don't know, Gramp. All I know is everyone's going away these days.

GRANDFATHER: Everyone's going away? Hear that, Dora? Everyone's going away.

NICK: [*Desperately*] An awful lot of people are going away! [*Pause*]

GRANDFATHER: I didn't go away.

NICK: I know, Gramp.

GRANDFATHER: Didn't even go to Country Day. Went to the old P.S. 36 down on Huron Street.

NICK: Yes, Gramp.

GRANDFATHER: Didn't finish, either. Father died, and I had to go to work. Had to support my mother.

NICK: I know that, Gramp.

GRANDFATHER: My father didn't go to school at all. Learned Greek at the plow.

NICK: You told us, Gramp.

GRANDFATHER: Yes well I didn't do too badly. Without a High Episcopal boarding school, and an indoor hockey rink.

NICK: But you're a self-made man, Gramp.

GRANDFATHER: Oh, is that what I am? And what are you? Don't you want to be self-made? Or do you want other people to make you? Hmmm? Hmmm? What've you got to say to that?

NICK: [*Squashed*] I don't know. . . .

GRANDFATHER: Everyone wants to go away. Me? I went away twice. Took two vacations in my life. First vacation, took a week off from work to marry your grandmother. Went to Hot Springs, Virginia. Bought this table. Second vacation: Europe. 1928. Again with your grandmother. Hated the place. Knew I would. Miserable meals. Took a trunkload of shredded wheat along. Came back when it ran out. Back to this table. [*Pause*] They're all leaving us, Dora. Scattering like birds.

DORA: Yes, sir.

GRANDFATHER: We're small potatoes these days.

DORA: Yes, sir.

GRANDFATHER: This one wants to go to one of those fancy New England boarding schools. He wants to play ice hockey indoors with that crowd from Long Island and Philadelphia. He'll come home talking with marbles in his mouth. We won't understand a word, Dora.

DORA: Yes, sir.

GRANDFATHER: And we won't see much of him, Dora. He'll go visiting in New York and Baltimore. He'll drink liquor in the afternoon and get mixed up with women who wear lipstick and trousers and whose only thought is the next dance. And he wants me to pay for it all. Am I right?

NICK: No, Gramp! No I don't! I don't want to go! Really! I never wanted to go! I want to stay home with all of you!

[*Pause*]

GRANDFATHER: Finish your greens. They're good for your lower intestine.

[*They eat silently. From stage right, a man named* PAUL *enters. He's in his mid-thirties and wears an open shirt. He starts carefully examining the dining room chairs along the left wall, one by one, turning them upside down, testing their strength.*

Finally, with a sigh, to NICK]

No. You go. You've got to go. I'll send you to Saint Whoozie's, and Betsy to Miss Whatsie's, and young Andy to Whatever-it's-called. And Mary can go to Europe this summer, and Tony can have a car, and it's all fine and dandy.

[*He gets slowly to his feet.* NICK *gets up too.*] Go on. Enjoy yourselves, all of you. Leave town, travel, see the world. It's bound to happen. And you know who's going to be sitting here when you get back? I'll tell you who'll be sitting right in that chair. Some Irish fella, some Jewish gentleman is going to be sitting right at this table. Saying the same thing to *his* grandson. And your grandson will be back at the *plow.* [*Starts out the door, stops, turns*] And come to think of it, that won't be a bad thing, either. Will it Dora?

DORA: No, sir.

[*He exits.* DORA *starts clearing off.* NICK *stands in the dining room.*]

Well, go on. Hurry. Bring him his checkbook before he falls asleep.

[NICK *hurries offstage right.* DORA *goes off with plates stage left.* PAUL *begins to check the table. A woman, about forty, call her* MARGERY, *appears in the hall doorway. She watches* PAUL.]

MARGERY: What do you think?

PAUL: [*Working over a chair*] You're in trouble.

MARGERY: Oh, dear. I knew it.

PAUL: It's becoming unglued.

MARGERY: I know the feeling.

PAUL: Coming apart at the seams.

MARGERY: Do you think it's hopeless?

PAUL: Let me check the table. [*He crawls under the table.*]

MARGERY: It shakes very badly. I had a few friends over the

226

other night, and every time we tried to cut our chicken, our water glasses started tinkling frantically. And the chairs creaked and groaned. It was like having dinner at Pompeii.

PAUL: [*Taking out a pocket knife*] I'm checking the joints here.

MARGERY: It's all very sad. How things run down and fall apart. I used to tell my husband—my *ex*-husband—we have such lovely old things. We should oil them, we should wax them, we should keep them up. But of course I couldn't do everything, and he wouldn't do anything, and now here you are to give us the *coup de grâce*.

PAUL: [*Still under table*] Hey look at this.

MARGERY: What?

PAUL: Look under here.

MARGERY: I don't dare.

PAUL: I'm serious. Look.

MARGERY: Wait till I put on my glasses. [*She puts on her glasses which are hanging from a chain around her neck; then she bends down discreetly*] Where? I can't see.

PAUL: Under here. Look. This support. See how loose this is?

MARGERY: I can't quite . . . Wait. . . . [*She gets down on her knees.*]

PAUL: Come on.

MARGERY: All right. [*She crawls under the table.*]

PAUL: See? Look at this support.

MARGERY: I see. It wiggles like mad.

[*They are both crawling around under the table now.*]

PAUL: [*Crawling around her*] And look over here. I'll have to put a whole new piece in over here. See? This is gone.

MARGERY: [*Looking*] I see.

PAUL: [*Crawling back*] And . . . excuse me, please . . . this pedestal is loose. Probably needs a new dowl. I'll have to ream it out and put in another. . . .

MARGERY: Do you think so?

PAUL: Oh, sure. In fact your whole dining room needs to be rescrewed, reglued, and renewed. [*His little joke. He comes out from under.*]

MARGERY: Hmmmm. [*She is still under the table.*]

PAUL: What's the matter?

MARGERY: I've never been under a table before.

PAUL: Oh, yeah?

MARGERY: It's all just . . . wood under here, isn't it?

PAUL: That's all it is.

MARGERY: [*Fascinated*] I mean you'd think a dining room *table* was something special. But it isn't, underneath. It's all just . . . wood. It's just a couple of big, wide . . . boards.

PAUL: That's right.

MARGERY: [*Peering*] What's this, here?

PAUL: What's what?

MARGERY: Well you'll have to come back under here to see. There's some writing here, burned into the wood.

PAUL: [*Crawling under*] Where?

MARGERY: Right here. [*She reads, carefully.*] "Freeman's Furniture. Wilkes-Barre, Pa., 1898."

PAUL: [*Under the table*] Oh, that's the manufacturer's mark.

MARGERY: 1898?

PAUL: That's what it says.

MARGERY: But that's not so old.

PAUL: Not if it was made in 1898.

MARGERY: That's not old at all. It's not even an antique. [*Pause*] It's just . . . American.

PAUL: There's a lot of these around. They used to crank them out, at the end of the nineteenth century.

MARGERY: Now aren't I dumb? For years, we've been thinking it's terribly valuable.

PAUL: Well it is, in a sense. It's well made. It's a solid serviceable copy. Based on the English.

MARGERY: Well I'll be darned. You learn something every day.

[*They are both sitting, side by side, under the table. She looks at him.*]

You know a lot about furniture, don't you?

PAUL: I'm beginning to.

MARGERY: Beginning to. I'll bet your father was a cabinet-maker or something.

PAUL: My father was a banker.

MARGERY: A *bank*er?

PAUL: And I was a stockbroker. Until I got into this.

MARGERY: I don't believe it.

PAUL: Sure. I decided I wanted to see what I was doing. And touch it. And see the results. So I took up carpentry.

MARGERY: I am amazed. I mean, I *know* some stockbrokers. [*Embarrassed pause. She looks at the strut.*]
Is this the support that's bad?

PAUL: That's the one.

MARGERY: What if you put a nail in here?

PAUL: Not a nail. A screw.

MARGERY: [*Crawling over him*] All right. And another one over here. Or at least some household cement.

PAUL: Well, they have these epoxy glues now. . . .

MARGERY: All right. And maybe cram a matchbook or something in here.

PAUL: Not a matchbook.

MARGERY: A wedge then. A wooden wedge.

PAUL: Good idea.

MARGERY: See? I can do it too.
[*In her intensity, she has gotten very close to him physically. They both suddenly realize it and move away, crawling out from under the table on either side, and brushing themselves off.*]
So. Well. Will you be taking the table away? Or can you fix it here?

PAUL: I can fix it here. If you want.

MARGERY: That might make more sense. My husband used to ask for written estimates. Materials and labor.

PAUL: I'll write one up.

MARGERY: Suppose I helped. On the labor.

PAUL: I never worked that way. . . .

MARGERY: I should learn. I shouldn't be so helpless.

PAUL: OK. Why not?

MARGERY: Besides, it's not an antique. If I make a mistake, it's not the end of the world, is it?

PAUL: Not at all.

MARGERY: When could we start?

PAUL: Today. Now, if you want.

MARGERY: Then we're a partnership, aren't we? We should have a drink, to celebrate.

PAUL: OK.
[*From offstage right, we hear voices singing the Thanksgiving hymn "Come, Ye Thankful People, Come."*]

A. R. GURNEY, JR.

MARGERY: What'll we have? Something snappy? Like a martini?

PAUL: No, I gave them up with the stock market. How about a beer?

MARGERY: Fine idea. Good, solid beer. If I've *got* it.

[*They go off into the kitchen, as* NANCY, *in her thirties, comes out, carrying a stack of plates and a carving knife and a fork. She calls back over her shoulder.*]

NANCY: I've got the plates, Mrs. Driscoll. You've got your hands full with that turkey.

[*She sets the plates and carving utensils at the head of the table and calls toward the hall.*] We're ready everybody! Come on in!

[*The singing continues as* FRED, BEN, *and* BETH *begin to come into the dining room, to celebrate Thanksgiving dinner. The oldest son,* STUART, *has his mother on his arm. She is a very vague, very old* OLD LADY.]

STUART: . . . Now, Mother, I want you to sit next to me, and Fred, you sit on mother's left, and Ben, you sit opposite her where she can see you, and Nancy and Beth hold up that end of the table, and there we are.

[*Genial chatter as everyone sits down. The two sons push in their mother's chair. After a moment the* OLD LADY *stands up again, looking around distractedly.*]

What's the matter, Mother?

OLD LADY: I'm not quite sure where I am.

STUART: [*Expansively; arm around her; seating her again*] You're *here*, mother. In your own dining room. This is your table, and here are your chairs, and here is the china you got on your trip to England, and here's the silver-handled carving knife which father used to use.

OLD LADY: Oh, yes. . . .

[*Genial laughter; ad-libbing: "She's a little tired. . . ." "It's been a long day. . . ." The* OLD LADY *gets up again.*]

But who are these people? I'm not quite sure who these people are.

[*She begins to wander around the room.*]

STUART: [*Following her around*] It's me, Mother: Stuart. Your son. And here's Fred, and Ben, and Nancy, and Beth. We're all here, Mother.

NANCY: [*Going into the kitchen*] I'll get the turkey. That might help her focus.

STUART: Yes. [*To* OLD LADY] Mrs. Driscoll is here, Mother. Right in the kitchen, where she's always been. And your grandchildren. All your grandchildren were here. Don't you remember? They ate first, at the children's table, and now they're out in back playing touch football. You watched them, Mother. [*He indicates the "French doors."*]

OLD LADY: Oh, yes. . . .

[*She sits down again at the other end of the table.* NANCY *comes out from the kitchen, carrying a large platter. Appropriate Oh's and Ah's from* GROUP]

STUART: And look, Mother. Here's Nancy with the turkey. . . . Put it right over there, Nancy. . . . See, Mother? Isn't it a beautiful bird? And I'm going to carve it just the way father did, and give you a small piece of the breast and a dab of dressing, just as always, Mother. [*He sharpens the carving knife officiously.*]

OLD LADY: [*Still staring out into the garden.*] Just as always. . . .

STUART: [*As he sharpens*] And Fred will have the drumstick—am I right, Fred?—and Beth gets the wishbone, and Ben ends up with the Pope's nose, am I right, Ben?

[*Genial in-group laughter*]

NANCY: Save some for Mrs. Driscoll.

STUART: I always do, Nancy. Mrs. Driscoll likes the second joint.

OLD LADY: This is all very nice, but I think I'd like to go home.

STUART: [*Patiently, as he carves*] You are home, Mother. You've lived here fifty-two years.

BEN: Fifty-four.

BETH: Forever.

STUART: Ben, pass this plate down to Mother. . . .

OLD LADY: [*Getting up*] Thank you very much, but I really do think it's time to go.

NANCY: Uh-oh.

BETH: Oh, dear.

STUART: [*Going to her*] Mother. . . .

OLD LADY: Will someone drive me home, please? I live at Eighteen Summer Street with my mother and sisters.

BETH: What will we do?

STUART: It's not there now, Mother. Don't you remember? We drove down. There's a big building there now.

OLD LADY: [*Holding out her hand*] Thank you very much for asking me. . . . Thank you for having me to your house. [*She begins to go around the table, thanking people.*]

FRED: Mother! I'm Fred! Your son!

OLD LADY: Isn't that nice? Thank you. I've had a perfectly lovely time. . . . Thank you. . . . Thank you so much. [*She shakes hands with* NANCY.]
It's been absolutely lovely. . . . Thank you, thank you.

STUART: Quickly. Let's sing to her.

BETH: Sing?

STUART: She likes singing. We used to sing to her whenever she'd get upset. . . . Fred, Ben. Quickly. Over here.

OLD LADY: [*Wandering around distracted*] Now I can't find my gloves. Where would my gloves be? I can't go out without my gloves.

BEN: What song? I can't remember any of the songs.

STUART: Sure you can. Come on. Hmmmmm.
[*He sounds a note. The* OTHERS *try to find their parts.*]

BEN *and* FRED: Hmmmmmmmmm.

OLD LADY: I need my gloves, I need my hat. . . .

STUART: [*Singing*]

As the blackbird in the spring . . .

OTHERS: [*Joining in*]

'Neath the willow tree . . .
Sat and piped, I heard him sing
Sing of Aura Lee . . .

[*They sing in pleasant, amateurish corny harmony. The* OLD LADY *stops fussing, turns her head, and listens. The other women remain at the table.*]

MEN: [*Singing*]

Aura Lee, Aura Lee, Maid of Golden Hair . . .
Sunshine came along with thee, and swallows in the air.

OLD LADY: I love music. Every person in our family could

play a different instrument. [*She sits in a chair along the wall, downstage right.*]

STUART: [*To his* BROTHERS] She's coming around. Quickly. Second verse.

MEN: [*Singing with more confidence now; more daring harmony*]

In thy blush the rose was born,
Music, when you spake,
Through thine azure eye the morn
Sparkling seemed to break.
Aura Lee, Aura Lee, maid of golden hair,
Sunshine came along with thee, and swallows in the air.

[*They hold a long note at the end. The* OLD LADY *claps. Everyone claps.*]

OLD LADY: That was absolutely lovely.

STUART: Thank you, Mother.

OLD LADY: But now I've simply got to go home. Would you call my carriage, please? And someone find my hat and gloves. It's very late, and my mother gets very nervous if I'm not home in time for tea. [*She heads for the hall.*]

STUART: [*To no one in particular*] Look, Fred, Ben, we'll drive her down, and show her everything. The new office complex where her house was. The entrance to the thruway. The new Howard Johnson's motel. Everything! And she'll see that nothing's there at all.

FRED: I'll bring the car around.

STUART: I'll get her coat.

BEN: I'm coming, too.

STUART: We'll just have to go through the motions.

[*The brothers hurry after their mother.* NANCY *and* BETH *are left alone onstage. Pause. Then they begin to stack the dishes.*]

NANCY: That's scary.

BETH: I know it.

NANCY: I suddenly feel so . . . precarious.

BETH: It could happen to us all.

NANCY: No, but it's as if we didn't exist. As if we were all just . . . ghosts, or something. Even her own sons. She walked right by them.

BETH: And guess who walked right by *us*.

NANCY: [*Glancing offstage*] Yes. . . . [*Pause*] Know what I'd like?

BETH: What?

NANCY: A good stiff drink.

BETH: I'm with you.

NANCY: I'll bet Mrs. Driscoll could use a drink, too.

BETH: Bet she could.

NANCY: [*Deciding*] Let's go out and ask her!

BETH: Mrs. Driscoll?

NANCY: Let's!

[*Pause*]

BETH: All right.

NANCY: Let's go and have a drink with Mrs. Driscoll, and then dig into this turkey, and help her with the dishes, and then figure out how to get through the rest of the goddamn day!

[*They go offstage into the kitchen. The table is clear, the dining room is empty.*]

END OF ACT I

ACT II

The dining room is empty. The light suggests that it is about three in the afternoon. After a moment SARAH's *voice is heard offstage right, from the front hall. She is about 16 or 17.*

SARAH'S VOICE: Mom? MOM? Anybody home? [*Silence; then more softly*] See? I told you. She isn't here.

[SARAH *appears in the doorway, with* HELEN *behind her.*]

HELEN: Where is she?

SARAH: She works. At a boutique. Four days a week. And my father's away on business. In Atlanta. Or Denver or somewhere. Anyway. Come on. I'll show you where they keep the liquor.

HELEN: My mom's always there when I get home from school. Always.

SARAH: Bummer.

HELEN: And if she isn't, my grandmother comes in.

SARAH: The liquor's in the pantry.

[SARAH *goes out through dining room door, stage left.* HELEN *stays in the dining room.*]

HELEN: [*Taking in the dining room*] Oh. Hey. Neat-o.

SARAH'S VOICE: [*From within*] What?

HELEN: This *room.*

SARAH'S VOICE: [*Over clinking of liquor bottles*] That's our dining room.

HELEN: I know. But it's viciously nice.

SARAH: [*Coming out of kitchen, carrying two bottles*] Which do you want? Gin or vodka?

HELEN: [*Wandering around the room*] You decide.

SARAH: [*Looking at bottles*] Well there's more gin, so it's less chance they'll notice.

HELEN: Gin, then.

SARAH: But the reason there's more gin is that I put water in it last week.

HELEN: Vodka, then.

SARAH: Tell you what. We'll mix in a little of both.
[*She goes into the kitchen.*]

HELEN: OK. . . . Do you *use* this room.

SARAH'S VOICE: Oh, sure.

HELEN: Special occasions, huh? When the relatives come to visit?

SARAH'S VOICE: Every night.

HELEN: Every *NIGHT*?

SARAH'S VOICE: Well at least every night they're both home.

HELEN: Really?

SARAH: [*Coming in, carrying two glasses*] Oh, sure. Whenever they're home, my father insists that we all eat in the dining room at seven o'clock.
[*Hands HELEN her drink*]
Here. Gin and vodka and Fresca. The boys are bringing the pot.

HELEN: [*Drinking*] Mmmm . . . It must be nice, eating here.

SARAH: [*Slouching in a chair*] Oh, yeah sure you bet. We have to lug things out, and lug things back, and nobody can begin till everything's cold, and we're supposed to carry on a decent conversation, and everyone has to finish before anyone can get up, and it sucks, if you want to know. It sucks out loud.
[*They drink.*]

HELEN: We eat in the kitchen.

SARAH: Can you watch TV while you eat?

HELEN: We used to. We used to watch the local news and weather.

SARAH: That's something. At least you don't have to talk.

HELEN: But now we can't watch it. My mother read in *Family Circle* that TV was bad at meals. So now we turn on the stereo and listen to semiclassical music.

SARAH: My parents said they tried eating in the kitchen

when I went to boarding school. But when I got kicked
out, they moved back in here. It's supposed to give me
some sense of stability.

HELEN: Do you think it does?

SARAH: Shit no! It just makes me nervous. They take the
telephone off the hook, so no one can call, and my
brother gets itchy about his homework, and when my
sister had anorexia, she still had to sit here and *watch*,
for God's sake, and my parents spend most of the meal
bitching, and the whole thing bites, Helen. It really
bites. It bites the big one. Want another?

HELEN: No thanks.

SARAH: I do. . . . You call the boys and tell them it's all
clear.

[SARAH *goes back into the kitchen.*]

HELEN: [*Calling toward kitchen*] Sarah. . . .

SARAH'S VOICE: [*Within*] What?

HELEN: When the boys come over, can we have our drinks
in here?

[KATE, *a woman in her mid-forties, comes out. She carries
a small tray containing a teapot, two teacups, sugar, and
creamer. She sits at the table and watches the teapot.*]

SARAH'S VOICE: [*Within*] In the *dining* room?

HELEN: I mean, wouldn't it be cool, sitting around this
shiny table with Eddie and Duane, drinking gin and
Fresca and vodka?

SARAH: [*Coming out from the kitchen*] No way. Absolutely
no way. In here? I'd get all up tight in here. [*She heads
for the hall.*] Now come on. Let's *call* them.

[HELEN *starts after her.*]

Having *boys* in the *dining* room? Jesus, Helen. You
really are a wimp sometimes.

[*They go out, right,* HELEN *looking back over her shoulder
at the dining room.*]

KATE: [*Calling toward hallway*] I'm in here, Gordon. I made
tea.

[GORDON *comes in from the hall. He is about her age. He is
buttoning his shirt, carrying his jacket and tie slung over
his shoulder.*]

GORDON: Tea?

KATE: Tea.

GORDON: Why tea?

KATE: Because I like it. I love it. [*Pause*] Or would you like a drink?

GORDON: No thanks.

KATE: Go ahead. Don't worry about me. I'm all over that. We even have it in the house, and I never touch it.

GORDON: No thanks, Kate.

KATE: Then have tea. It's very good. It's Earl Gray.

GORDON: I ought to be getting back.

KATE: Gordon, please. Have tea.

· [*Pause*]

GORDON: All right.

KATE: Thank you. [*She begins to pour him a cup.*]

GORDON: [*Ironically*] Tea in the dining room.

KATE: Where else? Should we huddle guiltily over the kitchen table?

GORDON: No.

KATE: Then tea in the dining room. . . . What would you like? Lemon or milk?

GORDON: Whatever.

KATE: Gordon.

GORDON: Milk, then. No sugar.

KATE: Milk it is. [*She hands him a cup.*] Well sit down, for heaven's sake.

GORDON: [*Not sitting*] I thought I heard a sound.

KATE: Oh, really? And what sound did you hear? A distant lawn mower? A faulty burglar alarm?

GORDON: I thought I heard a car.

KATE: What? A car? On this godforsaken street? Should we rush to the window? Cheer? Wave flags?

GORDON: Go easy, Kate.

KATE: Well I doubt very much that you heard a car.

GORDON: [*Listening*] It stopped.

KATE: The sound?

GORDON: The *car*. The car stopped.

KATE: All right, Gordon. You heard a car stop. But it's not Ed's car, is it? Because Ed, as you and I well know, is in Amsterdam, or Rotterdam, or who-gives-a-damn until next Tuesday. [*Reaches for his hand*] Now sit *down*. Please. Let's have tea, for heaven's sake.
[*He sits on the edge of his chair.*]
Now when can we meet again?

GORDON: [*Jumping up*] I heard a car door slam.

238

KATE: Oh, really. That's because cars have doors. And people when they get really frustrated feel like slamming them.

GORDON: I'm going.

KATE: I see how it is—a quick tumble with the bored wife of your best friend.

GORDON: Someone's at the front door.

KATE: No. . . .

GORDON: Yes. Someone with a key!

[KATE *jumps up. They listen.*]

KATE: [*Whispering*] Now you've got to stay.

[GORDON *quickly puts on his coat.* CHRIS's *voice is heard calling from the hall.*]

CHRIS'S VOICE: Mom!

KATE: Lord help us.

CHRIS'S VOICE: I'm home, Mom!

KATE: [*grimly to* GORDON] Now you've got to have tea.

CHRIS'S VOICE: Mom?

KATE: [*Calling out*] We're in the dining room, dear.

[CHRIS *slides into view from stage right. He is about seventeen, carries a duffel bag.* KATE *goes to him effusively.*] Darling! How'd you get here?

CHRIS: I took a cab from the bus station.

[KATE *embraces him. He looks at* GORDON.]

KATE: You look marvelous! Taller than ever! Say hello to Uncle Gordon.

GORDON: Hi, Chris. Welcome home.

CHRIS: [*Coolly*] Hi.

KATE: What's this? Is this what they teach you at Deerfield? Not to shake hands? Not to call people by name?

CHRIS: Hello, Uncle Gordon.

[*They shake hands.*]

GORDON: Hi, Chris.

KATE: But what brings you home, my love? I expected you Saturday.

CHRIS: I got honors.

KATE: Honors?

CHRIS: You get out two days early if you get an over-eighty-five average.

KATE: But then you should have telephoned.

CHRIS: I wanted to surprise you.

[*Pause*]

GORDON: I ought to go.

KATE: Nonsense. Have more tea. Chris, would you like tea? I was taking a nap, and Gordon stopped by, and we thought we'd have tea. Have some tea, dear. Or a Coke. Have a Coke. Or shall I get you a beer? How about a beer for a big boy who gets honors?

CHRIS: No, thanks.

GORDON: I'd really better go.

KATE: You won't have more tea.

GORDON: Can't. Sorry.

KATE: All right, then. Good-bye.

GORDON: [*Shaking hands with her stiffly*] Good-bye. . . . Good-bye, Chris.

[*He tries to shake hands with* CHRIS.]

CHRIS: [*Turning away*] Good-bye.

[GORDON *goes, quickly, offstage right.* KATE *starts to put the tea things back on the tray.*]

KATE: He wanted to talk to me about stocks. I inherited some stock he thinks I should sell, and so he stopped by—

CHRIS: Where's Dad?

KATE: He's in Europe, darling. As I think I wrote you. He'll be home Tuesday.

[*She starts for the kitchen with the tray.*]

CHRIS: Oh, Mom.

KATE: [*Stopping, turning*] And what does that mean, pray tell? "Oh, Mom."

[*He turns away.*]

I'd like to know, please, what that means?

[*He shakes his head.*]

I happened to be having *tea*, Christopher. It happens to be a very old custom. Your grandmother used to have tea at this very table with this same china every afternoon. All sorts of people would stop by. All the time. I'd come home from school, and there she'd be. Serving tea. It's a delightful old custom, sweetheart.

[*He starts for the hall.*]

Where are you going? I asked you a question, please. We don't just walk away.

[CHRIS *walks out of the room. A young man named* TONY *comes in from the kitchen, decked out with a camera and various pieces of photographic equipment. He begins to test the room with his light meter.* KATE *calls after* CHRIS.]

Chris, I am talking to you. I am talking to you, and I am your mother, and the least you can do is . . .

[*She follows him out into the hall, still carrying the tray.* TONY *finds an area by a chair which pleases him. He calls toward the kitchen.*]

TONY: Would you mind setting up over here, Aunt Harriet? I want to get you in the late afternoon light.

[AUNT HARRIET, *a woman of about sixty, appears at the kitchen door, carrying another tray, glittering with old china and crystal.*]

AUNT HARRIET: [*Beaming proudly*] Certainly, Tony.

[*She goes to where he indicates, puts down her tray, and begins to set a place at the table.*]

Now I thought I'd use this Irish linen place-mat with matching napkin that my husband—who was what? Your great uncle—inherited from his sister. They have to be washed and ironed by hand every time they're used.

[*She places the place-mat; he photographs it.*]

And then of course the silver, which was given to us as a wedding present by your great-grandmother. You see? Three prong forks. Pistol-handled knives. Spoon with rat-tail back. All Williamsburg pattern. This should be polished at least every two weeks.

[*She sets a place as he photographs each item. She becomes more and more at home with the camera.*]

And then this is Staffordshire, as is the butter plate. All of this is Bone. The wine glasses are early Steuben, but the goblets and finger bowls are both Waterford. None of this goes in the dishwasher, of course. It's all far too delicate for detergents.

[*The place is all set. She surveys it proudly.*]

TONY: Finger bowls?

AUNT HARRIET: Oh, yes. Our side of the family always used finger bowls between the salad and the dessert.

TONY: Would you show me how they worked?

AUNT HARRIET: Certainly, dear.

[*He continues to snap pictures of her as she talks.*]

You see the maid would take away the salad plate—like this—[*She puts a plate aside to her right.*] And then she'd put down the finger bowls in front of us. Like this. [*She does.*] They would be filled approximately halfway with

241

cool water. And there might be a little rose floating in it. Or a sliver of lemon. . . . Now of course, we'd have our napkins in our laps—like this. [*She sits down, shakes out her napkin, puts it discreetly in her lap.*] And then we'd dip our fingers into the finger bowl . . . gently, gently . . . and then we'd wiggle them and shake them out . . . and then dab them on our napkins . . . and then dab our lips . . . then, of course, the maids would take them away. . . . [*She moves the finger bowl aside.*] And in would come a nice sherbet or chocolate mousse!

[*She beams at the camera, at last used to it. He snaps her picture.*]

TONY: Thanks, Aunt Harriet. That was terrific. [*He begins to pack up his photographic gear.*]

AUNT HARRIET: You're welcome. Now, Tony, dear, tell me again what all this is for. I didn't quite understand over the telephone.

TONY: This is a classroom project. For Amherst.

AUNT HARRIET: Oh, my. A project. [*She stands up.*] In what, pray tell.

TONY: Anthropology, actually.

AUNT HARRIET: Anthropology. Heavens! [*She starts to return items to her tray.*] What does that have to do with this?

TONY: Well you see we're studying the eating habits of various vanishing cultures. For example, someone is talking about the Kikuyus of northern Kenya. And my roommate is doing the Cree Indians of Saskatchewan. And my professor suggested I do a slide show on us.

AUNT HARRIET: Us?

TONY: The Wasps. Of northeastern United States.

[*Pause*]

AUNT HARRIET: I see.

TONY: You can learn a lot about a culture from how it eats.

AUNT HARRIET: [*With increasing coldness*] Such as what?

TONY: Well. Consider the finger bowls, for example. There you have an almost neurotic obsession with cleanliness, reflecting the guilt which comes with the last stages of capitalism. Or notice the unnecessary accumulation of glass and china, and the compulsion to display it. Or the subtle hint of aggression in those pistol-handled knives.

AUNT HARRIET: I think I'll ask you to leave, Tony.

TONY: Aunt Harriet . . .

AUNT HARRIET: I was going to invite you to stay for a cocktail, but now I won't.

TONY: Please, Aunt Harriet. . . . [*He begins to gather up his equipment.*]

AUNT HARRIET: Out! Right now! Before I telephone long-distance to your mother!

[TONY *backs toward the hallway.*]

Vanishing culture, my eye! I forbid you to mention my name in the classroom! Or show one glimpse of my personal property! And you can tell that professor of yours, I've got a good mind to drive up to Amherst, with this pistol-handled butter knife on the seat beside me, and cut off his anthropological balls!

[TONY *runs hurriedly from the room.* AUNT HARRIET *returns to her tray proudly, and carries it back into the kitchen. As she goes, an older man, called* JIM, *comes in from the hall, followed by his daughter,* MEG. *He is in his late sixties; she is about thirty.*]

MEG: Where are you going now, Daddy?

JIM: I think your mother might want a drink.

MEG: She's reading to the children.

JIM: That's why she might want one.

MEG: She wants no such thing, Dad.

JIM: Then I want one.

MEG: Now? It's not even five.

JIM: Well then let's go see how the Red Sox are doing. [*He starts back out.*]

MEG: Daddy, *stop!*

JIM: Stop what?

MEG: Avoiding me. Ever since I arrived, we haven't been able to talk.

JIM: Good Lord, what do you mean? Seems to me everybody's been talking continuously and simultaneously from the moment you got off the plane.

MEG: *Alone,* Daddy. I mean *alone.* And you *know* I mean alone.

JIM: All right. We'll talk. [*Sits down*] Right here in the dining room. Good place to talk. Why not? Matter of fact, I'm kind of tired. It's been a long day.

MEG: I love this room. I've always loved it. Always.

JIM: Your mother and I still use it. Now and then. Once a

week. Mrs. Robinson still comes in and cooks us a nice dinner and we have it in here. Still. Lamb chops. Broilers—

MEG: [*Suddenly*] I've left him, Daddy.

[*Pause*]

JIM: Oh, well now, a little vacation. . . .

MEG: I've left him permanently.

[*Pause*]

JIM: Yes, well, permanently is a very long word. . . .

MEG: I can't live with him, Dad. We don't get along at all.

[*Pause*]

JIM: Oh, well, you may think that now. . . .

MEG: Could we live here, Dad?

[*Pause*]

JIM: Here?

MEG: For a few months.

JIM: With three small children?

MEG: While I work out my life.

[*Pause.* JIM *takes out a pocket watch and looks at it.*]

JIM: What time is it? A little after five. I think the sun is over the yardarm, don't you? Or if it isn't, it should be. I think it's almost permissible for you and I to have a little drink, Meg.

MEG: Can we stay here, Dad?

JIM: Make us a drink, Meggie.

MEG: All right.

[*She goes into the kitchen; the door, of course, remains open.*]

JIM: [*Calling to her*] I'd like Scotch, sweetheart. Make it reasonably strong. You'll find the silver measuring gizmo in the drawer by the trays. I want two shots and a splash of water. And I like to use that big glass with the pheasants on it. And not too much ice. [*He gets up and moves around the table.*]

MEG'S VOICE: [*Within*] All right.

JIM: I saw Mimi Mott the other day. . . . Can you hear me?

MEG'S VOICE: [*Within*] I can hear you, Dad.

JIM: There she was, being a very good sport with her third husband. Her third. Who's deaf as a post and extremely disagreeable. So I took her aside—can you hear me?

MEG'S VOICE: [*Within*] I'm listening, Dad.

JIM: I took her aside, and I said, "Now, Mimi, tell me the

truth. If you had made half as much effort with your first husband as you've made with the last two, don't you think you'd still be married to him?" I asked her that. Point blank. And you know what Mimi said? She said, "Maybe." That's exactly what she said. "Maybe." If she had made the effort.

[MEG *returns with two glasses. She gives one to* JIM.]

MEG: That's your generation, Dad.

JIM: That's every generation.

MEG: It's not mine.

JIM: Every generation has to make an effort.

MEG: I won't go back to him, Dad. I want to be here.

JIM: [*Looking at his glass*] I wanted the glass with the pheasants on it.

MEG: I think the kids used it.

JIM: Oh.

[*Pause. He drinks, moves away from her.*]

MEG: So can we stay, Dad?

JIM: I sleep in your room now. Your mother kicked me out because I snore. And we use the boys' room now to watch TV.

MEG: I'll use the guest room.

JIM: And the children?

MEG: They can sleep on the third floor. In the maids' rooms.

JIM: We closed them off. Because of the oil bills.

MEG: I don't care, Dad. We'll work it out. Please.

[*Pause. He sits down at the other end of the table.*]

JIM: Give it another try first.

MEG: No.

JIM: Another try.

MEG: He's got someone else now, Dad. She's living there right now. She's moved in.

JIM: Then fly back and kick her out.

MEG: Oh, Dad. . . .

JIM: I'm serious. You don't know this, but that's what your mother did. One time I became romantically involved with Mrs. Shoemaker. We took a little trip together. To Sea Island. Your mother got wind of it, and came right down, and told Betty Shoemaker to get on the next train. That's all there was to it. Now why don't you do that? Go tell this woman to peddle her papers elsewhere. We'll sit with the children while you do.

MEG: I've got someone too, Dad.

[*Pause*]

JIM: You mean you've had a little fling.

MEG: I've been going with someone.

JIM: A little fling.

MEG: I've been living with him.

JIM: Where was your husband?

MEG: He stayed with his girl.

JIM: And your children?

MEG: Oh, they . . . came and went.

JIM: It sounds a little . . . complicated.

MEG: It is, Dad. That's why I needed to come home.

[*Pause. He drinks.*]

JIM: Now let's review the bidding, may we? Do you plan to marry this new man?

MEG: No.

JIM: You're not in love with him?

MEG: No. He's already married, anyway.

JIM: And he's decided he loves his wife.

MEG: No.

JIM: But you've decided you don't love him.

MEG: Yes.

JIM: Or your husband.

MEG: Yes.

JIM: And your husband's fallen in love with someone else.

MEG: He lives with someone else.

JIM: And your children . . . my grandchildren . . . come and go among these various households.

MEG: Yes. Sort of. Yes.

JIM: Sounds extremely complicated.

MEG: It is, Dad. It really is.

[*Pause. He drinks, thinks, gets up, paces.*]

JIM: Well then it seems to me the first thing you do is simplify things. That's the first thing. You ask the man you're living with to leave, you sue your husband for divorce, you hold onto your house, you keep the children in their present schools, you—

MEG: There's someone else, Dad.

[*Pause*]

JIM: Someone else?

MEG: Someone else entirely.

JIM: A third person.

MEG: Yes.

JIM: What was that movie your mother and I liked so much? *The Third Man?* [*He sits, downstage left.*]

MEG: It's not a man, Dad.

[*Pause*]

JIM: Not a man.

MEG: It's a woman.

JIM: A woman.

MEG: I've been involved with a woman, Dad, but it's not working, and I don't know who I am, and I've got to touch *base,* Daddy. I want to be here.

[*She kneels at his feet. Pause.* JIM *gets slowly to his feet. He points to his glass.*]

JIM: I think I'll get a repair. Would you like a repair? I'll take your glass. I'll get us both repairs.

[*He takes her glass and goes out to the kitchen, leaving the door open.*]

MEG: [*Moving around the dining room*] I'm all mixed up, Dad. I'm all over the ball park. I've been seeing a crisis counselor, and I've taken a part-time job, and I've been jogging two miles a day, and none of it's working, Dad. I want to come home. I want to take my children to the zoo, and the park lake, and the art gallery, and do all those things you and mother used to do with all of us. I want to start again, Dad. I want to start all over again.

[JIM *comes out from the kitchen, now carrying three glasses.*]

JIM: I made one for your mother. And I found the glass with the pheasants on it. In the trash. Somebody broke it. [*He crosses for the doorway.*] So let's have a nice cocktail with your mother, and see if we can get the children to sit quietly while we do.

MEG: You don't want us here, do you, Dad?

JIM: [*Stopping*] Of course we do, darling. A week, ten days. You're most welcome.

MEG: [*Desperately*] I can't go back, Dad!

JIM: [*Quietly*] Neither can I, sweetheart. Neither can I.

[*He shuffles on out.* MEG *stands for a moment in the dining room, then hurries out after him as* EMILY, *a woman of about thirty-five, comes in and looks at the table.*]

EMILY: [*Distractedly*] I don't know whether to eat or not.

[*Her son* DAVID *comes in. He's about fourteen.*]

247

DAVID: What's the trouble, Mother?

EMILY: I don't know whether to eat or not. Your father and I were sitting in the living room, having a perfectly pleasant cocktail together, when all of a sudden that stupid telephone rang, and now he's holed up in the bedroom, talking away. [*She closes the kitchen door.*]

DAVID: Who's he talking to?

EMILY: I don't know. I don't even know. I think it's someone from the club.

[CLAIRE, *her daughter, enters. She's about sixteen.*]

CLAIRE: Are we eating or not?

EMILY: I simply don't know.

[BERTHA, *the maid, sticks her head out of the kitchen door.*]

I don't know whether to go ahead or not, Bertha. Mr. Thatcher is still on the telephone.

CLAIRE: Couldn't we at least start the soup?

EMILY: I don't know. Oh, let's wait five more minutes, Bertha.

BERTHA: Yes, Mrs.

[BERTHA *disappears.* EMILY, DAVID, *and* CLAIRE *sit down.*]

EMILY: Honestly, that telephone! I could wring its neck! It should be banned, it should be outlawed, between six and eight in the evening.

[*The* FATHER *comes in hurriedly from the hall. His name is* STANDISH.]

STANDISH: I've got to go.

EMILY: [*Standing up*] Go? Go where?

STANDISH: Out.

[BERTHA *comes in with the soup tureen.*]

EMILY: You mean you can't even sit down and have some of Bertha's nice celery soup?

STANDISH: I can't even finish my cocktail. Something very bad has happened.

EMILY: Bertha, would you mind very much putting the soup back in a saucepan and keeping it on a low flame. We'll call you when we're ready.

BERTHA: Yes, Mrs.

[BERTHA *goes out.* STANDISH *takes* EMILY *aside, downstage.*]

EMILY: [*Hushed tones*] Now what on earth is the matter?

STANDISH: Henry was insulted down at the club.

EMILY: Insulted?

CLAIRE: [*From the table*] *Uncle* Henry?

STANDISH: [*Ignoring* CLAIRE; *to* EMILY] Binky Byers made a
remark to him in the steam bath.

EMILY: Oh, no!

DAVID: What did he say, Dad?

CLAIRE: Yes, what did he say?

STANDISH: I believe I was speaking to your mother.
[*Pause. The children are quelled.*]
Binky made a remark, and apparently a number of the
newer members laughed. Poor Henry was so upset he
had to put on his clothes and leave. He called me from
mother's.

EMILY: Oh, no; oh, no.

STANDISH: I telephoned the club. I spoke to several people
who had been in the steam bath. They confirmed the in-
cident. I asked to speak to Binky Byers. He refused to
come to the phone. And so I've got to do something about
it.

EMILY: Oh, dear; oh, dear.

DAVID: Won't you tell us what he said to Uncle Henry, Dad?

STANDISH: I will not. I will not dignify the remark by repeating it.

DAVID: Oh, come on, Dad. We're not babies.

EMILY: Yes, Standish. Really.

STANDISH: He said— [*Checks himself*] Claire, I want you to
leave the room.

CLAIRE: Why? I'm older.

EMILY: Yes. She should know. Everybody should know.
These are different times.
[BERTHA *comes out.*]
We're not quite ready yet, Bertha.
[BERTHA *goes back in.*]

EMILY: Now go on, Standish. Be frank, This is a family.

STANDISH: [*Hesitatingly; looking from one to the other*] Mr.
Byers . . . made an unfortunate remark . . . having to do
with your Uncle Henry's . . . private life.
[*Pause. The children don't get it.*]

EMILY: I'm afraid you'll have to be more specific, dear.

STANDISH: [*Taking a deep breath*] Mr. Byers, who had obviously been drinking since early afternoon, approached

Uncle Henry in the steam bath, and alluded in very specific terms to his personal relationships.

CLAIRE: What personal relationships?

STANDISH: His—associations. In the outside world.

[*Pause*]

DAVID: I don't get it.

EMILY: Darling, Mr. Byers must have made some unnecessary remarks about your Uncle Henry's bachelor attachments.

DAVID: You mean Uncle Henry is a *fruit?*

STANDISH: [*Wheeling on him*] I WON'T HAVE THAT WORD IN THIS HOUSE!

DAVID: I was just . . .

EMILY: He got it from school, dear.

STANDISH: I don't care if he got it from God! I will not have it in this house! The point is my own *brother* was *wounded* at his *club!*

[*Pause*]

EMILY: But what can you do, dear?

STANDISH: Go down there.

EMILY: To your mother's?

STANDISH: To the *club!* I'll demand a public apology from Binkie in front of the entire grille.

EMILY: But if he won't even come to the telephone. . . .

STANDISH: I'll have to fight him.

EMILY: Oh, Standish.

STANDISH: I have to.

CLAIRE: Oh, Daddy. . . .

STANDISH: I can't let the remark stand.

DAVID: Can I come with you, Dad?

STANDISH: You may not. I want you home with your mother. [*He starts for the door.*]

EMILY: Standish, for heaven's sake!

STANDISH: No arguments, please.

EMILY: But Binky Byers is half your age! And twice your size!

STANDISH: It makes no difference.

EMILY: I think he was on the boxing team at Dartmouth!

STANDISH: No difference whatsoever.

EMILY: What about your bad shoulder? What about your hernia?

STANDISH: I'm sorry. I imagine I shall be seriously hurt. But I can't stand idly by.

CLAIRE: [*Tearfully*] Oh, Daddy, please don't go.

[BERTHA *comes out of the kitchen.*]

BERTHA: The lamb will be overdone, Mrs.

EMILY: And it's a beautiful *lamb*, Standish!

STANDISH: [*Shouting them down*] Now *listen* to me! All of you!

[BERTHA *has been heading back to the kitchen.*]

And you, too, Bertha!

[*He points toward a chair on the side.* BERTHA *crosses, as everyone watches her. She sits on the edge of the chair. Everyone turns back to* STANDISH.]

There is nothing, nothing I'd rather do in this world, than sit down at this table with all of you and have some of Bertha's fine celery soup, followed by a leg of lamb with mint sauce and roast potatoes. Am I right about the sauce and the potatoes, Bertha?

BERTHA: Yes, sir.

STANDISH: There is nothing I'd rather have than that. But I have to forego it. My own brother has been publicly insulted at his club. And that means our family has been insulted. And when the family has been insulted, that means this table, these chairs, this room, and all of us in it, including you; Bertha, are being treated with scorn. And so if I stayed here, if I sat down with all of you now, I wouldn't be able to converse, I wouldn't be able to laugh, I wouldn't be able to correct your grammar, David, I wouldn't be able to enjoy your fine meal, Bertha. [*Turning to* EMILY] I wouldn't even be able to kiss my handsome wife good-bye.

[*He kisses her. It's a passionate kiss.*]

Good-bye, dear.

EMILY: Good-bye, darling.

[*He kisses* CLAIRE.]

STANDISH: Good-bye, Winkins.

CLAIRE: Good-bye, Daddy.

[*He shakes hands with* DAVID.]

STANDISH: Good-bye, David.

DAVID: So long, Dad. Good luck.

STANDISH: Good-bye, Bertha.

BERTHA: Good-bye, sir. God bless you.

A. R. GURNEY, JR.

STANDISH: Thank you very much indeed.

[*He goes out. Pause*]

EMILY: [*Now all business*] Of course we can't eat now, Bertha. Have something yourself, and let people raid the icebox later on.

BERTHA: Yes, Mrs.

EMILY: And the children can have lamb hash on Saturday.

BERTHA: Yes, Mrs.

[BERTHA *goes offstage.*]

EMILY: David: You and I will drive down to the club, and wait for the outcome in the visitor's lounge.

DAVID: OK, Mother.

EMILY: So get a book. Get a good book. Get *Ivanhoe*. We could be quite a while.

DAVID: OK.

[*He exits.*]

EMILY: And Claire: I want you to stay here, and hold the fort.

CLAIRE: All right, Mother.

EMILY: Get on the telephone to Doctor Russell. I don't care whether he's having dinner or in the operating room. Tell him to be at the club to give your father first aid.

CLAIRE: All right, Mother.

EMILY: And then study your French.

CLAIRE: All right. [*She starts out, then stops.*] Mother?

EMILY: [*Impatiently, in the doorway*] What, for heaven's sake?

CLAIRE: Is it true about Uncle Henry?

EMILY: Well it may be, sweetheart. But you don't say it to *him*. And you don't say it at the *club*. And you don't say it within a ten-mile radius of your *father*. Now good-bye. [EMILY *rushes offstage right, followed by* CLAIRE. *An* OLD MAN *and his middle-aged son come on from stage right. The old man is* HARVEY, *his son is* DICK. *The light is dim in the dining room now except downstage, by the "French doors."*]

HARVEY: [*As he enters*] We'll talk in here. No one will disturb us. Nobody comes near a dining room anymore. The thought of sitting down with a number of intelligent, attractive people to enjoy good food, well cooked and properly served . . . that apparently doesn't occur to people anymore. Nowadays people eat in kitchens, or in living rooms, standing around, balancing their plates like jugglers. Soon they'll be eating in bathrooms. Well why not? Simplify the process considerably.

DICK: Sit down somewhere, Pop.

HARVEY: [*Coming well downstage, pulling a chair down, away from the table*] I'll sit here. We can look out. There's a purple finch who comes to the feeder every evening. Brings his young.

[DICK *pulls up a chair beside him. Behind, in the dim light, three women begin to set the table, this time for an elaborate dinner. A great white tablecloth, candles, flowers, the works. The process should be reverential, quiet, and muted, not to distract from the scene downstage.* HARVEY *takes an envelope from his inside pocket.*]

Now. I want to go over my funeral with you.

DICK: Pop—

HARVEY: I want to do it. There are only a few more apples left in the barrel for me.

DICK: You've been saying that for years, Pop.

HARVEY: Well this time it's true. So I want to go over this, please. You're my eldest son. I can't do it with anyone else. Your mother starts to cry, your brother isn't here, and your sister gets distracted. So concentrate, please, on my funeral.

DICK: All right, Pop.

HARVEY: [*Taking out a typewritten document*] First, here is my obituary. For both newspapers. I dictated it to Miss Kovak down at the office, and I've read it over twice, and it's what I want. It's thorough without being self-congratulatory. I mention my business career, my civic commitments, and of course my family. I even touch on my recreational life. I give my lowest score in golf and the weight of the sailfish I caught off the Keys. The papers will want to cut both items, but don't you let them.

DICK: OK, Pop.

HARVEY: I also want them to print this picture. [*He shows it.*] It was taken when I was elected to chair the symphony drive. I think it will do. I don't look too young to die, nor so old it won't make any difference.

DICK: All right, Pop.

HARVEY: [*Fussing with other documents*] Now I want the funeral service announced at the end of the obituary, and

to occur three days later. That will give people time to
postpone their trips and adjust their golf games. And I
want it at three-thirty in the afternoon. This gives people time to digest their lunch and doesn't obligate us to
feed them dinner. Notice I've underlined the word
church. Mr. Fayerweather might try to squeeze the service into the chapel, but don't let him. I've lived in this
city all my life, and know a great many people, and I
want everyone to have a seat and feel comfortable. If you
see people milling around the door, go right up to them
and find them a place, even if you have to use folding
chairs. Are we clear on that?

DICK: Yes, Pop.

[*By now the table has been mostly set behind them. The
women have gone.*]

HARVEY: I've listed the following works to be played by
Mrs. Manchester at the organ. This Bach, this Handel,
this Schubert. All lively, you'll notice. Nothing gloomy,
nothing grim. I want the service to start promptly with a
good rousing hymn—"Onward, Christian Soldiers." And
then Fayerweather may make some brief—underlined
brief—remarks about my life and works. Do you plan to
get up and speak, by the way?

DICK: Me?

HARVEY: You. Do you plan to say anything?

DICK: I hadn't thought, Pop. . . .

HARVEY: Don't, if you don't want to. There's nothing more
uncomfortable than a reluctant or unwilling speaker.
On the other hand, if you, as my eldest son, were to get
on your feet and say a few words of farewell . . .

DICK: [*Quickly*] Of course I will, Pop.

HARVEY: Good. Then I'll write you in. [*He writes.*] "Brief remarks by my son Richard." [*Pause: looks up*] Any idea
what you might say?

DICK: No, Pop.

HARVEY: You won't make it sentimental, will you? Brad
Hoffmeister's son got up the other day and made some
very sentimental remarks about Brad. I didn't like it,
and I don't think Brad would have liked it.

DICK: I won't get sentimental, Pop.

HARVEY: Good. [*Pause: shuffles documents; looks up again*]

254

On the other hand, you won't make any wisecracks, will you?

DICK: Oh, Pop. . . .

HARVEY: You have that tendency, Dick. At Marcie's wedding. And your brother's birthday. You got up and made some very flip remarks about all of us.

DICK: I'm sorry, Pop.

HARVEY: Smart-guy stuff. Too smart, in my opinion. If you plan to get into that sort of thing, perhaps you'd better not say anything at all.

DICK: I won't make any cracks, Pop. I promise.

HARVEY: Thank you. [*Looks at documents; looks up again*] Because you love us, don't you?

DICK: Yes, Pop.

HARVEY: You love us. You may live a thousand miles away, you may have run off every summer, you may be a terrible letter-writer, but you love us all, just the same. Don't you? You love me.

DICK: [*Touching him*] Oh, yes, Pop! Oh, yes! Really!
[*Pause*]

HARVEY: Fine. [*Puts his glasses on again; shuffles through documents*] Now at the graveside, just the family. I want to be buried beside my brothers and below my mother and father. Leave room for your mother to lie beside me. If she marries again, still leave room. She'll come back at the end.

DICK: All right, Pop.

HARVEY: Invite people back here after the burial. Stay close to your mother. She gets nervous at any kind of gathering, and makes bad decisions. For example, don't let her serve any of the good Beefeater's gin if people simply want to mix it with tonic water. And when they're gone sit with her. Stay in the house. Don't leave for a few days. Please.

DICK: I promise, Pop.

[ANNIE, *the maid from the first scene, now quite old, adds candlesticks and a lovely flower centerpiece to the table.*]

HARVEY: [*Putting documents back in the envelope*] And that's my funeral. I'm leaving you this room, you know. After your mother dies, the table and chairs to you. It's the best thing I can leave you, by far.

DICK: Thanks, Pop.

255

[ANNIE *exits into the kitchen.*]

HARVEY: Now we'll rejoin your mother. [*He gets slowly to his feet.*] I'll put this envelope in my safe-deposit box, on top of my will and the stock certificates. The key will be in my left bureau drawer. [*He starts out, then stops.*] You didn't see the purple finch feeding its young.

DICK: [*Remaining in his chair*] Yes I did, Pop.

HARVEY: You saw it while I was talking?

DICK: That's right.

HARVEY: Good. I'm glad you saw it.

[*He goes out slowly.* DICK *waits a moment, lost in thought, and then replaces the chairs. The lights come up on the table, now beautifully set with white linen, crystal goblets, silver candlesticks, flowers, the works.* ANNIE *begins to set plates as a hostess—*RUTH—*comes in from stage right.*]

RUTH: [*Surveying the table*] Oh, Annie! It looks absolutely spectacular.

ANNIE: Thank you, Mrs.

RUTH: [*As she begins to distribute place cards carefully around the table*] Now make sure the soup plates are hot.

ANNIE: I always do, Mrs.

RUTH: But I think we can dispense with butter-balls. Just give everyone a nice square of butter.

ANNIE: I'll do butter-balls, Mrs.

RUTH: Would you? How nice! And keep an eye on the ashtrays, Annie. Some people still smoke between courses, but they don't like to be reminded of it.

ANNIE: I know, Mrs.

RUTH: And let's see . . . Oh, yes. Before people arrive, I want to pay you. [*She produces two envelopes from the sideboard.*] For you. And for Velma in the kitchen. It includes your taxi. So you can both just leave right after you've cleaned up.

ANNIE: Thank you, Mrs.

RUTH: There's a little extra in yours, Annie. Just a present. Because you've been so helpful to the family over the years.

ANNIE: Thank you, Mrs.

RUTH: And now I'd better check the living room.

ANNIE: Yes, Mrs.

[RUTH *starts out stage right, then stops.*]

RUTH: Oh, Annie. I heard some strange news through the grapevine.

[ANNIE *looks at her.*]

Mrs. Rellman told me that you won't be available anymore.

ANNIE: No, Mrs.

RUTH: Not even for us, Annie. We've used you more than anyone.

ANNIE: I'm retiring, Mrs.

RUTH: But surely special occasions, Annie. I mean, if we're desperate. Can I still reach you at your nephew's?

ANNIE: He's moving away, Mrs.

RUTH: But then where will you go? What will you do?

ANNIE: I've got my sister in Milwaukee, Mrs.

RUTH: But we'll be lost without you, Annie.

ANNIE: You'll manage, Mrs.

RUTH: [*Indicating the table*] But not like this. We'll never match this.

ANNIE: Thank you, Mrs.

RUTH: I think I heard the bell.

ANNIE: I'll get it, Mrs.

RUTH: Women's coats upstairs, men's in the hall closet.

ANNIE: Yes, Mrs. [ANNIE *starts out.*]

RUTH: [*Suddenly*] Annie!

[ANNIE *stops.* RUTH *goes to her and hugs her.* ANNIE *responds stiffly.*]

Thank you, Annie. For everything.

ANNIE: You're welcome, Mrs.

[ANNIE *goes offstage right to answer the door.* RUTH *goes to the sideboard, gets a book of matches. She lights the two candles on the table as she speaks to the audience.*]

RUTH: Lately I've been having this recurrent dream. We're giving this perfect party. We have our dining room back, and grandmother's silver, before it was stolen, and Charley's mother's royal blue dinner plates, before the movers dropped them, and even the finger bowls, if I knew where they were. And I've invited all our favorite people. Oh, I don't mean just our old friends. I mean everyone we've ever known and liked. We'd have the man who fixes our Toyota, and that intelligent young couple who bought the Payton house, and the receptionist at the doctor's office, and the new teller at the bank.

And our children would be invited, too, and they'd all come back from wherever they are. And we'd have two cocktails, and hot hors d'oeuvres, and a first-rate cook in the kitchen, and two maids to serve, and everyone would get along famously! [*The candles are lit by now.*] My husband laughs when I tell him this dream. "Do you realize," he says, "what a party like that would cost? Do you realize what we'd have to *pay* these days for a party like that?" Well, I know. I know all that. But sometimes I think it might almost be worth it.

[*The rest of the cast now spills into the dining room, talking animatedly, having a wonderful time. There is the usual gallantry and jockeying around as people read the place cards and find their seats. The men pull out the women's chairs, and people sit down. The* HOST *goes to the sideboard, where* ANNIE *has left a bottle of wine in a silver bucket. He wraps a linen napkin around it, and begins to pour people's wine. The conversation flows as well. The lights begin to dim. The* HOST *reaches his own seat at the head of the table, and pours his own wine. Then he raises his glass.*]

HOST: To all of us.

[*Everyone raises his or her glass. As their glasses go down, the lights fade to black. The table is bathed in its own candlelight. Then the two downstage actors unobtrusively snuff the candles, and the play is over.*]

THE END

Also by A. R. Gurney, Jr.

Plays

THE GOLDEN FLEECE
THE LOVE CURSE
THE OLD ONE-TWO
THE OPEN MEETING
THE PROBLEM
THE RAPE OF BUNNY STUNTZ

Published by Samuel French Co.

THE COMEBACK
THE GOLDEN AGE
THE WAYSIDE MOTOR INN
WHAT I DID LAST SUMMER
WHO KILLED RICHARD CORY?

Published by Dramatists Play Service

Novels

ENTERTAINING STRANGERS
THE GOSPEL ACCORDING TO JOE
THE SNOW BALL

BARD BOOKS DISTINGUISHED DRAMA

BENT Martin Sherman	75754-0/$3.95
BROKEN PROMISES: FOUR PLAYS David Henry Hwang	81844-2/$3.95
CHRISTOPHER DURANG EXPLAINS IT ALL FOR YOU Christopher Durang	82636-4/$3.95
FANTASTICKS Jones Schmidt	00915-3/$2.95
FIVE PLAYS by Ronald Ribman	40006-5/$4.95
FOUR PLAYS: Scenes from American Life, Children, The Middle Ages, The Dining Room A.R. Gurney, Jr.	89498-X/$4.95 US /$5.95 CAN
GREAT SCENES FROM THE WORLD THEATRE Vol. I James L. Steffenson Jr., Ed.	00793-2/$3.95
GREAT SCENES FROM THE WORLD THEATRE Vol. II James L. Steffenson Jr., Ed.	01220-0/$4.95
GREATEST REVUE SKETCHES Donald Oliver, Ed.	79194-3/$4.95
KEY EXCHANGE Kevin Wade	61119-8/$2.50
MASS APPEAL Bill C. Davis	77396-1/$2.50
OUR TOWN Thornton Wilder	00557-3/$2.25
PETER PAN, OR THE BOY WHO WOULD NOT GROW UP James M. Barrie	57752-6/$2.95
SCENES FOR YOUNG ACTORS Lorraine Cohen	69829-3/$4.95 US /$3.95 CAN
THE IMPORTANCE OF BEING EARNEST Oscar Wilde	01277-4/$1.95
THE RING: FOUR PLAYS FOR CHILDREN Adapted by Philip Caggiano	79434-9/$2.50
THREE PLAYS BY THORNTON WILDER Thornton Wilder	00527-1/$2.50
THREE PLAYS BY TINA HOWE Tina Howe	05001-X/$4.95
UNCOMMON WOMEN AND OTHERS Wendy Wasserstein	45997-4/$2.95
WHOSE LIFE IS IT ANYWAY? Brian Clark	52407-4/$2.95
YOUNG PLAYWRIGHTS FESTIVAL COLLECTION Compiled & Edited by the Foundation of the Dramatists Guild, Inc.	83642-4/$3.95

AVON BARD PAPERBACKS

Buy these books at your local bookstore or use this coupon for ordering:

- -

CAN—Avon Books of Canada, 210-2061 McCowan Rd., Scarborough, Ont. M1S 3Y6

US—Avon Books, Dept BP, Box 767, Rte 2, Dresden, TN 38225

Please send me the book(s) I have checked above. I am enclosing $ _____
(please add $1.00 to cover postage and handling for each book ordered to a maximum of
three dollars). Send check or money order—no cash or C.O.D.'s please. Prices and num-
bers are subject to change without notice. Please allow six to eight weeks for delivery.

Name _____

Address _____

City _____ State/Zip _____